SPLENDID LEGACY

VIRGINIA M. ESPOSITO, *Editor*

JOSEPH FOOTE, *Associate Editor*

ANDY CARROLL, *Project Manager*

THE GUIDE TO CREATING YOUR FAMILY FOUNDATION

Library of Congress Cataloging-in-Publication Data

Splendid legacy : the guide to creating your family foundation /
edited by Virginia M. Esposito.
    p. cm.
Includes bibliographical references and index.
    ISBN 1-929455-06-2 (alk. paper)
1. Endowments—United States—Handbooks, manuals, etc.
2. Charitable uses, trusts, and foundations—United States—
Handbooks, manuals, etc. 3. Family—United States. I. Esposito,
Virginia M., 1952- II. National Center for Family Philanthropy (U.S.)
    HV41 .S75 2002
    361.7'632—dc21

                        2002008329

Printed in the United States of America

National Center for Family Philanthropy
1818 N Street, NW, Suite 300
Washington, DC 20036
Tel: 202.293.3424
Fax: 202.293.3395
www.ncfp.org

"Starting a family foundation isn't rocket science."

JAYLEE MEAD

Research Astronomer, *NASA/Goddard Space Flight Center*
Co-Founder, *Gilbert and Jaylee Mead Family Foundation*

CONTENTS

PREFACE

My role at the National Center for Family Philanthropy offers me all kinds of wonderful opportunities and satisfaction. After all, what could be better than working with donors and their families as they create and sustain philanthropic programs? I get to meet those who have been given great gifts and who choose to share those gifts with others.

One of the greatest joys has to be my chance to talk with founders of family foundations. The conversations usually take many twists and turns. There is excitement about the possibilities of doing good, there is anxiety about doing what's right, and there is optimism about doing both well. In all of this, there is enthusiasm and commitment.

Inevitably, the request comes to send the new foundation founder some materials to help in the start-up phase. Fortunately, the National Center has been able to publish a pretty substantial library of resources in its first few years. Several of us on staff have worked on or are familiar with other publications as well. However, since nothing has ever existed before to give donors, their families, and advisors a comprehensive guide to creating a family foundation, I apologetically pack up a daunting array of specialized resources and mail them off to soon-to-be-overwhelmed founders — in a big box!

If you pack that big box often enough, you begin to dream about a single resource that covers the range of issues thought-fully and thoroughly enough to get founders off to a great start. The dream for *Splendid Legacy* began just that way. And the dream? An introduction to all you want and need to know about starting a family foundation: the challenges and the opportunities; the creativity and the discipline; the basic facts and the stories of other new family foundations. It would cover governance and grantmaking, funding the foundation and finding the family's role, investments and integrity. It would be inspiring and instructional and fill a need for thousands of family members and advisors. I am delighted that you hold in your hands the result of that dream.

It is yet another great privilege to welcome you to the world of family foundations. It may be surprising to you that there are those of us who celebrate your decision to create a family foundation for reasons other than the dollars you will invest in our communities. It may also be surprising that so many in the field of family philanthropy want to support your efforts. But it is like welcoming the new voices and visions that will renew a glorious tradition. Our welcome and encouragement are sincerely offered and, I hope, to be found throughout this book.

I believe *Splendid Legacy* speaks to the practical information you will need as you create your family foundation, the more intangible goals you bring, and the support you are also likely to need. Many of your philanthropic colleagues will encourage you to develop clear goals and outcomes, make levelheaded choices and conduct solid evaluation. That's good advice. The more you can tie your work to expectations and outcomes, the easier and more effective your grantmaking is likely to be.

Yet, there is another aspect to the family foundation, an aspect born of human connections and passions. There is no more emotional bond than that of family and no more emotional satisfaction than that which comes from working in service to your community. And that is as it should be. Philanthropy does derive from the Greek for love of mankind. There will be times you will need to do what is reasoned and efficient and there will be times when your feelings, instinct, and even human empathy will drive your decisionmaking.

This dichotomy was best described in a speech by Ambassador James A. Joseph, former president of the Council on Foundations, when he declared that "the vision of philanthropy in this new age must continue to be a matter of both the heart and head. Pascal said that the mind builds walls and the heart jumps over them. To be in philanthropy is to refuse to accept the heart and the mind as antagonists." Your family foundation will most assuredly require the commitment of both heart and head.

Countless people have been involved in making the dream of *Splendid Legacy* a reality. The National Center is indebted to each and every one, and no one feels that sense of gratitude more than this editor/author.

We began with a dynamic and experienced advisory committee who reviewed our plans, amended them (turned them on end, actually), and reviewed our progress along the way. They were excited and cautious. "Tell stories." "Don't overwhelm them." "It should look and be inviting." "If you don't have to know it right away, don't include it." "Speak English — no legal-ese or philanthropy-speak." And, "can you finish it by next week?" A list of these remarkable volunteers is included in the Acknowledgments section.

The David and Lucile Packard Foundation reviewed our plans and made a grant to support the editorial and curriculum development of the book. Knowing that the book would take several years didn't detract from their enthusiasm, and we are grateful for their faith and patience. The National Center Friends of the Family made an enormous contribution through their gifts, guidance, and encouragement.

From the beginning, I hoped to include a diverse group of authors in developing *Splendid Legacy*. I believed, and the Advisory Committee agreed, that having strong voices —

experts — in each area would make the book that much more substantive and more specific. Finding the right group and giving the book one voice out of many individual styles and perspectives were the challenges. The authors worked for months — they were and are creative, smart, talented, and committed to the value of this book and to serving philanthropic families. Please take a look at the Authors and Contributors section for brief biographical sketches of these writers.

As with many publications I have been proud to be part of, I was blessed with the literary talents and personal encouragement of Joseph Foote, associate editor. Joe has a special affinity for family philanthropy that helps you both understand and feel the family's story. Joe manages to work on about six essays at a time — keeping families and authors straight! It is a wonderful gift and he is a gift to family foundations everywhere. Andy Carroll served as project manager and brought an extraordinary commitment to *Splendid Legacy*. Andy's special blend of steel and gentleness, combined with a capacity to sort through thousands of minute details, made him the bedrock and hall monitor of authors and editors alike.

The staff of the National Center for Family Philanthropy brought it all together. Besides writing and editing, they checked sources, developed special features, handled marketing and orders, and waded through mountains of paper and details professionally, pleasantly, and promptly!

Splendid Legacy also reflects the contributions of many mentors and teachers in this field. The Board of Directors of the National Center has guided both the development of a new organization and the vision for our mission and programs, including this book. Many other individuals read portions of the manuscript and offered critical appraisal and thoughtful suggestions. I am proud that two of the first people to teach me about philanthropy — Alice Buhl and Bob Hull — served as reviewers for the entire manuscript — yeoman's work and a gesture that can only be attributed to an act of love and pity. My friend and former colleague at the Council on Foundations, John Edie, provided a review of several portions of this manuscript and gave us permission to include a few excerpts from his own terrific publications for family foundations.

Whenever I became mired in the details of starting a family foundation, in danger of losing sight of the goal, I had only to read from the writings of Margaret Mahoney, David Dodson, Curtis Meadows, Bruce Sievers, Jack Murrah, Ambassador James Joseph, John Nason, and Paul Ylvisaker to remind me why I do what I do and love to do it.

Developing this book constantly renewed my appreciation for what remarkable families can accomplish. I sometimes joke that it may be easy to love what I do because I don't have to do it with my own family. But I also know how important it is to be supported and encouraged by your family and mine is pretty terrific. And they have taught me how, in turn, to support and encourage the philanthropic families I meet.

With great gratitude and even more respect, this book is dedicated to two men who have worked selflessly and tirelessly for many years in support of family philanthropy.

Joel Fleishman brings intellectual rigor, an encouraging personal style, and grand passion to his work in philanthropy. He is rare in his extraordinary individual gifts and in his delight in supporting the work of others rather than commanding a much-earned personal stage for himself. The National Center and this book owe much to his vision and encouragement, as do I.

Tom Lambeth was also an early advocate for family foundations, and remains an ardent, if humble, one to this day. It wasn't so long ago that extolling the special qualities and contributions of family foundations was unheard of in nonprofit circles. Tom helped start those conversations and did it with integrity, grace, and grit. As founding chairman of the National Center for Family Philanthropy, he brought those qualities and more to making a home, a resource center, and a cheering section for those who participate and believe in family philanthropy.

The legacy of these two philanthropic leaders is, indeed, splendid.

Finally, this book is offered in memory and anticipation of philanthropic families everywhere. Thank you for sharing your stories, your hopes and frustrations, your accomplishments and your goals for your family and your communities. May your philanthropic family always be faithful to your vision and your trust, may you all bring what John Nason calls "practical wisdom" to the work of the foundation, and may your work together be inspired and guided by the dedicated community leaders and colleagues you will meet along the way.

And do I really believe that can happen? Absolutely! My experience with philanthropic families — the struggling and the soaring — gives me hope. As Ambassador Joseph continued in that 1995 speech:

> "Despite all the reasons for concern, even dismay, I am hopeful about the future of our society because I am hopeful about the potential of philanthropy; but it is the kind of hope that Vaclav Havel had in mind when he wrote in 1990 that 'I am not an optimist because I am not sure that everything ends well. Nor am I a pessimist, because I am not sure that everything ends badly. Hope is a feeling that life and work have a meaning...I cannot imagine that I could strive for something if I did not carry hope in me. It is as big a gift as life itself'."

It is also my hope that this book will prove to be a gift to you as you begin to build your own splendid legacy. Please let me know how you are doing.

Virginia M. Esposito
Washington, DC, June 2002

FOREWORD

When I was asked "why" I created my family foundation, the answer, for me, is quite simple. I created the Brainerd Foundation as a way to give back and support the causes that my family and I cared for deeply.

As a native of Oregon, I grew up hiking, wandering in the forests, and enjoying the outdoors. Conservation of the Pacific Northwest environment was something I felt strongly about...it was a "heart felt" connection. The Brainerd Foundation is focused specifically on environmental protection of the Northwest. The geographic and programmatic focus made sense given my roots and passion for preserving the greatness of this region.

My sister, Sherry, shared my interests in the environment so her involvement on the Board has been a wonderful way we could work together as adults. This work over the past seven years has proven to be invigorating, challenging, and extremely rewarding, though there is a lot of work left to be done.

I first considered forming the Foundation when I was ready to leave my career in the high-tech world. At the time, there were a lot of important decisions to consider- how to structure the foundation, how to define the focus, tax and legal implications. I sought out the help and advice of many people. I talked to people in the environmental community about the focus of the foundation. I spoke with lawyers and accountants. I also talked to other families about their experiences in establishing a family foundation...what they had learned, what they would advise.

I wish I had a copy of *Splendid Legacy* back then. It would have been an invaluable resource. The book brings together a wealth of information and offers insightful guidance from people at the top of the field. It is a comprehensive guide for families as they consider the important, lasting decisions of forming a family foundation.

In the course of my conversations with those experts and families back in the mid-90s, I was also asking them what I could do to play a broader role in helping to engage more families in philanthropy in our region. It took me only a few lunches to realize that there was a real opportunity to create some innovative avenues for newer families to get more engaged in their community and to enable them to become more philanthropic. I had a strong personal conviction about not only my personal responsibility, but my role in encouraging other families and individuals to get into philanthropy.

That feeling and what I heard people say led me to found Social Venture Partners (SVP) back in late '97. The dual mission of SVP is to provide financial and human capital to local nonprofits to help them build their organizational capacity and to act as a catalyst and stimulus for accelerating individual and family philanthropy. The idea has taken off in ways we never could have expected, and there are now hundreds of members in Seattle and SVP groups in about 20 cities around North America. Many SVP members have newly formed giving vehicles or are in the process of forming family foundations to further the causes they care about and leave a lasting legacy.

It has been inspiring to watch other families create and further their philanthropic work. Without any strategic plan to tell them to, a number of families have created a giving circle called Social Venture Kids to involve their own teenaged kids in philanthropy at an early age. When we asked SVP Seattle members "If you were having a great experience in SVP in 3–5 year what would you be doing?" one of the most frequent answers given was to "involve my family and kids in philanthropy more fully." And at the conclusion of a seminar we offered last year on family philanthropy, one of our members remarked, "I got everything I wanted and more. I walked away with illuminating clarity as to my philanthropy mission for the first time in my life. It all came together."

One of the unexpected things we have learned through SVP is the power and value of a peer network in which families can learn from and collaborate with each other. I would strongly encourage you to find lots of peers that are going through the same decisions you are exploring as you read *Splendid Legacy*.

To bring all of this full circle, my wife, Debbi, and I had an idea. About 4 years ago, we walked around a 255-acre patch of second growth forest, wetlands, and abandoned streams on Bainbridge Island across Elliott Bay from our home in Seattle. And now for the past 4 years, we have worked with hundreds of local citizens and families to bring the Puget Sound Environmental Learning Center to life on those 255 acres.

For Debbi and me, the PSELC is a wonderful and humbling way to bring together our love of the environment, the joy of seeing kids learn and develop a sense of stewardship, and our passion for engaging more and more people in their communities, the environment, and philanthropy. We hope you will come visit us on Bainbridge Island if you ever come to Seattle! I have come full circle from where my sister, Sherry, and I started almost a decade ago now. And I hope my philanthropy will enable me to create even more new circles in the decades ahead.

Paul Brainerd

Founder, Brainerd Foundation, Social Venture Partners Seattle,
& Puget Sound Environmental Learning Center

CREATING YOUR FAMILY FOUNDATION

Values, Mission, and Family Involvement

I

FIGURES

THE FOUNDER'S HOPES
From Values to Vision

by Virginia M. Esposito

Congratulations! You're establishing a private grantmaking foundation and you've decided to share the process with members of your family. The potential to meet and support wonderful people and organizations doing important work fills you with anticipation; you'll have the opportunity to contribute to society in ways few ever experience. You are about to enjoy what the late family foundation trustee, Paul Ylvisaker, called a "rare privilege." You've begun to appreciate what a tremendous personal responsibility and awesome public trust your new venture represents. And then, the self-questioning begins:

- Should I put my trusted legal advisor on the board?
- Who will help with staff duties?
- Should I accept proposals or seek out grantees?
- Should my foundation exist in perpetuity?
- How will I manage investments?
- Should my foundation make a few large grants or a greater number of smaller ones?

And so on.

As you begin to look for answers to these and the other questions you will likely have, you will quickly discover that no "one size fits all" solutions exist. Founders, families, and the community interests they serve determine the individual character of every family foun-

dation. Practices that work well for one family — even one with similar asset size and program interests — may not work for you. But that doesn't mean you have to start from scratch or even that you're on your own. Although the perfect solution for one family foundation may not be right for you, knowing the range of common practice is a great benefit. When you consider all the foundation policies and practices detailed in this guidebook, you will likely find some that feel like they might work for you. Or, you might even decide to experiment with a new way of doing things that no one has tried before.

But, by what measure will you make those decisions? And, how can you make

sense of all the issues that surround such decisions?

No ready-made answers fit all situations, but a set of questions does exist that can provide a framework for considering all your philanthropic options and opportunities. By thinking through your feelings and wishes about each of these questions — either alone or together with those you hope to involve in your new endeavor — you will be designing a blueprint for the foundation you are creating. And although you may not yet know how you feel about all the options (you may not even know all the decisions you must make), the best place to start is with the motivation that brought you to create the foundation in the first place. Some of the questions and issues you will be addressing include:

- Questions of values: understanding what inspires and motivates you;
- Questions of mission: linking decisionmaking to your goals;
- What are you trying to accomplish?
- How would you like to be involved in and manage your giving?
- What is your giving style and what are your giving interests?
- Questions of family involvement: bringing others into this work with purpose and integrity;
- Creating a community of concern;
- What kind of support will you need?
- Creating a splendid legacy.

Questions of Values:
Understanding What Inspires and Motivates You

Why are you interested in philanthropy and community involvement?

At the heart of your decision to start a family foundation — and the best place to start your philanthropic inquiry — is determining what motivated you to take the initial step. Why are you interested in philanthropy and in being involved in your community? Your motivation is likely to play a big part in determining what you'll do and how you'll do it.

For some, establishing a private foundation came about as a result of financial planning. Our American public policy, including our tax code, encourages private initiatives for the public good. But tax planning alone may not be enough to sustain the energy and commitment a family foundation requires. As a California donor once reported, "taxes got me in the door, but they didn't keep me in the room."

Consider other motivations that may be at play. What is it — in your character, background, and experience — that prompted you to pursue a charitable mission? In talking with hundreds of donors, six personal characteristics are most often mentioned:

- **Faith and spirituality.** Every religious or faith-based tradition includes tenets that encourage concern for others. Whether referred to as charity, tzedakah, sadaqah, or even love — traditions of faith call on those who share a spiritual heritage to give to others. More and more, donors are articulating the spiritual link between their faith and the decision to give as well as to the choices they will make in that giving.

- **Traditions.** Many foundation founders talk about the family traditions that shaped their charitable conscience — even if they are the first member of their family to create a foundation. A fourth generation family foundation trustee remembers the three boxes on her childhood bookshelf. Each box held an equal portion of her allowance: one-third for spending; one-third for savings; and one-third for charity. Her earliest understanding of money was that it had three, equally important, purposes. A Texas donor talks about his family tradition of celebrating holidays by participating as a family in a volunteer, community service project. Whatever your particular traditions, they play a powerful role in initiating a lifetime commitment.

- **Mentors.** Most of us can point to people in our pasts who had a profound impact on our lives. A grandparent, a parent, a relative, a teacher, a colleague, or a neighbor — someone who provided encouragement at an important

"To give away money is an easy matter and in any man's power, but to decide to whom to give it and how large and when, and for what purpose and how, is neither in every man's power nor an easy matter. Hence, it is that such excellence is rare, praiseworthy, and noble."

— ARISTOTLE

moment, counseled during a difficult situation, helped with a career move, or taught simply, but deeply, by personal example. Interviews with foundation donors reveal that most mentors are an immediate family member (often a grandparent) and that a great many are not persons of great wealth.

Personal interests and experiences. Many founders note that their philanthropic point-of-entry came through an issue of special, personal importance or an event that was deeply felt and, therefore, transforming. A lifelong interest in the arts or the environment might motivate the desire to give dollars and time. A personal experience such as the death of a loved one to breast cancer or receiving a much-needed educational scholarship are examples of life events that can lead someone to appreciate the value of private giving and compel them to charitable action.

Community involvement and volunteering. Many entrepreneurs who eventually become generous philanthropists were active in their communities long before they had the potential or inclination to give away significant amounts of money. Some speak eloquently about volunteer experiences that began in their childhood. Volunteering at a homeless shelter, serving as a docent for a museum or historical site, serving on a nonprofit board, or sharing a family custom of working at a soup kitchen at Thanksgiving — all indicate a charitable inclination and can also indicate a philanthropic tradition to come.

Business skills and experience. In a 1998 series of interviews with new donors, many mentioned that a business colleague who was already an active donor prompted their interest in philanthropy. The willingness of their colleague-donors to talk about their experiences had encouraged them to think about what they might accomplish as a donor. The power of these stories may be an indication that the 21st century workplace will play a role in stimulating charitable interest and provide a ready-made network of philanthropic support — much like churches, temples, and mosques have done in the past. One of the great opportunities family foundations often offer donors is the chance to use their business skills in different ways and for different purposes. Just as your education, professional skills, and experience contributed to your financial success, they may now be used to contribute to your community in a different way.

What Donors Name as Guiding Values

The sum of these possibilities — personal influences, interests, and experiences — together with the source of inspiration and motivation for charitable giving may very well be your guiding values. Compassion, justice, fairness, and respect for others are just a few of the values most frequently named by donors as guiding values.

Interestingly, in cases where family members and others inherit responsibility for a foundation where no specific instructions have been left behind,

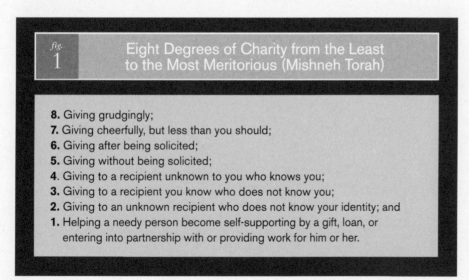

fig. 1 Eight Degrees of Charity from the Least to the Most Meritorious (Mishneh Torah)

8. Giving grudgingly;

7. Giving cheerfully, but less than you should;

6. Giving after being solicited;

5. Giving without being solicited;

4. Giving to a recipient unknown to you who knows you;

3. Giving to a recipient you know who does not know you;

2. Giving to an unknown recipient who does not know your identity; and

1. Helping a needy person become self-supporting by a gift, loan, or entering into partnership with or providing work for him or her.

> *"Over time, family members change and program priorities change; what holds the family and its philanthropy together is the legacy of its values. This legacy provides continuity and our donor family believes it is that continuity — the family values — that gives the family philanthropy its special character."*
>
> — BRUCE SIEVERS executive director, Walter and Elise Haas Fund (1983-2002)

many successfully engage in a process of considering the donor's values. Values can offer insight and guidance as to the direction of the philanthropy. Similarly, in the second and third generations of family foundations, when a family is trying to determine what they can best pursue as a family, understanding both the founder's and their own shared values can be more helpful than the more elusive process of finding shared program interests.

Questions of Mission:
Linking Decisionmaking to Your Goals

What are you trying to accomplish? How would you like to be involved in and manage your giving? What is your giving style and what are your giving interests?

Just as you had many motivations for considering establishing a family foundation, you probably had just as many — usually more than one — reasons to follow through. There are hundreds of decisions you'll make about your foundation and your grantmaking. Understanding your goals — what you

are trying to accomplish — is critical to making sense of those decisions.

A West Coast family foundation donor regrets the first few years of his family foundation. He recounts how he stumbled through his grantmaking pretty much in the same way he had before the foundation was established. He reports he had been, "sold his family foundation as a financial planning tool." He had no idea what it was, what it could do, or what he wanted to do with it. In this case, a single, external factor had prompted the formation of the foundation. After several years, he met another donor who introduced him to a family foundation conference, grantmaking colleagues and the world of possibility. Together with his family, they

began a process of thinking about what they wanted to do and how they wanted to do it. Today, they are enthusiastically active in managing their foundation, in working with their grantees, and in finding creative grantmaking opportunities.

What Are You Trying to Accomplish?

When hundreds of family foundation donors were asked what they hoped to accomplish through their foundation, the responses were strikingly consistent. Six of the most often cited responses were:

- **Give back**. Without a doubt, most donors said they hoped to give back. For some this meant giving back in a universal sense; they have been fortunate, and hope to share that good fortune with others.

> *"One day Alice came to a fork in the road and saw a Cheshire cat in a tree. 'Which road do I take?' she asked. 'Where do you want to go?' was his response. 'I don't know,' Alice answered. 'Then,' said the cat, 'it doesn't matter.'"*
>
> — LEWIS CARROLL, *Through the Looking Glass*

5

For many, it meant giving back to the community where the family grew up and prospered. In such cases, donors wanted to acknowledge and show appreciation for the region that is the family's, and therefore, the foundation's hometown. In a recent survey by the Council on Foundations, about two-thirds of the family foundations in the survey sample stated that they make grants in the county where the wealth was made. Many of today's second- and third-generation family foundations, particularly those whose family members have moved away, perhaps entirely, from the hometown, are balancing the goal of giving back to their hometown with the logistical constraints of their current situation.

■ **Create a vehicle for working with family.** Some of the great advantages of choosing a family foundation include: the opportunity to accomplish something for and with your family; to instill a charitable ethic; to promote individual volunteering and giving; to balance issues of great wealth and privilege with social concern and responsibility; to raise responsible, community-minded children; to create a legacy of family giving that may extend over several generations; and to provide a place where the family can work together on issues of great importance — beyond the circumstances of the family and other family enterprises.

"Building a Foundation on the fragile relationships that characterize any family is a precarious enterprise, but the returns are worth the risk and all the tensions that go with it."

— PAUL YLVISAKER

In choosing to establish a family foundation, a donor implicitly acknowledges two sets of goals: goals for sharing the experience with family members and goals for their community involvement. The ongoing dynamism and challenge is to keep those goals in balance and in context. Family is intensely personal and complex. The decision to serve a foundation involves a significant personal commitment — a commitment to a public trust and to an institution created as a result of public policy to serve a public good. The potential conflicts of this dynamic are obvious. But so should be the joys and benefits. After all, it is this same dynamic upon which our own democracy depends.

■ **Express your values and explore your interests.** The values we profess and cherish guide our everyday decisions and actions. Our personal interests often drive our career choices and how we spend our free time. Philanthropy is a remarkable opportunity for those who wish to give practical expression to their values or to explore a special interest beyond a career or hobby. The pursuit of social justice or an interest in advancing medical research both can be sources of charitable purpose.

■ **Avoid taxes.** Yes, among all this talk of donors who come to philanthropy out of selflessness and greater purpose, some also come principally as an estate-planning vehicle. And if it starts that way, isn't our tax policy doing exactly what the framers intended? Those trying to get a private philanthropic tradition started in other countries envy the fact that the American system encourages such action. But, as noted above, although an effective catalyst, taxes are poor motivation for sustaining a philanthropic program. And, although tax benefits may be sufficient to keep the interest of the original donor (who enjoyed the tax advantage), other motivations are required for succeeding generations.

■ **Use your talents and skills for a different purpose.** Although donors may have been very successful in a profession or business, many are very new to grantmaking. As a consequence, they may be uncertain about the "rules" and feel a little hesitant about moving forward. Still, most have enormous confidence in the talent or skill that helped make them successful. You may see great possibilities in applying your skills to the nonprofit world. The communications entrepreneur may want to contribute that expertise, the investment banker can lend that skill, and so on. One of the many unsung gifts of high technology donors is their real appreciation for the back-office costs nonprofit organizations face. Donors who know the value of computer systems, phone service, and websites may be more likely to understand the value of making grants for operating costs.

■ **Support the people and institutions that have been important to you.** Many donors establish a foundation to provide a framework or structure for their giving. They have been active in the community, in their church, their alma mater, and involved in a variety of causes. All of this involvement has provided the opportunity and reason for their giving. The advent of a foundation doesn't change that; donors know what issues and institutions they believe are important and intend to continue to support them. Consider the new foundation donor who makes a generous gift to her university or the donor whose foundation makes a grant to the homeless shelter on whose board he has served for many years. Your goal for your family foundation may include support for causes you have supported for some time; whether and how you are made aware of other opportunities and what will happen in future generations may be questions you want to consider.

Regardless of the goal or goals founders may have for their family foundations, they often cite one other intention: to make a difference. What this means varies from donor to donor. For some, it implies specific kinds of grants and measurable outcomes. For others, it may be the more intangible, but just as personally satisfying, feeling that comes from trying to do something worthwhile. And, although the desire to make a difference may not come with step-by-step instructions, the implied potential and promise make it the perfect goal and hope for a new family foundation.

How Would You Like to Be Involved in and Manage Your Giving?

Now that you've had the chance to consider why you're doing this and what you hope to accomplish, the next question is *how*. The question of your personal involvement is important. Your personality, time constraints, style, and the availability of a trusted network of family members and advisors are all likely to determine your preferences. Similarly, the management style you've brought to other tasks, business pursuits, even your home life, will likely be reflected in your management of the foundation. A few questions to get you thinking:

■ **Are you a hands-on person?** Many entrepreneurs are successful because of their careful attention to detail. They see every aspect of their business through and are involved in every decision. Most "first generation" foundations report that founders continue that hands-on approach when they take on their role in the family foundation. Other founders like to provide general guidance (set policy, review procedures, take part in the voting, etc.) but are content for others to play an equally or even more active role. Still others take a hands-off approach: they are content to see others with the passion, interest, or time take the lead and give shape to the foundation's future. Understanding your own style — with both candor and integrity — can have an important effect on early management of the foundation and how others learn and participate in the process.

■ **Are you more comfortable with a formal or informal atmosphere?** As a new donor, you may prefer the comfort of structure and procedure. Some donors like forms, want to see a set grants schedule, and find having a well-specified plan helps in effective decisionmaking. Others see their foundation as an opportunity to be responsive and spontaneous. You like to get a phone call about a promising new nonprofit and go off to visit them. You want to make grants as need and opportunities arise. In either case — or more likely some combination of the two — understanding your style and communicating it appropriately to those involved with the foundation are fundamental to many other management decisions.

Will your decisionmaking be donor driven, by consensus, or democratic? Many family foundations begin life with a strong — dominant — patriarch or matriarch. Others take their foundation participation cues from their expected roles in the family or other business matters. But even in cases where the founder genuinely wants the full participation of others, fellow trustees, advisors, and family members may defer to the founder out of respect and affection.

In other family foundations, making decisions by consensus allows for both good discussion and minimal hard feelings. In such cases, decisions will be reached based on what all agree they can live with. Board decisions are reached by mutual consent and no one is so uncomfortable as to "veto." In the democratic family foundation, majority vote rules the day and the decision. No extended discussion or process, although the

potential for "you vote for mine, I'll vote for yours" always exists.

How long will the foundation exist? It has only been in recent years that the life expectancy of family foundations has become a frequent topic for discussion. In the past, it was assumed that donors chose to create private foundations — in part— because of the ability to establish a permanent philanthropic legacy. In fact, when the rare family foundation chose to spend down over a predetermined, limited time, or split into multiple, smaller foundations, it was generally considered to be the result of some problem or failure. No more.

Overwhelmingly, founders still say they created their private family foundation with the intention that it exist in perpetuity, but it is increasingly common for founders to raise the question of perpetuity in the earliest years of foundation existence. And you, the donor, do have options.

One option is to establish the foundation for a limited period. Some founders who want to make a significant impact on a problem or program area choose to concentrate giving in a specific timeframe; 10 years is a common example of such a timeframe. Others choose to establish the foundation for their lifetime, their lifetime plus 10 years, or the lifetime of their children. These donors

are interested in an experience that can be shared with those they know and love. They may also feel that those who knew them can best carry out their intentions for the foundation.

Those who choose to establish their foundation in perpetuity are warmed by the thought of something that links the family across time and generations, creating a legacy of giving for their family and the good work they will do over the years. These families are challenged to consider goals and policies that can stand the test of time when establishing the foundation. For example, a policy that every blood relative should have the opportunity to serve on the foundation board may not be workable with a foundation established in perpetuity.

Do you like to work collaboratively or independently? In this case, your preferences may indicate whether you seek donor collaboratives and other opportunities to work together with other funders or choose " to go it alone."

Do you want to seek out or be responsive to grantmaking opportunities? Some donors are very active in their communities and know the organizations or types of organizations they want to fund. They may enjoy the exploration process of matching their interests with possible grantee organizations. Others claim that the great learning and fun in the giving process is hearing about all the wonderful things nonprofit organizations are doing. The "over the transom" applications provide the interest and the appeal of funding. Both cases imply different time demands and management strategies.

What Is Your Giving Style and What Are Your Giving Interests?

As you prepare to make your first grants or learn more about the process by doing, earlier questions of goals and involvement prepare you for very specific decisions about grantmaking. None of these decisions is hard and fast. You may choose to have a foundation "toolbox" that allows you to make many different kinds of grants to many different kinds of organizations for many different reasons. Still, it may be helpful to understand your options because they can provide good guidance for your grants review and send clear messages to those you hope to fund.

- **Are you more interested in issues or institutions?** Some donors are driven to contribute to the arts, public education, or other program areas of special interest. Others feel most comfortable getting to know and support institutions and organizations — a university, nonprofit clinic, or children's museum might be the recipient of regular support. Your preferences will determine the kind of background information you'll

need to make grants, and the relationships you develop.

- **Do you want to fund special projects or operating costs?** At some point you are going to think about how to focus spending of the precious philanthropic dollars you steward. Will you choose to fund only the special programs and projects nonprofits offer? Or will you go beyond?

Some donors believe their philanthropic dollars are best spent taking advantage of these project opportunities. Because they see how limited their grants dollars are, they don't want nonprofits to come to rely on them for support of day-to-day operations.

In recent years, grantmakers have focused attention on the need to ensure that good nonprofits have the organizational capacity to do good work. Some have added grant dollars to a project to help with marketing and communications, human resources and fundraising — even general operating support. After all, they reason, what good does it do for the women's shelter to run a great prenatal healthcare program if they can't pay the light bill? Other foundations are doing both: they make a special project grant and add a percent on top for general administrative costs/overhead.

- **Seed grants or sticking with it?** Some foundations love being in on

the beginning of a great thing. They have a tolerance for risk and the sense of possibility to help something get started. Others prefer to identify a number of grantee organizations and stick with them. They fund them over a longer period — even when times are bad — reasoning that it may just be during the bad times that a good organization needs help the most.

Family foundations are more likely to be loyal to a grantee over a longer period than other types of foundations. Yet some family foundations worry that providing funding over too long a period may generate a feeling of dependency; the grantee may take the foundation funding for granted and not seek new funding sources. A confounding dilemma until your experiences reveal the pattern you're most happy with.

- **Will you identify grantees or accept proposals?** The answer to this question plays a major role in determining the kind of grantmaking you'll do and the management you'll need. Accepting proposals means communicating your interests and availability to prospective grantees and having a system in place to manage the proposal review process. Seeking out grantees requires a greater effort to research your interests and relevant organizations.

Questions of Family Involvement:
Bringing Others into this Work with Purpose and Integrity

Whom would you like to involve? Why? How? And, what kind of support will you need?

The fact that you've chosen to establish a private family foundation suggests that you plan to include family members in the enterprise. You have other options if that is not your intention. You might have chosen to be an individual advisor to a fund in a public foundation or established a private foundation for your lifetime. You could have endowed a favorite nonprofit organization directly. Or you might have created a private foundation or other giving vehicle and involved members of your business or personal circle, community leaders, or program experts in your areas of interest. Many other possibilities are available to help you achieve your charitable goals — each rich in potential.

You may also wish to share in the joy and responsibility of the foundation — and the decisionmaking process — with non-family members. Most family foundations report having a non-family member on the board, usually a trusted legal, financial, or business advisor. Many others involve non-family members not only as trustees but also as staff, advisors, consultants, and contract help.

Identifying your trusted circle of advisors or governors is a critical early step. And, because this area of establishing the foundation deals directly with those you love and value, this is often an especially significant source of concern, not just in the early days of the foundation but also in ways that can play out over many generations.

Many donors report that they were asked to name board members before they had a chance to give serious thought to what they needed and were looking for in the governing body. For this reason, and natural inclination, many founders focus first on who is going to serve and less on why they will ask them to serve and how they might provide that service. Countless founders don't share their intentions to name close individuals as trustees and advisors much less share their reasons and hopes for doing so.

Creating a Community of Concern

In surrounding yourself with the expertise, encouragement, and energy you'll need to fulfill your charitable purpose, family foundation trustee David Dodson says you are "creating a community of concern."

As you create your community of concern, think about all the possible voices that can add to both the quality of the process and your ability to serve your community:

- **The founder.** While seemingly obvious, few founders actually think about the role they want to play, particularly with regard to others. How will power and responsibility be shared? How well understood and articulated are your intentions? What are your expectations for adherence to your giving patterns and interests after you step down? Who will chair the foundation board? What sort of leadership plan — including identifying future leaders, training, and transition planning — would you like to see?

- **Spouses.** Frequently, a donor couple rather than an individual donor starts a family foundation. If that is the case with your foundation, how will you work together in leadership roles? Will you serve as equal leaders or will authority rotate? Are intentions and plans jointly established? What about succession? And, a sensitive and difficult question: what happens in the event of divorce or death?

- **Children.** The decision to involve children in the foundation may present both the most complicated and rewarding issues you'll face as you consider foundation leadership and involvement. As parents, we want to ensure that our children have a good home, a good education, and some

fig. 2 — Suggestions for Involving Others in the Family Foundation

- **Be clear about the roles and expectations each person will play.** Writing down roles and expectations and making them understood — even before the invitation is extended — can save confusion and pain later on.

- **Consider developing a statement of board qualifications and expectations.** The universe of people that might be included is vast; it may not seem like it in the earliest days of the foundation, but it gets larger as time goes on. Board qualifications can help family members and others understand what they must bring to the table; board expectations can help them understand what they must do in service to the foundation.

- **Plan early.** Determining whether your children's spouses will be eligible for board service, or age limits for board membership, is always easier when neither possibility is in the immediate offing. It becomes more difficult when you're talking about real possibilities and real people. If you are forced to create policy in the face of an immediate need, you don't have the chance to consider thoughtfully and objectively what's in the best interest of the foundation. At that point, it becomes very personal, very awkward, and potentially very painful.

- **Visit the question of managing both your hopes for your family and the giving** — reinforcing the foundation's responsibility as a public trust — early and often. Appointing family members to the board can be the first time that individual family member's interests might compete with the philanthropic interests of the giving program.

- **Consider setting a terms and rotation policy for service on the board.** Such a policy can help to renew the giving program, refresh the participants, and allow many more people to participate.

- **Recognize that there are lots of ways others can be involved — beyond board service.** Committee membership, site visit participation, and advisory boards are just a few of the creative ways founders have engaged a creative circle. If participation in the philanthropy is perceived to be limited to board service, sheer logistical constraints will force you to disappoint many people. Moreover, you'll also miss the opportunity to engage a range of thoughtful, experienced voices.

- **Consider engaging an experienced family foundation consultant to help you and your board work through these issues.** Working with someone who is familiar with foundation practices, and sensitive to family dynamics and process, can help you to get off to a good start, set the stage for the quality of your future interaction, and let you participate fully in the conversation.

measure of financial well being — the good things. But we also want to ensure that we do what we can to raise good children. Founders speak movingly of their hope that the foundation can provide an experience that fosters generosity, community involvement, empathy, and responsibility.

All these good intentions can be realized, but success is most likely if children are well introduced to the foundation and the family shares the goal of community service. At what age should that introduction occur? Opportunities abound for introducing children to giving and volunteering beginning in early childhood. They can appreciate the message of *The Giving Tree*, understand why you're leaving for the weekend to attend a foundation retreat, participate in a community service project or go along on an age-appropriate site visit … the possibilities are as

fig. 3	Creating a Community of Concern: Reflections of a Family Foundation Trustee

David Dodson, a trustee of the Mary Reynolds Babcock Foundation, a family foundation in North Carolina, and a close observer of the Irwin-Sweeney-Miller family giving programs in Indiana, observes that a family's values and motivations are critical to the family foundation. But, he continues, the great purpose of a family foundation should not be the perpetuation of family interests but the impulse to be of value to something beyond the family circle.

Dodson believes that what characterizes the two family foundations he knows best are the curiosity and compassion with which they approach their foundation work. What families choose to commit to and support should reflect their passions, he advises. But it doesn't end there. Dodson encourages creative family foundations to ask themselves how they can take what they care about and use it to build a community of concern that is alert and responsive to changing circumstances. What the family knows and loves is the logical place to begin a rich process of philanthropic inquiry into what the community needs and how they can serve it.

Dodson notes that the Miller and Babcock families don't seek to perpetuate old ways of doing things but strive in each generation to understand the needs and opportunities facing their communities of interest. The issues may change or they may stay the same, but what a family foundation perpetuates is their posture of caring and compassion.

Dodson observes that the family foundation that is able to construct a view of their giving with the community to be served firmly in the center is able to surround that core with an even more vibrant family circle. He says that such families are motivated to be of service outside the family and are likely to be both curious and compassionate in identifying ways to use their assets.

Those assets may even include advisors and networks outside the immediate family. He cites his fellow Babcock trustee, Carol Zippert, and her assertion that family foundations can include those who are members of the "family of blood" and those who are members of the "family of the heart" — related by interests and values but not genealogy. But, he cautions, if families think a foundation may be the instrument to save a troubled family, this is not it.

endless as your imagination and commitment. Begin when you think it appropriate for your family, but don't wait too long.

Between the ages of 18 and 35, your children are working on their education, establishing careers, even starting families. Free time and vacation days are in short supply. Build a community conscience in them early, and work with them to determine if their busy schedules and a role in the foundation can peacefully and satisfactorily co-exist. If that's not possible, let them know they'll be welcome when their circumstances and interests change.

Sadly, it is all too common that adult children of foundation donors only "discover" the family foundation and their responsibility for it — a recipe for confusion, distress, even resentment — in their 40s and 50s. They may even be dealing with the death of a parent. What may be most sad is the opportunity missed; the opportunity parents and children might have shared in building a tradition of charitable service.

Will all your children serve? Will there be opportunities to inform and involve them beyond board service? Will there be a board qualifications/expectations process or will all children serve based on birthright? What about adopted or stepchildren? And, again, a related but painful question: how does the philanthropy affect other financial plans for or expectations of the children?

Open communication about money matters can prevent a situation where adult children feel anger that their "inheritance" was the philanthropy rather than a personal bequest, and they didn't know about it. Visiting troubling issues of power, money, and poor communication on a nascent foundation distorts and detracts from the public purpose and will likely torpedo the founder's hopes for a family endeavor.

- **Parents.** In an era of great fortunes made by the young, founders may wish to involve family, but have not yet committed to a partner or had children. These donors often involve their parents in the process. Parents may have long histories of community involvement, they may have retired and have more discretionary time available for philanthropic initiatives, and philanthropy may represent a wonderful new way for an entrepreneur and his or her parents to work together and get to know one another in a new, rewarding way. In such cases, again, role clarification is critical because the normal parent/child power dynamic may be altered.

- **Other family members.** In some cases, donors reach out to siblings, nieces, nephews, and cousins to involve them in the giving. This, too, can be a rewarding experience. Issues

of qualifications and responsibilities are much the same as they are for your children. A particular difference may arise in cases where the only significant family wealth is the founder's and that wealth will pass only to the founder's direct line. Then, sensitive issues can arise: power; prestige; even the ability to take time off and pay one's own expenses to participate in foundation meetings and activities.

- **Legal, financial, and program advisors.** The counsel offered by your circle of advisors is key to success. But what role will they play? A board role can be enormously helpful as advisors lend the expertise that strengthens your deliberations and builds your confidence. Advisors can also dominate if they use their expertise to "shut down" discussion. All new donors need expert legal and financial advisors. Program advisors can help by adding expertise in the areas to be funded. Talk candidly with your advisors about your relationship and your need for their guidance. Determine if the boardroom, an advisory committee, or a consultancy/contract is the best way to access that guidance.

- **Friends and colleagues.** An increasing number of donors engage business colleagues and trusted friends early in their philanthropy. Respect and trust gained over the years become important sources of encouragement and support.

- **Community representatives.** As a foundation donor, you have the extraordinary chance to engage those the philanthropy will seek to serve. If you're working in another part of the country (or world) or with a community or population group with which you are unfamiliar, the voices of your constituency groups can be powerful: keeping you both informed and sensitive to special circumstances and new developments.

What Kind of Support Will You Need?

Once your closest circle, your community of concern, is in place, the work of the foundation can begin. (A world of resources, educational offerings, and colleagues await you.) You will determine how grantmaking, governance, and finances will be managed. You'll also quickly realize that the field of organized philanthropy offers an increasing array of programs and services for grantmaking foundations.

A few questions to get you thinking about your support network:

- **What kind of staffing and administration will you need?** Based on your grantmaking goals, costs, and personal preferences, options can range from an office with multiple staff members dedicated to managing the giving, to shared staffing, or a part-time administrator, to taking advantage of the family business or family office. Law

Katharine Mountcastle, daughter of the founder of the Mary Reynolds Babcock Foundation, was once asked what it was like to have Paul Ylvisaker on the board of her family's foundation. Ylvisaker, internationally respected for his philanthropic experience and wisdom, was standing with Mountcastle and the questioner expected to hear a gushing tribute to his profound influence. "Oh, that's easy," *she quickly replied.* "We all behave better when he's in the room."

firms, community foundations and other public foundations, banks and other financial institutions, and many entities offer opportunities for foundation administration and support.

- **Will family members be available as staff — on a volunteer or paid basis?** Staffing with family members can provide wonderful synergy and continuity because family members often find it easy to trust those who share the heritage and circumstances of the family and the foundation. Still, the choice of family staff can also raise difficult questions of performance, accountability, and power sharing.

- **What kind of legal, financial (including investment management), and other organizational expertise will you need?**

- **How will expertise in the programs areas or communities you intend to fund be accessed?** Are advisory boards, guest speakers, community panels, or other options of interest to you?

- **How can the experiences of other foundations and families be helpful to you, and how will you reach out?** Your fellow foundation founders, trustees, and advisors are a generous group of people in every sense of the word. They are always willing to share their experiences, offer an idea, and welcome you to this important work. Regional and national associations of grantmakers, affinity (special interest) groups, donor collaboratives, and giving circles are just a few of the communities of grantmakers available to you.

- **How will you stay in touch with the nonprofit world?** Will you encourage your family and trustees to serve on boards and as volunteers? What about associations and organizations of nonprofits or those that specifically encourage grantmaker/grantee communications and learning?

- **Pages and pages of resource material** — both in print and on the web — are available to you. **How can that material be prioritized given the time you have available to read through it?**

Creating a Splendid Legacy

The framework of questions detailed in this chapter offers you a way to think through your hopes and your intentions. In a study and book on the development of family foundations to be released by the National Center for Family Philanthropy, researcher and author Kelin Gersick calls this critical early phase, *Mission and Dream.* He links the thoughtfulness of this phase to the path the family foundation will travel in succeeding generations.

"Providing the guidance of a statement of donor intent is not the 'dead hand of the past' as many claim. It is, once again, a 'helping hand' that provides insight into the values, vision, and purpose of the foundation."

— CHARLES HAMILTON Founder, The Hamilton Foundation

You are, in effect, articulating what some people have called *donor intent*. This has been a much-debated concept in past years. Some see donor intent as the "dead hand" (implying that the wishes and interests of founders can't possibly be relevant to current and future stewards). Others see it as "sacred shackles" (implying that there can't possibly be a good reason to re-visit, re-interpret, and renew the founder's vision).

Both positions miss something special to family foundations: the glorious complexity of motivations and hopes: some profound, others quirky, some perfectly understandable, others surprising or even puzzling. It is this complexity, so personal to each founder and so relevant to his or her interests and choices, that guides the governance, grantmaking, and management of the foundation. In starting this venture by considering — once again — your motivations, hopes, and dreams, you will discover the vitality, the commitment, and ultimately, the contribution of your philanthropic participation.

A richer and more dynamic phrase to describe these dreams is donor legacy. It gets to the heart of what you are trying to accomplish … and why. It can speak to your hopes for those you would like to be involved … and why. The dreams for the communities to be served — the grantmaking strategies and the program interests — can be found by exploring your hopes for the legacy you are about to create. And whether you will choose to articulate very definite intentions or choose to leave little specific guidance, legacy speaks to the process of renewal that reenergizes the foundation with each new family member, trustee, grantee, advisor, and colleague.

Moving On

Having moved from values to vision, you are now ready to proceed from vision to action. In the next chapter, you will see how the building blocks of your family foundation — a values statement, a mission statement, and a plan for family involvement — can be put in place. Your work will be illuminated by the experiences and stories of dozens of families who have gone before. As you move into this new and rewarding place, the hopes and strengths of your family will guide you each step of the giving way.

BUILDING ON YOUR BEST HOPES
From Vision to Action

by Joseph Foote and Dorna L. Allen

F amily values, philanthropic mission, involvement of family members — these are the three great building blocks of a family foundation. Serious consideration of each of these is essential for guidance and direction for the philanthropy. Every founder will find it not only desirable but also ultimately necessary to address each of these building blocks.

The first chapter examined the founder's best hopes for the foundation and family throughout the philanthropic journey. This chapter offers a guide to the beginning steps of building a lasting family foundation. This chapter focuses on ways in which the founder and family can explore their personal and family values. From the bedrock of those values, they can fashion a mission for the foundation. Then they can address involvement of family members. The National Center for Family Philanthropy encourages founders to consider gathering up this

From Vision to Action: A Grantmaker's Odyssey

fig. 1

STEP 1: What are my values and my family's values?
Education: I was the first in my family to go to college. Education got me where I am today and has greatly enriched my personal life. As a family, we highly value the importance of education in preparing young people to be self sufficient, training them to be good citizens, and giving them the tools to pursue personal growth.

STEP 2: What values do we want reflected in our philanthropy?
We value opportunity for underprivileged youngsters who show high promise.

STEP 3: What values do we want to pursue in the family foundation Mission Statement?
Our family foundation supports enrichment programs and teacher training in the metropolitan public school system, with an emphasis on schools in underserved neighborhoods.

STEP 3: How can we implement the Mission Statement in Grantmaking Guidelines?
Our foundation welcomes proposals from nonprofit organizations that develop elementary school enrichment programs and appropriate teacher training for implementation.

STEP 5: What specific grantees are best suited to carry out the Mission?
We award a grant to the Wing School for a pilot enrichment and teacher training project.

STEP 6: How can we evaluate grantee performance and help improve it?
We process evaluation by school administrators, teachers, students, and parents to help us review our grant and look at the program for the coming year.

effort into three written statements: Family Values, Mission, and Family Involvement Statements.

In guiding the founder and family through this process, this chapter addresses three fundamental questions:
- What are your family values?
- What are your philanthropic goals?
- How can family members be involved in the foundation?

Descriptions follow of ways to develop Family Values, Mission, and Family Involvement Statements, what the contents might be, and how some family foundations have prepared them.

What Are Your Family Values?

Values are what we hold to be of the greatest personal importance and worth. Although seldom talked about, they show up in everything we think, say, and do. They directly influence our lives — motivating, activating, and directing. A penetrating look at these deeply held values can bring you and your family members to a new understanding and appreciation of each other.

For each founder about to open the door to philanthropy and walk into the world of family giving, values can show the way to an effective and fulfilling family foundation enterprise. What are your values and those of family members? How can you link those values to

the foundation to mission? A foundation built on family values can stand the test of time. As we learn more about ourselves and those closest to us, the more incentives we have to write the legacy of a family foundation built on common goals and commitments.

How Can You Identify Your Family Values?

How can a founder and family go about identifying and cataloging their values? Deeply held values come from many places, such as faith and spirituality,

traditions, mentors, personal interests and experiences, community involvement, etc. Founders have used various techniques to articulate and capture family values. Here are five:
- **Encourage family talks:** Start conversations, often informally, around the dining table and encourage family members to talk about their values;

- **Make a leadership statement:** Circulate a piece of writing about your dreams and aspirations for the foundation, based on values you hold dear;

---

fig. 2

Sources of One Man's Compassion

I have had a lifelong interest in how compassionate values are developed, nurtured, and activated. The formal research for my book, *The Charitable Impulse*, a study of wealth and social conscience in communities and cultures outside the United States, began while I was in residence at Nuffield College at Oxford University and Mishkenot Sha Ananim in Jerusalem, but the moral curiosity, the informal search, began in my father's church in the bayou regions of Louisiana. It took me later to the professional study of theology and peaked during my 14 years as president of the Council on Foundations.

I share this personal note to make the point that my concern with faith and philanthropy has deep and enduring roots. Yet, there is something of an irony in my personal experience. In the black church in which I spent my early years, the rivers of compassion ran deep. When we were hungry, we shared with one another. When we were sick, we cared for one another. However, we did not think of what we gave to others as philanthropy, because it was an act in which both the giver and the receiver benefited. We did not think for what we did for others as volunteering, because it was as much a moral imperative as an act of free will.

SOURCE: James A. Joseph, "Building a Foundation for Faith and Family Philanthropy," *Faith and Family Philanthropy: Grace, Gratitude, and Generosity*. Washington, DC: National Center for Family Philanthropy, 2001.

- **Draw on important family circumstances:** Look close to home for matters of overriding importance and concern to family members, and build on those concerns;

- **Think creatively and expansively:** Create safe conditions so that family members can open up and talk about dreams, vision, values, hopes, aspirations — the whole ball of wax; and

- **Research the family and the founder:** Particularly in posthumously established foundations, family members can learn about the founder's life, values, and reasons for creating the foundation.

Encouraging Family Talks Pays Off

Family talks about major issues were not exactly an institution in the hustle and bustle of the busy family of Jerry Taylor and his wife Nancy Bryant. He ran MCI Corporation, and she had her hands full with family and community responsibilities. When he retired, they created their long-dreamed-of family foundation and finally found time to kick back and look at the big picture. "We talked informally at first," Nancy Bryant says. "We are not a family given to meetings.

When we first sat down, to discuss the focus of the foundation, it was the first time that we had all sat down together to discuss something like this. I took the lead and asked Jerry and our son to think about the kinds of things that they considered important and that the foundation might support. What subjects? Which organizations?" Family members found that their values rested on concern for the elderly, a belief in the importance of education, and a passionate vision that computers were essential for the growth and development of young people. These values would later morph into the direction the foundation would take.

Making a Leadership Statement

A founder may want to offer a leadership statement to family members. The statement might speak about the core of his or her vision, about the passion behind the idea of the foundation. In describing the origins of that core vision, that idea — be it a sense of caring, of giving back, of spiritually guided giving — the founder can share the deepest meaning of his or her philanthropy with the family. It's risky for a family leader who has seldom brought up values, but it can be inspiring to other family members, particularly the younger generation.

"Dad had a dream that he wrote out during his last month with us," Frank Gibney says. The "Dream" encourages us to meet periodically to share our lives, learn more about each other, and

---

fig. 3

Examples of Family Values

Here are some examples of typical family values:

"We believe strongly in family history and tradition. We have family reunions every few years. We all go to family moments — graduations, marriages, baptisms, and funerals. We all show up."

"Our family keeps in touch. We're on the phone and the Internet all the time with the grandparents, the parents. We help each other out with advice and support."

"Our family takes our name very seriously. We have a lot of pride in our ancestors. We have a history, and we're proud to be part of that history."

"We care about our community and take part in community affairs."

"We value diversity of opinion. Our family members represent a wide range of views."

"Our family values education. Any time any family member graduates from anything, it's a big deal."

become educated about how each of us might contribute in a meaningful way toward making life better for others. "The children are now taking his dream to a new level," Gibney says. The ones investing the time to better understand the challenges facing those who we are chartered to help will pave the way for others to follow. "The Family's diverse background will only help to strengthen our foundation and make our grants more effective."

GOOD ADVICE ➤ "The problem with oral tradition is that family members often have different memories."

CURTIS W. MEADOWS, JR. PRESIDENT EMERITUS, THE MEADOWS FOUNDATION

Drawing on Family Circumstances
Family circumstances can be so powerful that discussion of family values starts right there. Don and Jane O'Keefe have long been personally committed to helping the less fortunate, with special emphasis on children, health, and education of the deaf. With profound conviction, they value the lives of all children with special needs, believing that every child should have a chance at a full life. The idea of a family foundation arose when O'Keefe sold his business and found himself in an unexpectedly favorable financial position. "We have a special interest in the handicapped, since our youngest daughter is deaf and has cerebral palsy," O'Keefe says.

fig. 4

Writing a Letter to the Family

I always encourage the founding couple to take the time and make the effort to write a lengthy statement, almost like a letter to the family. I advise them to state their reasons for starting the family foundation, and their specific goals and objectives, and describe the results they would like to see for their community and for the family. They should also make clear the types of philanthropic interests that are of no interest to them. I suggest that they go through several drafts and at least a week to give them adequate time to reflect, consider, and make changes. If the children are willing to honor the wishes of their parents, and most are, the children have clear guidance as to what their parents really wanted. They receive a magnificent benefit from their parents – a gift, really – which is that they can thoughtfully carry out the wishes of their parents. That is more than a gift, it is a blessing, because the children feel good about doing it. The children also meet interesting people, learn, experience and enrich their lives. Only after doing the work for several years will they fully appreciate the magnitude of the "gift" from their parents.

I had a client whose father established a family fund at The Cleveland Foundation. Of his two sons, one became interested in carrying out his father's wishes, and the other was not interested. The one who is interested lives in California and comes to Cleveland at least two or three times every year to ensure that the goals his father set are being pursued and accomplished. His affection for his father and his loyalty are deeply touching to all of us who understand what he is doing.

Intent can create a connection that lasts the rest of your life. In philanthropy, you will meet wonderful people, you will do beautiful things, and you will gain great satisfaction. For this man, the happiest time of his life is to see the results of his father's wishes working well.

MAL BANK, GENERAL COUNSEL, THE CLEVELAND FOUNDATION

Thinking Creatively and Expansively
Thinking creatively and expansively is a characteristic of successful business people, of which John Colina is a good example, and it can lead to extraordinary results. He and his wife Nancy formed their Colina Family Foundation without much of any written Family Values, Mission, or Family Involvement Statement. Not long thereafter, their two daughters asked if they could be involved. The daughters were adults, married, with life interests and value systems of their own. Soon the family found itself drawn into a deepening discussion of

fig. 5 — How the Kennedys Linked Family to Mission

A statement of philosophy and values can emerge from family circumstances and lead to a Mission. When Ambassador Joseph P. Kennedy, Sr., established a foundation to honor his son, Joseph P. Kennedy, Jr., a heroic U.S. Army Air Corps pilot who died in World War II, he asked his daughter, Eunice, to find direction for the foundation. After lengthy research and consideration of family feelings toward her sister, Rose Mary who had mental retardation, Eunice Kennedy recommended basing foundation activities on concern for persons with mental retardation. Today, the foundation publishes this Values Statement.

The Joseph P. Kennedy, Jr., Foundation believes that persons with mental retardation have the ability to live, learn, work, recreate, and worship like everyone else. We recognize that people with mental retardation may need assistance to do these things. We believe that families of people with mental retardation, especially families of children with mental retardation, benefit from support and information to successfully include their family member with mental retardation in the everyday activities of their community. The foundation works to improve the lives of people with mental retardation and to prevent the causes of mental retardation.

fig. 6 — Wealth as a Value

One of the more important subjects in family discussion of values is (or can be) money. Among key questions that often arise in family talks are these:
- How do family members really feel about money and about the family wealth?
- How do they feel about allocating a portion of family wealth to philanthropy?
- How comfortable are family members talking about family wealth?
- How much to family members know about the origins of the family wealth?
- How much do they know about the founder's estate and will?
- What happens when the family wealth is more and more widely distributed with each new generation?
- What experience do family members have in discussing family financial matters?

Points that might come up in family discussions of money are these:
- The subject of money is usually fraught with emotional overtones;
- Money is the economy's way of recognizing certain kinds of accomplishment;
- Money may play a role in a person's self-esteem; and
- Inherited wealth can become an emotional burden and a handicap.

values that encompassed the foundation, the family, and society at large. Talks took place over months at get-togethers (the daughters had moved away) and by telephone, email, and letters. Talks covered many subjects and ranged far beyond the matter of the family foundation. What is beauty, and what role does it play in our lives and in society? asked one daughter, who is an artist. What responsibilities do we all have toward Nature and the environment? asked the other, who is an environmentalist. "Eventually, we got around to talking about the foundation," John Colina recalls. "We shared views that we'd never discussed before. Our daughters and their husbands had become involved in the foundation. We had all had a profound and enriching experience."

Researching Family and Founder Can Be Inspiring

Researching the family's history can be a deeply stirring and inspiring experience for family members. Many families have taken the opportunity afforded by formation of the family foundation to engage in deep genealogical research. The head of one large family foundation once took all interested family members back to the homestead in North Carolina where the family forebears had arrived from Europe and made their living generations before. The farm was still there, with its fields and forests amidst the gentle rolling hills. That was where the family started in America. It was moving moment and a powerful reminder to the younger generation of the responsibilities that accompany the accident of inherited wealth.

Research into the life and values of the founder, or the donor, can be important to the family. The Helen Bader Foundation in Milwaukee is a family foundation started by the two sons of Helen Bader a few years after her death in 1989. The foundation recently observed two milestones — its first 10 years in operation and its first $100 million in grants.

The two sons, Daniel and David, researched their mother's background to determine what values were closest to her heart. "Our mother was a dynamic woman," says Daniel Bader. "Among other values, she held community cohesion and development in high regard. She wanted to be involved in her life and times, and she encouraged other people to be involved. She believed strongly that those who have the resources should establish foundations." Daniel and David Bader learned much about their mother; they had a video made of her life. From that learning came personal understanding of and admiration for this remarkable woman on the part of family members. The Helen Bader Foundation is active in metropolitan Milwaukee affairs, in addition to its grantmaking; for example, it promotes community

---

fig. 7 — Values Drive Grantmaking and Money Pays for It

Money is a critical driver in grantmaking. Many founders make no bones about the importance on money in their philanthropy both in use of tax incentives and in use of money for doing good.

Two brothers, who prefer to remain anonymous, have done very well with their investments and have set up a family foundation. "We made a lot of money at a young age," says one brother. "We weren't sure where to direct our interests, and we thought a private foundation would at least defer the situation. So we set one up, with $1 million, which we later increased to $6 million. Then, as a favor, we let friends donate low-basis stock or cash to the foundation, on the assumption that they could recommend giving as long as we were comfortable with it."

"Then we looked at what we cared about," the brother continues. "Our parents have had bouts of cancer, and were treated at the Dana Farber Clinic in Boston. So a large amount of our giving has flowed to a doctor there, for research. My family is interested in conservation, while my brother is interested in the environment."

"It's a classic family philanthropy."

---

dialog. The foundation also promotes formal philanthropy.

Writing a Family Values Statement

The family exercise in considering values may be one of the more important activities in the early history of the family foundation.

Compassion, respect and support for others, improving people's lives, empowering others, communicating honestly and directly with those seeking help, fostering rich cultural expression, deepening our connections to nature, and fairness are just a few of the guiding values of family foundations. Perhaps these are some of your family's and your own values as well. Whatever your family values, a concerted effort to express those values can have lasting effect on the family and generations to come.

Once family values have been articulated, it is helpful to put them into a Family Values Statement as one piece of the ancient papyrus that will link family members forever.

Developing a Values Statement: A "Sample" Scenario

When members of the Sample family come to the table to draft a Values Statement for the Sample Family Foundation, they bring as many differing perspectives and opinions as any other family. Chairman Richard Sample appreciates the power of cultural activities to soothe the spirit and spark his imagination. Vice Chairman Maureen Sample is a former elementary school teacher and, together with her son, Michael, volunteers regularly for a variety of children's organizations. Patrick Sample, their son, is studying medicine and is keenly interested in alternative therapies. Their daughter, Louise, is autistic. All family members share a commitment to the principles of their faith, particularly those that encourage generosity and charity toward the poor and disadvantaged.

It takes a bit of work, but the Sample family agrees that their shared values embrace:
- Concern for children and youth;
- Support for the role of arts and culture in society;
- Desire to support the disadvantaged and most challenged among us; and
- Willingness to support creative solutions to difficult problems.

Such a statement of values could lead — with a bit more effort on the part of the family — to a Mission Statement. The Sample Family Foundation might find that support of arts enrichment programs for disadvantaged youth or arts therapy for ill and disabled children embraces their shared values and also speaks to the passions and concerns of all family members.

What Are Your Philanthropic Goals?

Once your Family Values Statement is in place, it is time to turn to the critical subject of philanthropic goals. Having gained insight into what you and family members hold to be important, the next building block — a Mission Statement — is ready to be cast.

Virtually every family foundation sooner or later develops a Mission Statement. Those that start operations with an unwritten mission almost invariably commit to a written document at some point. A Mission Statement is a necessity in issuing grant guidelines. More important at startup, however, is the creative process itself: developing the Mission Statement can be one of the truly thrilling moments in the life of your family foundation. Many founders find enormous satisfaction in writing the Mission Statement, which gives concrete purpose and direction to the foundation.

This section proposes a process that addresses four basic questions:
- Why have a Mission Statement?
- Who decides the final wording of the Mission Statement?
- How can you and your family create a Mission Statement?
- What does a Mission Statement contain?

Why Have a Mission Statement?

Let's consider the ways in which a Mission Statement can give direction to every aspect of family foundation.
- **Give guidance to trustees:** As the governors, policymakers, and guardians of the foundation, trustees need a basis for developing a long-range strategy for the foundation, and the Mission Statement provides it. Trustees can also use the Mission Statement to ensure that the foundation stays in focus, on task, and supported with appropriate resources (see Governance: Vision, Trust, and Moral Imagination in Trusteeship, p. 85).

- **Bring focus to grantmaking:** The core reason for the Mission Statement is to direct grants toward a particular field, social change, research activity, or other undertaking (see Establishing Grantmaking Interests and Priorities, p. 159).

- **Provide a framework for management:** Whoever manages foundation operations should start with a clear idea of the overall purpose of the enterprise. The Mission Statement offers a framework for setting up management activities (see Setting Up Shop, p. 115).

- **Drive portfolio investment:** Cash needs, risk tolerance, length of investment terms, program-related investments, and other dimensions of the investment strategy work best for foundation interests when they are tied directly to the time horizons, grantmaking levels, and policy outcomes expressed in the Mission Statement (see Fashioning an Investment Strategy, p. 137).

- **Shape communications:** Founders have wide latitude deciding what and how much to communicate about foundation or grantee activities. Founders may consider a communications program aimed at supporting the Mission (see Communicating: Enhancing Process, Participation, and the Public Face of Your Foundation, p. 191).

What Process Is Right for Your Family?

A family foundation's Mission Statement can reflect founder and family values. It

fig. **8**   **Key Questions in Developing a Mission Statement**

- Who will participate in conceptualizing the statement?
- Who will manage the process of developing the statement?
- What other voices might be sought, such as grantees, the community, and other family foundations?
- Who will write the draft statement?
- How will editing and finalization be conducted?
- How will the statement be communicated to family members?

can be cast in the founder's voice, the family's voice, or the foundation's voice. Some founders even want to add the community's voice. With individual family member insights providing direction, strength, and support for the philanthropic works, a family foundation can gain the momentum to endure and prosper for generations to come.

Experiences of family foundations demonstrate the diversity of approaches to determining the voice, the spirit, and the style of the Mission Statement. "We are four years old, and we're going slow on developing a grantmaking focus," says Alison Goldberg, trustee and daughter of the founder of the Robert P. and Judith N. Goldberg Foundation. "Why? We have young family members; non-family board members with different interests; diverse interests in general; and very different political perspectives. We're experimenting, feeling what's right, and learning from each other."

Mission Statements Are Woven in Many Colors

"When the board started its work six years ago, we deliberately went with a very broad mission," recalls David D. Weitnauer, executive director of the Rockdale Foundation in Atlanta, Georgia. "This left room to experiment and learn from our grantmaking. After three years of experience, we conducted a strategic planning retreat and developed a more specific mission statement. Now, two years later, we've just completed another planning retreat and it helped us tighten our focus even more."

Elliott Springs's hopes, values, and intentions were clearly defined from the beginning — he knew exactly what he wanted to do, well before establishing his family foundation. Early in his career as a textile magnate, he sought ways to improve the lives of people in upstate South Carolina, thousands of whom worked in his mills. In the midst of the Great Depression, he created a nonprofit organization to finance college education for local high school graduates. At the onset of World War II, he founded the Springs Foundations to "promote the general welfare of the residents" of Lancaster, Chester, and York counties. The foundation continues today as an important philanthropic force in that area.

How Can a Family Handle Differences in View?

What happens when family interests are so varied that difficulty arises in developing a single mission? Jerry Taylor and his wife, Nancy Bryant, faced this situation and worked out an imaginative solution that energized the Mission Statement.

They wanted to start a family foundation, the Jerry Taylor & Nancy Bryant Foundation, and to include their son, Galen Taylor. Differences in view about mission soon arose. Gerald wanted to address education. Nancy leaned toward eldercare. Galen was concerned about helping immigrants get started.

---

fig. 9 — What a Mission Statement Does

The mission clarifies what the family hopes to accomplish through their grantmaking, and in what areas it will make grants to get there. All founding documents for charitable vehicles include some sort of statement of purpose; the actual term can very from state to state. The law does not require a mission statement separate from this statement of purpose and many family philanthropies don't have one, especially in the formative years when the original donor is at the helm. The mission does state the purpose of the foundation or fund, but it goes far beyond that basic function.

The mission helps the family set a course that transcends generations. Older family members must ultimately hand over the torch to the young. Free and open conversations about the mission can give all the generations a chance to build upon the original donor's legacy, as well as express their hopes for the future and their vision for the family's philanthropy.

The mission enables the foundation to see where it is deviating from its expectations and goals so it can make course corrections. By including several goals in the mission, the family foundation can act more strategically, building in review of its goals in three or five years to see how far it has come, and whether it needs to revise its thinking.

The mission identifies gaps that the foundation or fund can fill. Most family foundations are small, with assets of less than $5 million. Taking time to think and talk about mission can focus the family on applying their resources where they can do the most good.

The mission enables the organization to be more strategic. For example, a mission can allow for grantmaking through collaboration and matching grants, thereby harnessing the power of larger organizations and compounding the impact of a family's grantmaking.

The mission ensures that the family members are truly in sync. Family trustees sometimes think they're in agreement when they may not be. The discussion around the mission early on can reveal and help reconcile important philosophical differences.

The mission strengthens the role of the family in the foundation. As family foundations grow and, sometimes, involve non-family members in the process, some families fear they will lose the family legacy and influence. By devising a clear mission, a family can assure that the foundation is headed in the direction that's right for them.

SOURCE: Virginia Peckham. *Grantmaking with a Purpose: Mission and Guidelines,* Practices in Family Philanthropy. Washington, DC: National Center for Family Philanthropy, 2000.

It fell to Nancy to iron out the differences. She went to work, gathered information, talked to people, and educated herself. She worked out a multi-purpose mission and a discretionary grantmaking arrangement that works just fine: Gerald directs a portion of grants to education; Nancy's field is eldercare and the arts; and Galen supports programs that provide computers for young people. Foundation grants are allocated to cover their multiple interests.

Some families may consider evolving from a multi-purpose mission to a more focused one. "Our family foundation has a large board made up

"It's important to give in an area where you have some special interest and passion"

— THOMAS KUBIAK
Founder, The Oliver B. Merlyn Foundation

entirely of family, including six of us siblings," says a family board member of a midwestern foundation. "My father established the foundation. Because so many of us are on the board, we don't now accept outside, unsolicited proposals. Talking with other family foundations in the Indianapolis area, however, one of the things I keep hearing is, 'Focus your grantmaking. The more narrow the focus, the more effective your foundation can be.' I hope our foundation will evolve from giving to diverse causes, based on the individual interests of board members, to more

focused grantmaking based on some shared family mission."

How Can You and Your Family Create a Mission Statement?

Approaches to drafting a Mission Statement are as varied as family styles. One founding couple will write out the essentials on the back of an envelope during a quiet dinner together. Another will convene a boisterous, high-energy family gathering, with everybody talking at once, and finally restore enough order to start a stream of ideas and suggestions from family members.

Here are some ideas for the drafting process, garnered from family foundation experiences:

- Hold a retreat at a family home, conference center, or place of historic importance in family history; the retreat might last a day or a few days. Many families work better together when they meet in low-stress settings, away from work, with no responsibilities for cooking and with ample facilities for the youngsters. The goal is to develop an atmosphere of trust in which family can focus on a subject that is sensitive

and important to all of them, well into the future.

- Appoint the founder, a family member, or a skilled outside person (an old friend, the trusted family lawyer, or a trustee of another family foundation) as discussion leader and facilitator. This person should be experienced at leading a group over emotional hurdles and toward consensus.

- Consider asking a neutral guide or professional facilitator to help the family develop its ideas and views. If a neutral guide is preferred, one with experience with family foundations would probably be more able to work with the family in this setting. (See When a Consultant Can Help, p. 110.)

- Try to keep everybody, including members of different generations, involved in the process. Grandparents may or may not want to be directly involved, but their counsel can lend a steadying tone to discussions. Siblings of the founding couple may want to be heard. Children and grandchildren, down to teenagers and younger, want to feel that they were present at the creation, and had a say. This experience can be a tremendously important learning opportunity, motivator, and life-direction experience for young people. They will observe how mature adults deal with complex emotional and value-rich issues that are consequential for the whole family.

■ Thank everybody for attending. Consider circulating your personal reflections on family values discussions, the foundation, and the mission talks. Include a draft Mission Statement for everyone's comments.

■ Keep family informed on your subsequent drafts of the Mission Statement, on efforts you have made to accommodate members' suggestions, on reasons why you have decided not to accept certain suggestions, and on the grand plan that your draft Mission Statement represents. The foundation is, after all, a product of the founder's dream, and the Mission Statement is simply a practical articulation of that dream — heated and blended in the crucible of family attention.

Philanthropy, like any new discipline, requires learning a new language, and creation of the Mission Statement offers a good opportunity to begin this learning. A founder and family might, for example, establish that one of their most basic values is family cohesion.

How to translate this value into an element of the Mission Statement? Family cohesion in grantmaking talk takes the form of "family-based support" or "programs for children, youth, and families." The Mission Statement might state the importance of family cohesion and say that the foundation supports nonprofit organizations that specialize in family-building programs.

Moving from Family Meeting to Mission
The England family found that intense discussion of family values opened the way to rapid resolution of views on Mission Statement. In 1994, Lois and Richard England, long-time community leaders and philanthropists, asked their immediate family to join them in establishing a family foundation. They formed a board of members of two generations of the family.

The Englands then held a two-day retreat at a conference center and hired a facilitator. "It was 9 to 5, both days," says Cathy England, the board chair. "Some of us were excited about the possibility of the foundation; others were nervous and wondered about family dynamics. The facilitator spent most of the two days talking about the family — family stories, common values, and common heritage. It was very structured, so we could talk about difficult things without getting hung up about them. I think it's really critical to use a facilitator. It goes beyond getting our ideas together. It's really a common together of the family to feel comfortable about the whole process."

The family did not reach the mission until the afternoon or the second day, but by then members were "ready to make a plan," says England. "My advice to new family foundations is to be strategic. You don't need a foundation just to write checks. A family foundation is a way for different people — who happen to be from the same family — to put their heads together. It's a group process where people think together about what most important."

Mission Statement of the Lois and Richard England Family Foundation:
Much of the Foundation's support for human services reflects its interest in comprehensive services that enable a low-income family or individual to become self-sufficient, to live independently, or provide employment and training to move toward the goal of independence.

In education, Foundation grants focus on pre-school, elementary and secondary education, and well as enrichment pro-

GOOD ADVICE ➤ When we were starting up, we organized a family retreat for my parents, my husband and myself. We hired a facilitator to guide the family through the process of developing a grantmaking program. We asked our parents to describe the reasons why they wanted to create a foundation, and we made an audiotape of my father's remarks — this was very wonderful. His words shed light on what's important to him, and they help other board members to focus. His remarks also will be helpful for future generations.

MICHELE GOODMAN, J.W. & H.M. GOODMAN FAMILY CHARITABLE FOUNDATION, HILLSBORO, OREGON

grams, particularly for children in under-served communities.

Arts and cultural program support is directed at local institutions, especially organizations with community outreach. Access to arts education for disadvantaged children is a key interest.

Board members have a strong commitment to strengthening Jewish life in the United States and Israel. Local grants support core community institutions; grants in Israel focus on peace and religious pluralism, and human rights. National Jewish grants support educational efforts to combat racism and anti-Semitism, as well as to support antipoverty work.

What Does a Mission Statement Contain?

Some family foundations choose brevity for their Mission Statement. The following are notable examples:

- **The Sobrato Family Foundation:** The mission of the Sobrato Family Foundation is to build a strong and healthy local community by supporting programs that have a lasting impact and to create opportunities that empower individuals to reach their full potential.

- **The McCune Foundation:** The mission of the McCune Foundation is to enable communities and nonprofit institutions to improve the quality and circumstances of life for present and future generations

- **The Mott Foundation:** The Charles Stewart Mott foundation affirms its founder's vision that each of us "is in a partnership with the rest of the human race" — that each individual's quality of life is connected to the well-being of the community, both locally and globally.

- **The Joseph P. Kennedy, Jr., Foundation:** The mission of the Joseph P. Kennedy, Jr., Foundation is to provide leadership in the field of mental retardation and service to persons with mental retardation, both those born and unborn, and their families.

A Mission Statement need not be limited to the grantmaking program. As described elsewhere in many places in *Splendid Legacy*, founders and family foundations have many ways to implement their philanthropic mission. "There's so much that family foundations can do beyond grant-making," says Anne Marie Kemp, director of the Greenlee Family Foundation in Boulder, Colorado. "Be listeners, offer help with strategic planning and board development, help nonprofits to diversify their funding base, refer grantseekers to other foundations." The Mission Statement can contemplate, and perhaps even state explicitly, that the foundation provides various forms of support in addition to grants.

Each of us has a personal mission, and when our missions come together to guide family giving, the outcome can be nothing less than spectacular. When the building block of philanthropic mission

---

fig. 10 — Elements of a Mission Statement

The elements of a Mission Statement are entirely up to the founder and family. Many family foundations combine some or all of the following elements with the Mission Statement:

- History of the family: its origins, values, patriarchs and matriarchs, business interests, public service, traditions of philanthropy, etc.

- History of the foundation: founder, when founded, funding source, etc.

- The field of interest of the foundation (education, environment, etc.) and what the foundation intends to accomplish;

- Program focus and specifics of where grants are targeted; and

- Key goals and desired outcomes.

has found its place in the foundation of family, it is the right time to look to how family members can be involved in and contribute to that mission.

How Can Family Members be Involved in the Foundation?

By now, your values and those of your family members have been articulated and expressed in a Family Values Statement. You have completed the crucial task of translating those values into a Mission Statement. The blueprint for the family foundation is complete and you are ready to begin construction.

What role do you want family members to play? How would you like to involve your children in this enterprise? And what about grandparents, grandchildren, inlaws, spouses, aunts and uncles, and cousins? This group might include some highly talented and experienced people who could help you. Finally, what about the next generation and generations beyond? What plans might you make for their involvement?

Founders give deep thought to these most sensitive and consequential of subjects. Some founders start the foundation with their spouse and perhaps a trusted friend or advisor as the board of trustees. The Bill & Melinda Gates

---

fig. 11   Founding Documents and the Mission Statement

It is important that your foundation's Mission Statement be in harmony with the founding and governing documents — the articles of incorporation or the statement of trust, as the case may be, and the foundation Bylaws. All these documents taken as a whole constitute the founder's legal and philosophical legacy and should be given much close attention (see Facing Important Legal Issues, p. 73, for an in-depth legal look at these subjects).

Foundation, for example, was started with the founding couple and Bill Gates, Sr., as the board (see One Family's Story: An Interview with Bill Gates, Sr., p. 50).

Many founders want to involve family members from the beginning. A process appropriate to family style is needed: perhaps a family meeting or a retreat, perhaps one-on-one contact, perhaps an open invitation for expressions of interest.

You may also want to pay particular attention to the role of family elders — your own or your spouse's parents, or even grandparents. Other considerations may evolve when two family members seek the same job; or when more family members seek board seats than are available.

Family Involvement Reflects Values and Style

Family involvement in the foundation is likely to flow from the work that family members did on preparing the Family Values Statement. It is also likely to reflect the style of the family — collegial, independent, loners. Involvement in a common enterprise, especially one aimed at the good of society, may be something of a new experience for the family.

Here are a few examples of real-life families.

"Our whole family is involved in the foundation," John Colina says. "From the very beginning, for my wife Nancy and me, the family foundation was a big plus. The very idea of the foundation encouraged us to hold family meetings and look for common interests."

With four children and 14 grandchildren, Don and Jane O'Keefe decided on a board of six, which consists of the two of them and their four children. (After the first five years of operation, the O'Keefes added the family lawyer to the board.) John and Nancy Colina have the same arrangement for the

(The following story has been fashioned to show how a family can unite around values, create a mission, and commit to involvement in the family foundation.)

1. Bob and Terry Austin, both in their 50s, have sold their software company and retired to enjoy the fruits of their labor. Now they want to form a family foundation with the proceeds of the sale, after providing for their three children: Anne, Tim, and Tom, who live in distant parts of the country. The Austins ask their children and spouses to take part in forming and managing the foundation.

Bob and Terry invite their children, as well as Anne's husband, Jim, and Tom's wife, Diane, to a daylong family retreat at a conference center near their home. They choose a quiet, neutral setting where everyone can focus on the family and the foundation, with special attention to three questions:

> **What does our family value?**
> **How can these values guide our family foundation?**
> **How can each of us be involved?**

2. **DEVELOPING A FAMILY VALUES STATEMENT**

Terry opens the family meeting by asking: *"What do you value in your life?"*

"What do you mean by value?" asks Anne. *"A value is something that has significant meaning for you,"* Terry responds. *"It can be an abstract thing, like honesty, but can also be expressed materially."*

Terry records each family member's responses on a flip chart. She asks members to prioritize their values and combines the top five values into a draft statement. Lively debate ensues, and by late morning the family agrees on this Family Values Statement:

> **The Austin Family values education of young people, social justice in our community, individual self-sufficiency, a healthy environment, and creative expression.**

3. **MOVING ON TO MISSION**

"How can we translate these values into the work of the foundation?" Terry then asks.

"I think we have the makings of a foundation purpose right in our values," Bob observes. *"Let's each write a Mission Statement using the Family Value Statement as a guide."*

After lunch, everyone shares his or her draft. A Mission Statement soon emerges, which the family discusses and edits. They adopt this final product:

> **The Austin Family Foundation is committed to enabling disadvantaged young people to achieve self-sufficiency, to protecting the natural environment, and to encouraging creative expression in the performing arts.**

"This statement represents our deepest family values," Bob says. *"It will guide our foundation in all aspects of its work."*

4. **FAMILY INVOLVEMENT STATEMENT**

Finally, it's time to talk about running the foundation.

"Mom, why don't you and Dad be co-chairs?" asks Tom. *"That suits us just fine!"* Bob responds.

"How can we be involved if we live all over the country?" Tim asks. *"Well, the board could meet only four times a year,"* Terry suggests, *"family members could carry out assignments from their home, we could correspond by email, and we'd have a website to keep everybody informed."*

In the late afternoon, in a rising spirit of good-natured cooperation and commitment, this Family Involvement Statement emerges:

> **The co-founders, and their children and spouses, will constitute the Board of Trustees of the Austin Family Foundation, with the co-founders serving as co-chairs. Tom will serve as Treasurer, Anne as Secretary, and Tim as Investment Advisor. Jim, a lawyer, will serve as General Counsel. Diane will serve as Office Manager. These appointments will remain in effect for 2 years, after which the Board will review assignments.**

In closing the meeting, Bob proposes a toast: *"To our unity as a family, to the good works to come, and to the legacy we have begun this day!"*

JUDITH K. HEALEY

Colina Foundation. Jerry Taylor, Nancy Bryant, and son, Galen Taylor, are their own board at the Jerry Taylor & Nancy Bryant Foundation.

The Gibney Family Foundation recently offered the entire extended family, over the age of 10, an invitation to make limited discretionary grants in order to raise the level of interest in philanthropy, family wide. The Grantmaking Guidelines were relaxed for these small grants. However, to keep the Foundation mission oriented, the greatest support will go to grant proposals that are closely aligned and most likely to be effective in accomplishing the Gibney Family Foundation Mission.

The communication "hub" for the foundation is its internal website, which provides information to family members about grant activity, stories that recognize the efforts of each family member, lessons learned, quick links to other useful information, family members, and foundation friends.

Ellis L. Phillips, founder of the family foundation bearing his name, chose strong immediate involvement for his family as soon as the foundation inaugurated its active life (16 years after it was established, having languished for lack of money). The founder named himself as president, his son as vice president, and his wife and a niece's husband as trustees (along with the founder's per-

---

fig. 13 — **Parent Involvement in the Foundation**

What do you do if a parent wishes to be involved in the family foundation? Here are some helpful hints for those who are considering this matter.

- Taking an objective look at the history of your relationship with your parent, how will his or her involvement help or hinder the formation of a family foundation?

- How well can you and your parent work together comfortably?

- How able are you to share decisionmaking easily with your parent?

- How capable is your parent? (What skills, expertise, and talents does he or she have?)

- Does there exist, or can you create, a contributing role for your parent that can be successfully accomplished?

- In the event that your parent's participation in the foundation doesn't work out, do you have a plan in mind to redefine or discontinue involvement?

If your responses to these considerations have been positive, capitalizing on your parent's capabilities, energies, and desire to be involved in the family foundation can bring much needed support and satisfaction. And an encouraging word, sprinkled with a bit of wisdom from the past, can mean a lot when it comes from such a close family member!

---

fig. 14 — **A Memorable Moment**

At one of his first board meetings in the chair, John S. Darrow, the great-grandson of the founder of Weiboldt Foundation in Chicago, was told by his mother, Anita Straub Darrow "Sit up straight, John." Family members might have been slightly surprised, but community board members were astonished. Today, the foundation uses the story to give prospective community members some understanding of how different a family board can be.

sonal legal counsel and four friends and colleagues). Moreover, Ellis L. Phillips, Jr., supplemented his father's gift of appreciated stock, which triggered activation of the foundation, with a healthy gift of stock of his own. Financial contributions certainly constitute one of the highest expressions of family involvement — and some family foundations require significant contribution as a prerequisite for board service.

A Family Involvement Statement can describe just how family members would contribute to and participate in the foundation and its mission. Such a statement can draw upon appropriate family resources to run the foundation (trustee duty, management, investment oversight, etc.), clarify roles of family members in foundation activities, and involve any number of family members (including next generations) on advisory committees or other vehicles. The statement can be amended and updated as necessary.

As parents themselves and as family leaders, many founders are careful not to characterize family involvement as a right or entitlement. For these founders, selection as a trustee brings certain expectations.

For example, trustees are expected to prepare for meetings, attend meetings, participate in discussions, work at committee assignments, make site visits, represent the foundation at public

fig. 15 — How Family Members Can Be Involved

- Serve as a trustee or board secretary (prepare board books, keep minutes, etc.).

- Serve as General Counsel.

- Serve as C.P.A. or help keep the books.

- Manage the grantmaking process (write checks, keep records, etc.).

- Administer the office or help answer the phone, reply to inquiries, etc.

- Advise on or manage the investment portfolio.

- Scout for charitable investment opportunities (program-related investments, low-interest loans to nonprofits, social venture capital collaborations, etc.).

- Take on communications responsibilities (help create a website, prepare a family newsletter, etc.).

- Serve on an Advisory Committee (for adult relatives or for members of the next generation) that can recommend grants, explore for new opportunities, accompany board members on site visits, etc.).

- Make financial contributions to the foundation endowment.

events when asked to do so, and so on. Younger family member might also be expected to learn about philanthropy — and perhaps other areas of life as well — by working with the founder or other older family member trustees.

Joining Family Involvement with Mission

One of Albert L. Gibney's dreams in founding The Gibney Family Foundation was to establish a "focus that Gibney family members could rally around." The founder wanted to

encourage his family to think beyond themselves and unite in efforts to help others. For the first 10 years, involvement on the part of the Gibney Family was primarily limited to occasional site visits, phone calls, and communications geared to increase their own understanding of the organizations and to ensure that they were comfortable with their use of foundation grants. In Frank Gibney's own words, "this approach met legal foundation requirements, but did not support the true intent of the Founder or serve to strengthen the foundation."

fig. 16 — Maintaining Active Family Participation

Curtis W. Meadows, Jr., president emeritus of The Meadows Foundation, was designated Distinguished Grantmaker by the Council on Foundations in 1997. He was interviewed by Thomas W. Lambeth, recently retired as executive director of the Z. Smith Reynolds Foundation, Inc., in Winston-Salem, North Carolina.

Lambeth: When did you first realize there was a Meadows Foundation?

Meadows: Well, my uncle formed it back in 1948 and he involved the family in it very, very early on. The foundation was essentially a gift Al Meadows was making to his family on behalf of others, because he was saying to the family, "I trust you above all others that I can think of to do this right and appropriately, and do it keeping with my interests and concerns."

Lambeth: How important is donor intent in The Meadows Foundation?

Meadows: After my uncle's death, when the family accepted the legacy of responsibility for governing and administering the foundation he created, I was really kind of overwhelmed with the sense of trust he placed in his family.

When I became president of the foundation, I hung my uncle's picture in my office and I got up every morning and looked at the picture and asked the question, Are we doing OK? Are we still on track with your values? Because the world has changed and the circumstances are so different. I always tried to be accountable to him.

Honoring donor intent is a trustee's first obligation, but it does not exist in a vacuum. It must be considered in the context of the changing times, public expectations, and other legal and moral responsibilities that are attendant to the existence of the foundation.

Lambeth: You have really made your board and staff about as family-oriented as you can. Why is that important?

Meadows: After my uncle's death, one of the first things I did was go around the country and look at foundations that had started with the family connection to see those that had sustained it over time and to ask the question, What did they do that made it sustainable?

What I found was that there was a natural evolutionary process away from family involvement that would occur in a family-based foundation if the family didn't work at maintaining a connection through active, direct participation.

Lambeth: How do you keep it from being in-bred?

Meadows: It is a great fallacy to believe that families — because they are family — are all going to be cookie-cutter replicas of the same mentality. They aren't — particularly a large family, scattered all over the United States, as we are.

So, there are very diverse views and interests, plus an accumulation of different life experiences within the family. But what united us as a family were the commonly held values such as responsibility, respect, caring, fairness, and a spiritual faith — not necessarily by denominations, though — but by a belief in the role of a Supreme Being in our lives.

The blood is why we are genetically related. The values we share make us a family.

But we realized that our life experience didn't prepare us to make judgments about all that was needed in terms of grantmaking, without help from others who had gone through experiences different from ours.

Once we decided upon an area of interest, then we would try to bring in people who had extensive experience in that kind of work to educate us, to help us look at what were successful models, and to try and find those models that worked as we went about doing the grantmaking. And so, that was one way to bring into the family a lifetime of experiences and learning that we needed to deal and cope with unfamiliar issues and solutions.

SOURCE: *Foundation News & Commentary*, Highlights, March/April 1997 Issue.

- Connect them with young people in other family foundations.
- Listen and respond to their ideas.
- Create a youth-friendly foundation organization.
- Make philanthropy accessible to young adults.

Adapted from "Opportunity of a Lifetime: Young Adults in Family Philanthropy," National Center for Family Philanthropy, 2002.

To better ensure attainment of the Founder's intent, the foundation recently developed four goals for family:

- Understand the basic challenges facing those whom the foundation intends to help;
- Increase family communication with a focus on helping others through the foundation;
- Employ more effective philanthropic processes by making new tools available; and
- Develop leadership in family foundation philanthropy.

Many family foundation founders have the same dream as Albert Gibney. What the Gibney foundation is doing to encourage family involvement and, equally important, strengthen familial bonds, is a wonderful lesson for all — within and outside the foundation world.

Involving Young Family Members

You may want to contemplate where the members of the next generation of the family might fit in, perhaps now, perhaps later. Many founders want to instill in the children and grandchildren a family tradition of philanthropy, a passing on of the legacy. They want to introduce the younger generations to the excitement and satisfaction of grantmaking. They want to prepare them for board service or other foundation duties. And they also want to benefit from the ideas and suggestions of the younger set.

Here are some suggestions for families that want to involve young adults:

- Be clear why you want the next generation to be involved, explain your reasons, and ask what their own reasons are for wanting to become involved.
- Discuss your philanthropic finances openly.
- Keep the young adults informed on foundation activities.
- Be clear about roles they can play.
- Allow them the opportunity to become involved while they are still young.
- Consider allocating discretionary funds to them.
- Encourage them to contribute personally, either through the foundation, some other family giving vehicle, or on their own.

Building an Enduring Foundation

The goal of this chapter has been to offer guidance in putting the basic building blocks of a family foundation in place. The most challenging and rewarding task of all is putting the family in the family foundation. When a family finally does surround and support the founder, and make the foundation its own, wonderful things can happen. Family strength and determination may in the long run prove to be the most valuable assets the foundation possesses. Family giving built on values, mission, and family involvement will stand and endure in this changing world. With these resources and supports, as generations come and go, the foundation will remain as a splendid legacy to those who came before.

FAMILIES CAN FIND MISSION IN THEIR DREAMS

by Jonathan Hopps and Chris Payer

Experience tells us that most family foundations begin with the donor/founder or a donor couple establishing the vision and mission. Increasingly, new family foundations include all family members (and others who are expected to play a role) in determining the shared sense of purpose. The opportunities described throughout Splendid Legacy are relevant to those in both situations. However, little has been written specifically about the experience of families who choose to work together in this effort. The following essay describes the reasons why some families chose a shared process, how they went about it, and what the results have been.

The Mission Statement is, for many families, the heart and soul of their foundation because it captures the family's dreams for the betterment of themselves and others. They take great care to ensure that it accurately embraces and articulates the family's vision and inner sense of gratitude.

Moving from dream to mission is, for many families, not all that difficult. What may prove difficult, rather, is speaking the dream itself and giving due regard to each family member's vision and values.

Every founder, by definition, holds a powerful feeling about philanthropy. Similarly, every family member probably holds his or her own vision about philanthropy, a personal feeling they may or may not easily express. Family members' feelings may parallel or diverge sharply from those of the founder. Some may harbor feelings about the use of family resources for philanthropy in the first place. Others may have long held a hope that family resources would be applied to address a community, national, or international problem of great importance to them.

A vehicle to raise this awareness to a more conscious level can be richly rewarding. This vehicle can be an invitation for family members to come together for the purpose of shar-

"[The family foundation provides] a new dimension of communication among our family members — one that focuses on collectively trying to make a difference in our local community, actively engaging in the causes we are passionate about, and approaching life with appreciation and gratitude. Our goal is to pass this family legacy of giving to future generations."

— LISA SOBRATO SONSINI daughter of the founder,
Sobrato Family Foundation

ing dreams and shaping mission, thereby bringing deeper meaning to the life of their foundation.

Sharon Daloz Parks, author of Big Questions — Worthy Dreams, asserts, "We need to be able to make some sort of sense out of things; we seek pattern, order, coherence, and relation in the disparate elements of our experience." Here is an opportunity to put dreaming into action (or put action where your dreams are) in the initial stages of family foundation creation.

The addition of a simple, clear, dream step can be one of the more rewarding steps in foundation creation. A well-articulated vision, a long-cherished dream, will pull you to higher ground — inspiring, motivating, and supporting you and your family through the times of challenge.

Family Meetings May Stir New Visions

The dream step can take many forms, depending on family style, but for many families it involves a meeting or series of meetings called by the founder. One family returned to the homestead of the first generation that had come to this country from Europe, settled in the South, begun life as farmers, and started what became a dynasty. The visitors sensed the simple and powerful values of their forebears in earlier times: directness of purpose, hard work, a cohesive family, faith. Other families simply let a natural and informal discussion unfold over the dinner table.

Storytelling can be a tool to help you both uncover your family's values and extract purpose and meaning from a lifetime of disparate yet common experiences. If you listen carefully to the stories your family tells from their life — the stories of heritage, vision, hopes, and wisdom gained from a lifetime of experience — you will uncover the important values. You will also uncover your family's own unique sense of care giving. The importance of the family story comes from listening carefully, connecting the patterns of the past, and re-interpreting them to inform the future. Values, vision, and story combine to create the future dream.

For Sarah Russell Cavanaugh, the youngest of the second generation involved in The Russell Family Foundation, one story stands out among many others — one told to her by her mother ("the motivator for most of our philanthropy"). Sarah's grandmother would come to the house once a week to care for the four Russell children to encourage her daughter to do volunteer work in the community. Sarah adds, "My mother's first experience was teaching swimming to disabled kids at the YMCA. She would come home from her day being thankful that her children were blessed with good health. The time her mother gave her allowed her to give to others, even during this busy time in her life. This was the beginning of philanthropy."

The three years it took to move from a corporate pass-through foundation to an endowed family foundation allowed Sarah's family members the time to get their values and mission statements in order, as well as to understand their dynamics as adults. Sarah encouraged her parents and siblings to write a personal mission statement, asking them to describe their current personal charitable activities, and where they would most likely give a significant amount of financial support if they could.

The family met and Sarah handed out the mission statements with no names attached. "The first thing everyone wanted to do was identify whose was whose … it put everyone on an even playing field. It opened the door to what we believe as individuals, what we would love to strive for as a group, and created an environment of mutual trust and respect … it was the best family discussion around money and philanthropy that we ever had."

---

fig. 1 Four Useful Principles

Here are four principles from Frederick M. Hudson's book, The Adult Years: The Art of Self-Renewal, to consider when drafting a dream plan:

- Keep the dream central to the plan.
- Construct a plan that draws on strengths (individuals and family).
- Honestly face up to one's limits and underdeveloped abilities.
- Continuously adapt your dream to the changing realities.

Respect All Family Voices

A family gathering where members are allowed to share their dreams without judgment can lead to increasing candor, expressions of imagination, and suggestions for the Mission Statement. The founder and family members alike may find that direction for the family foundation begins to take on a life of its own. Techniques developed during the dream step can have a lasting effect in other ways as well. As part of each Russell Family Foundation board meeting, for example, trustees pass around a meaningful object. Cavanaugh explains, "Each person holds the object and is able to speak uninterrupted. They may choose to pass it on, but often the most important things are said at this time. This again is to ensure every voice is heard."

For each family approaching this process, the story will have its unique character, one that reflects the family and family dynamics. Sarah Russell Cavanaugh's family sought "first, to explore our family dynamics, just to be aware of what they were, and to make sure that all voices were heard. Every family has its history, but if you are going to have a future, you must have all voices at the table heard." Her experience is not uncommon when the family embraces a process from the beginning.

However, as John Abele, founder of the Argosy Foundation points out, one must be careful how the process is presented to the family members. He believes everyone should feel they have a voice of contribution. "The process needed to create a family held vision for the foundation depends obviously on the psyche of the family, but in my experience, ask them [family members] before you do it. If you want me on the landing, include me on the take-off. It is a wonderful learning opportunity if everyone is involved." Cavanaugh agrees, "It is very important that it is not a forced march to the table — that everybody wants to be there."

John Abele remembers growing up in a family where he "felt blessed by having to struggle. I saw people from wealthy families who didn't do well and that concerned me. From a family point of view, suddenly there was wealth in the family and I wanted to make sure that we as a family talked with each other and were involved in philanthropy together. I believe wealth is an extraordinary opportunity to be creative and give to society."

Keep the Family and the Dream Central

Allow yourself and your family the space, time, flexibility, and creativity to explore your boldest, most imaginative dream for your family and the world in which they interact. It is from this dream that the passion and enthusiasm flow. It is imperative that the dream stays central in all foundation activity to inform the purpose and meaning behind the actions and family interactions. Rushworth Kidder, president of the Institute for Global Ethics, urges people to "develop a code that's vibrant and very specific to the kinds of things that align with your passion."

Educate family members about the family history and family foundations. Encourage the Mission Statement to embody family values. Sarah Russell Cavanaugh arranged for members of her family to visit with eight foundations or family members of foundations. During the visits, Sarah just sat back and listened to the questions her siblings and parents were asking. "It was an incredible learning experience for all of us together."

GOOD ADVICE➤ For Nancy Brain, of the Frances Hollis Brain Family Foundation, a conference on family foundations communicated the message loud and clear. "If one generation hoards all the power and doesn't share any of the responsibility, that wouldn't be good. It will be hard for them to take over. That is when we decided that the next generation would get involved at 16."

The Russell Family Foundation hosts a family website with antique photographs of family members, and they have created a family tree "that enabled us to see where we came from and where we are going." Learning more about our

Allow yourself and your family the space, time, flexibility, and creativity to explore your boldest, most imaginative dream for your family and the world in which they interact. It is from this dream that the passion and enthusiasm flow.

families helps us to know more about ourselves and our dreams. Our visions may even echo voices from the past.

Discovering a Deeper Family Meaning

In the process of taking the dream step, of identifying your dreams and values and determining direction for your family foundation, you may be pleasantly surprised at the unexpected personal and family inner gifts that appear. The level of family closeness can influence the heights that you can achieve, as well as the speed at which you can progress. What matters most, however, is that the process be inclusive, inspiring, broadening, and fulfilling.

Although the dream step is only the beginning, it may help to elevate and focus the founder's and the family's sights, thereby giving a higher and more lasting vision to the family foundation. This kind of family mission offers the fullness of philanthropic gifting to the givers as well as those who receive.

WHY DID I MAKE ALL THIS MONEY?
Values and Ethics in Family Foundations

by Rushworth M. Kidder

Donors who create successful family foundations generally begin by addressing three kinds of issues. The first are immediate and worldly — tax consequences, legal relationships, family involvement, public visibility, and so forth. The second are a pair of searching issues that every donor must answer: Why did I make all this money? And, what do I want to do with it?

If the answer to the last question is, To be charitable, a third range of issues arises. Because philanthropy seeks to serve others, it lives within the precincts of some of the deepest moral and metaphysical soul-searching about core values. Successful startup boards can explore those values by asking some of the big questions: Who are we? Why are we here? How do we understand our purpose? What is our obligation to others? What can we do to make a difference?

The act of creating a foundation, then, is the act of translating deeply held values into practical action. Thus, one of the most useful frameworks for a new foundation is a code of values — a statement of the attributes that should characterize the foundation's work. Such a code is generally brief, sometimes comprising only a few key words. It is aspirational rather than descriptive in nature — a promise of what the donor wants the foundation to be, rather than a declaration of how good he or she thinks it already is. It is also broadly shared, hammered out in discussions with all the relevant participants.

A code of values is not, however, a mission statement which, going back to the Latin meaning of *mission*, tells the foundation board and staff (if one exists) what it has been sent to do. Nor is it a strategic plan, which is a blueprint of the steps needed to fulfill the foundation's mission. Nor is it just

a motto, a generalized inspirational saying that hints at some popular sentiment without committing to any particulars. A code of values, by contrast, tells *how* staff and board are to accomplish the foundation's mission, implement strategy, and commit to reaching ideals.

Because shared values underlie the ethical culture of any group, articulating a code of values is important for any organization. For a foundation, having such a code goes beyond important to essential. Why? For two reasons. First, the public holds the nonprofit and charitable sector in high regard, expecting from it a more lofty ethical standard than it expects from the commercial or public sectors. The concern about lapses in ethical conduct touches every part of society, wrote Brian O'Connell, former executive director of Independent Sector, in a seminal 1991 report on ethics for nonprofits. "But, the public expects the highest values and ethics to be practiced habitually in the institutions of our charitable, nonprofit sector. Because these institutions, fundamentally, are dedicated to enhancing basic human values, expectations of them are particularly high. *Those who presume to serve the public good assume a public trust.*" [emphasis in original][1]

Second, foundation executives and trustees generally recognize these moral expectations — and realize that more needs doing to fulfill them. In a series of interviews by the Institute for Global Ethics staff with 40 foundation executives and trustees in 1998, [2] they found that:

- Fully 95 percent believe ethics is very or somewhat important as a topic of public concern these days;
- Nearly 98 percent said ethics is very or somewhat important within the foundation community;
- Only 55 percent, however, felt that ethics played a very extensive role in their organizations; and
- Only 10 percent believed that people are clear about what is meant by the word ethics.

One of the foremost tasks for a new family foundation, then, is to establish with some clarity, foundation values, what they mean, and how they can be applied in practical ways when ethical issues arise.

Is ethics important? Without a doubt. Is it being applied? Somewhat. Is it well understood? Hardly. One of the foremost tasks for a new family foundation, then, is to establish with some clarity, foundation values, what they mean, and how they can be applied in practical ways when ethical issues arise.

Whose Values?

While trustees may agree on the importance of a code of values, they may stumble over an old canard: Whose values will we adopt? The question presupposes that each of us has a different set — that we're all so different that we can't possibly agree on something as basic as our moral values.

In fact, the opposite is true. A decade of research at the Institute for Global Ethics strongly suggests that wherever you ask people to define the core moral values they would most like to see on a code of ethics for the global future, they articulate five things: *honesty, responsibility, respect, fairness, and compassion.* So universal are these five ideas that they appear across nationalities, cultures, races, religions, genders, economic strata, and political alignments. The Institute has verified these findings in survey work, in focus groups, and through a Values Definition Process in seminars around the world.[3]

These five values may or may not be the ones your foundation chooses to carve in stone. Even if they are, they'll require further work to make them operational and applicable to the foundation's particular circumstances. But they suggest an important point: If foundation board members settle for the notion that arriving at a set of shared values is impossible because we're all so different, they haven't pushed far enough. Individuals differ on huge numbers of things. But on core values there is wide agreement on a few key things. Finding that common ground gives trustees, in the startup as well as the operational phases, the courage to differ from one another over matters of mission, objectives, strategy, and tactics — while still respecting the core values that hold the foundation together.

Once a code of values is in place, one of the clearest ways to understand ethics is to recognize that ethical issues arise in two (and really only two) ways. First, they result from violations of a key value — when, for instance, someone is found being dishonest in an organization that regards honesty as a core value. In that case, ethics becomes (as it is most popularly thought to be) a matter of right versus wrong. Sometimes the wrongdoing rises to the threshold of illegality. The family-office manager who takes home old computers to sell for his or her personal benefit, the executive director who cooks the books to pocket unwarranted compensation, the trustee who fiddles foundation funds to pay for family vacations, are all violating the law.

But some profoundly unethical behaviors may or may not be legal: A personnel officer who advertises widely for a position he or she knows will be filled by someone inside the foundation, a program officer who delays responding to a request for funding until the applicant has gone out of business, or a board chair who tells only some of the trustees about a key meeting and leaves the others in the dark until the last minute. Although there is not always something *illegal* about these actions, ethically, the actions are just plain wrong.

The second way in which ethical issues arise is more complex — and more significant. They can come about from a clash between two core values already on the code — when, for example, we have a choice to make between fairness and compassion. In that case, ethics has nothing to do with right versus wrong. It's a matter of right versus right. Such an issue lies at the heart of the dilemma, based on a real-life example, that faced the hypothetical Francine Michaud Family Foundation (see below). Given the strength of the donor's pro-life views before she passed away two decades ago, and the concern among her descendants on the board about the current need for family planning, what should the foundation do? We can make a powerful case for "right" on both sides. Yet we can't do both. That's where ethics gets tough.

When Generations Disagree[4]
George is a trustee of the Francine Michaud Family Foundation. The foundation was created by George and his siblings as a memorial to George's mother, her values and ethics, and the way she helped people during her lifetime. While the formal grantmaking guidelines are fairly general, the foundation's key criterion boils down to a question: Would Mom have made these grants?

George's mother was Catholic, and had agreed with the church's position on abortion. Among her many volunteer activities, she had put her pro-life beliefs into action by serving as a telephone hotline contact person for young women with unexpected pregnancies. Since its founding, the foundation has provided funding for similar hotlines and information services for years, and has also provided modest support for other human services programs.

Twenty years after Francine Michaud's death, the grandchildren have begun to join the foundation's board. Several of them, however, are much more comfortable with family planning than their elders, some even favoring legal abortion.

One of George's sisters feels so strongly about pro-life issues that she is proposing that they concentrate virtually all of the foundation's resources in that one area. She is convinced that her mother felt more strongly about this issue than any other, and that the only way to honor her memory is to provide maximum funding to anti-abortion activities, from counseling to advocacy to policy research.

The grandchildren haven't asked to allocate foundation funds directly to pro-choice issues; however, several are balking at putting large amounts into fairly militant pro-life activities. They argue that were she alive today, their grandmother would want the foundation to take a temperate approach to this issue, and also to broaden support of other areas of growing community need such as education and job development.

Which side should George support? Should he support his sister's commitment to spend everything, powerfully, on this one issue? Or should he side with the grandchildren, tempering pro-life grants with expanded funding in other program areas?

What Is an Ethical Organization?
Ethics is so often thought of as right versus wrong that, for many people, it has come to mean little more than compliance with rules and regulations. And so it is — in part. There is no question that an ethical organization must, at the

most basic level, live by the law. It is imperative that the trustees and staff of family foundations understand the relevant legal frameworks for their activities. They must know the right and avoid the wrong.

But knottier aspects of ethics can arise where *both* sides are right and where the best resolution may lie beyond the guidance of the law.. When the Institute's survey of foundations asked respondents to share their principal ethical concerns, they responded with 12 key topics — almost all of which involved an interplay between right-versus-wrong and right-versus-right issues:

- Self-dealing;
- Conflict of interest;
- Transparency;
- Diversity and pluralism;
- Nepotism;
- Ethical investing;
- Abuse of power and privilege;
- What to fund — charity or systemic change;
- Arrogance in dealings with nonprofits;
- Inside information about nonprofits;
- Lack of candor, and how to temper unbounded optimism; and
- Spending — long-term versus short-term.

The first of these, *self-dealing*, is clearly illegal. It involves the deployment of foundation resources for the personal gain of one of its trustees or staff. Not always obvious, it can come in some tricky disguises, as when a trustee is part-owner of the public relations firm the foundation wants to hire, or when a family member leases office space to the foundation in a building he or she owns. No matter how efficient these may appear, they remain illegal.

Three other issues can also have strong legal overtones:
- *Conflict of interest.* Should a foundation trustee sit on the board of a grantee? Doing so can provide great insight into the grantee's activities and, depending on the nature of the

activity, can be a tremendous learning experience for a trustee who may have deep interest in that particular field. But when that trustee begins to argue for the grantee's interests at the expense of the foundation's concerns, there can be real conflict. This issue can have legal ramifications if it skates too close to self-dealing, although in many instances it may be more a matter of ethics than of law.
- *Transparency.* This, too, can be a legal issue, as in the requirement of full disclosure in such documents as Form 990 of the Internal Revenue Service. But what about publishing an annual report: Are scarce foundation resources better spent on shining a light on internal workings or on making more grants?
- *Diversity and pluralism.* Some foundations strive to ensure that trustees, staff, and grantees reflect the multiple cultures of the communities they serve. Others focus on single cultures in particular need of help. When the issue of diversity and pluralism touches on fair hiring and promotion practices, it has legal ramifications. In general, however, decisions to fund within a broader or narrower cultural bandwidth are ethical rather than legal.

But what about these others, where the law allows more latitude?
- *Nepotism.* Is it right to invite family members to serve in key positions within a family foundation, since they have such a strong stake in upholding the legacy and intent of the donor? Or do such family ties create managerial entanglements that impede the smooth functioning of the organization?
- *Ethical investing.* Is it right to invest the corpus with an eye solely for financial considerations, seeking the best return regardless of the nature of the stock to maximize the potential for programmatic giving? Or should trustees invest only in firms that don't operate in sectors they feel are unethical — as tobacco, armaments, and gambling are seen by some to be — even if that restriction lowers the return and limits the charitable impact of the foundation? (Trustees are, of course, also held to the Prudent Investor

and IRS rules that require them to protect the assets of the foundation.)

- *Abuse of power and privilege.* When a trustee steers funding to a certain nonprofit to win a seat on its prestigious board and move in more exalted social circles, that's abusive — though it may not be illegal. But when a foundation uses some of its resources to elevate its public profile and attract better grantees and partnerships, isn't that an acceptable use of power and privilege?

- *What to fund — charity or systemic change.* This question, a variant on the give-a-man-a-fish platitude, poses a tough dilemma. Do you ensure that foundation funds go directly to the worst hunger cases, the most gripping public health situations, and the neediest classrooms? Or, do you use them to build better nonprofits capable of strategically addressing the underlying causes of these ills — even if some of today's sufferers get no relief?

> *Ethics is so often thought of as right versus wrong that, for many people, it has come to mean little more than compliance with rules and regulations. And so it is — in part.*

- *Arrogance in dealings with nonprofits.* Not returning phone calls from potential grantees, brushing off well-meaning inquiries, and spending more time telling charities how to behave than listening to their perspective — these things are not illegal and may not noticeably harm a foundation's early record of success, though they surely speak of arrogance. Yet if a budding foundation is to protect its time and resources to focus on first-intensity issues, must it not find ways to limit the energy spent responding to queries, pleas, and inappropriate proposals?

- *Inside information about nonprofits.* How much information about grantees should a foundation share with other foundations? If a particular grant was unsuccessful, does that give a family foundation the right to blackball the grantee with a few negative words? Yet if the foundation discovers serious problems in a nonprofit's accounting, honesty, or competence, doesn't it have an obligation to warn other potential funders?

- *Lack of candor, and how to temper unbounded optimism.* Learning to say No nicely is just as difficult in the foundation world as in other walks of life. On some occasions, a delayed No can lead to huge expenditures of time and energy on the nonprofit's part — not to mention a hopefulness that will only be shattered. But on other occasions, a too-quick denial may shut off a promising project that, with coaching and fine-tuning, could become one of the foundation's finest grants.

- *Spending — long-term versus short-term.* One of the Institute's survey respondents put it neatly when he said, "If we look to the long term, we will conserve what we have today for tomorrow's problems. But such are the problems today, that it can be argued that we must spend more of our wealth now." Which is right for a particular foundation?

These issues raise tough moral questions. How does a foundation decide which is the higher right? A framework for decisionmaking, put in place as the foundation is developing, can help trustees and staff recognize ethical issues as they appear. It can help the foundation identify the basic paradigms into which right-versus-right issues tend to fall — truth versus loyalty, individual versus community, short-term versus long-term, and justice versus mercy — where clashes between good values become the drivers of the foundation's toughest ethical challenges. And it can help the foundation to apply some of the key resolution principles from moral philosophy — the ends-based principle of Utilitarianism, the rule-based principle anchored in Immanuel Kant's categorical imperative, and the care-based principle rooted in the Golden Rule.[5]

The capacity for this kind of moral decisionmaking referred to by the Institute as Ethical Fitness™ starts with the core

In the end, there are two intuitional tests for foundation ethics. Is the foundation doing things right? And, is the foundation doing the right things?

values of the foundation. Experience suggests that, where such values are embedded at the outset, the ethical issues will be far less problematic. Values won't prevent such issues from arising: Far from it. Having a focus on values tends to highlight moral concerns that, in a less values-driven culture, might slip past unseen. But a focus on values, and a commitment to address ethical issues courageously and robustly as they arise, help ensure that no unethical seedlings are allowed to grow into the kinds of stifling entanglements that can divide families and paralyze good grantmaking.

Is the Foundation Doing Things Right? Doing the Right Things?

In the end, there are two intuitional tests for foundation ethics. Is the foundation doing things right? And, is the foundation doing the right things? The first holds the foundation to the highest standards of ethical behavior and motivation. The second requires that foundation board and staff apply right-versus-right tests to every programmatic decision — separating the merely worthwhile from the absolutely essential, aligning funding with mission, and ensuring that the efforts of the foundation are in the service of its most enduring values which, after all, was why the donor made all that money.

[1] Independent Sector, "Obedience to the Unenforceable: Ethics and the Nation's Voluntary and Philanthropic Community," Washington, DC: Independent Sector, 1991, p.5.

[2] Graham Phaup, "Navigating the Waters in Today's Philanthropy: An Ethical Compass," Camden, ME: Institute for Global Ethics, 1998, pp. 5-7.

[3] Rushworth M. Kidder, "Chapter 8." *Shared Values for a Troubled World: Conversations with Men and Women of Conscience*. Camden, ME: Institute for Global Ethics.

[4] Dilemma prepared by Institute for Global Ethics staff for *Foundation News & Commentary* July/August 2001, p. 40. Reprinted by permission of the Council on Foundations.

[5] For a full explanation of this decision-making process, see Rushworth M. Kidder, *How Good People Make Tough Choices: Resolving the Dilemmas of Ethical Living*, New York: Simon & Schuster, 1997. For specific application of these concepts to family foundations, see *Ethics for Family Foundations*, a CD-ROM-based interactive ethics module and accompanying workbook (Camden, ME: Institute for Global Ethics, 2001). See www.foundationethics.org for more information.

ONE FAMILY'S STORY
A Conversation with Bill Gates, Sr.

Bill Gates, Sr., is no ordinary father, and Bill Gates III is no ordinary son. But their experiences in creating the Bill & Melinda Gates Foundation are ordinary to all families beginning the journey into family foundation grantmaking. Bill Gates, Sr., who was present from the first idea of the foundation, talked about its origins and formation with Virginia M. Esposito and Joseph Foote.

The earliest conversations about the advantages of a private foundation as against random personal giving were between my son and his professional advisors. There really wasn't anything you would call a family discussion. I was a part of it because I was a member of the law firm from which he was getting some of his advice. He and I did talk about it from time to time.

Bill resisted it for a long, long time because his view of life was that every time you create some kind of organization, it adds minor complications to your daily agenda. He was very reluctant to have to deal with another entity in this life. So, in spite of the financial advantages, he and Melinda were quite resistant to this idea.

Difficulties Keeping Up With Charitable Requests

After Bill's mother died in 1994, I had a conversation with him and Melinda about the fact that they were not doing a very acceptable job of keeping up with charitable requests that were being made of them personally. They didn't answer letters, they didn't get back to people. It wasn't a matter of lack of interest. It was a matter of priority. My son felt that the most important thing he had to do was to see to it that

his company succeeded, that he brought in a lot of very bright, energetic young people as employees, and that they created products that are of value to the world at large. Those things were a clear preoccupation for him.

Bill's Father Makes a Suggestion

I had become less active in my law firm, and suggested to Bill that I could serve as a sort of screen and responding mechanism for some of those letters and requests. He and Melinda thought that was a terrific idea. Activity flowed from that moment very, very quickly. Now it made sense to have an entity, a foundation, because he had somebody to manage it, and it would actually subtract from his burden. Not very long after I started to help with these affairs and the mail started to be shunted over to me, we did form a foundation for their personal philanthropy. That's the beginning of the story.

First Formal Structure Is Set in Place

The foundation was created in the form of a trust. There is no Mission Statement, or at least there wasn't when Bill funded it with something in the neighborhood of $200 million. Very shortly after that, we got into some discussion about things he and Melinda cared about, such as family planning. We then decided to become more proactive than we had contemplated. I did a survey, and invited proposals. We did select a couple of interesting projects to fund.

Discussion of Perpetuity Is Ongoing

In terms of planning, there has been a continuous discussion of how long this foundation was going to last, and how ultimately it might be brought to a close. We don't yet know what the right answer is. It's very hard to think in terms of perpetuity. I don't know how rational it is, but there is a hesitancy about the idea of perpetual institutions.

The other consideration is that there is an attraction to having something like this for your heirs to participate in. This involves a risk, because you don't know much about the per-

The central challenge of the decades ahead will be to share lifesaving advances such as vaccines and new medicines, as well as the benefits of the revolution in information technology, with those who need them most.

— LETTER FROM BILL & MELINDA GATES
Bill & Melinda Gates Foundation website

sonality of your heirs, particularly the second generation. But if you assume that they are going to be quality human beings, then the idea of having this kind of an activity for them to be involved in is a very attractive thing.

We looked at the Rockefeller family philanthropy, a perpetual entity, which is an argument for perpetuity, because in our judgment it has continued to operate in a very imaginative and effective way. On the other hand, you can see models where family purposes have been diverted. The foundation gets diverted from what the person who started it, whose money it was, wanted to have happen.

Bill and Melinda Gates Find a Cause

Back to history: events imposed upon us the need for goal setting, and a more thoughtful approach to what we were about. These were not things we sat down and thought about in a preliminary way or in preparation for what we were doing. They were imposed on us by circumstances and our operations. We had an unbelievably large number of proposals coming in which we had to sort on the basis of what was most important to Bill and Melinda.

Then, in late 1995 or early 1996, Bill and Melinda read an article in *The New York Times* talking about the disease burden in the underdeveloped world, about how many people were dying from diseases that had long since been eradicated in the industrial world. Bill sent that article to me and asked if possibly we could do something about this.

That article showed the egregious inequity that a human being, by the accident of birth, is in a situation where a lifetime of good health is relatively hopeless compared with somebody in the United States, for whom good health care is virtually assured. That inequity is so gigantic that it does shake one's sense of justice. This was clearly the most directional event that happened in the history of the foundation. The size of the foundation began to increase hugely following that. In the course of about 12 months, Bill and Melinda contributed something in the neighborhood of $20 billion. That infusion of funds, plus Bill's developing interest in the problems of global health, gave us a very definite focus. That focus continues to narrow.

There is a lesson here of general applicability, which is that anybody who launches on an activity of this kind will find themselves modifying and probably narrowing their focus and goals and the kinds of things they take an interest in. It's clear to me that, over time, as we have experience with the things we support, we may well modify even the relatively set ideas we have now. We will see the successes and non-successes.

fig. 1

Current Foundation Programs and Initiatives

GLOBAL HEALTH INITIATIVE ➢ This Initiative is now more than half of what we do. It started almost casually with Bill and Melinda reading that article that caught their fancy, and now it has clearly developed a life of its own.

LIBRARY TECHNOLOGY PROGRAM ➢ This activity was carried out by the Microsoft Corporation. My son recognized that is was going to become too big for the company to support, so he spun it off to a personal activity, which was an operating foundation. It was later merged with the activity I was conducting, so now there is just one foundation. This program brought a very precise second focus, a completely definable kind of objective — to bring technology at some level to every library in the United States, with librarians trained and equipped to use it.

EDUCATIONAL REFORM PROGRAM ➢ This initiative came along at about the same time that the foundation was being grown so radically. It is making some very significant awards and grants, particularly addressed to structural problems in public education.

GOOD CITIZEN ROLE IN THE NORTHWEST ➢ We are a substantial supporter of capital campaigns and civic activities in the Pacific Northwest. The focus is largely geographic.

Founder and Foundation Affect One Another

The array of interests and even prejudices that people have is so vast that, to somebody, the creation of an art museum, or the development of a symphony, or the enhancement of the quality of a school are things that appeal to personal passions — in very much the way that global health has caught on with my son and his wife.

That's the great beauty of private philanthropy — the enormous diversity of it. The amplification of one's charitable

The Bill & Melinda Gates Foundation is dedicated to improving people's lives by sharing advances in health and learning with the global community.

Bill & Melinda Gates Foundation website

urges has a value of its own. It imposes a discipline on the activity that is very positive. It requires you to think about compliance with regulations, such as the business of minimum distributions — which I happen to be sympathetic to. It generates and continues to give a focus to what you're doing. The business of having an entity almost uniformly brings a third party, an objective player, into the mix, which is a very valuable contribution that weighs against indiscriminate, momentary passions or interests that a donor might be subject to. Almost everybody has, either within the family or in a circle of professional help, mentors and advisors, lawyers and accountants, people they talk with about important things. In that circle, there's bound to be constructive guidance and constructive day-to-day support.

Then there is the business of the contribution that the history of your activity makes to your own evaluation of what you're doing and your own sense of doing it in the best, most effective way — that's an enormously positive contribution.

This new century brings with it exciting advances in health and learning.
We all share the responsibility of ensuring that these opportunities are not
out of reach for the people who need them the most.

— LETTER FROM BILL & MELINDA GATES
Bill & Melinda Gates Foundation website

Grantmaking Style Develops with Experience

By and large, the creation of a family foundation is a positive thing to do. It's a positive contribution and something that people should approach with optimism. I would certainly encourage people to go into it with some degree of flexibility, recognizing that actually conducting a foundation over a period of time will very likely have a significant effect on one's views about what they want to do.

There are process choices here, as well as subject choices. There is something of a dichotomy between a rather freewheeling gifting of money to responsible entities to perform on, and a more staffed, programmed, controlling approach where, to a large extent, activities are carried out or closely followed by people on foundation staff. When you get to a certain size, you have a choice between whether you do the work or the grantee does the work.

A Father Finds Gratification in His Son's Philanthropy

My gratification from involvement in my son's foundation is almost self-evident. It is such a joy to be a party to his philanthropy, and such a joy to see what he and Melinda are wanting to do and to be a part of it. No one should be surprised by the joy that flows from that.

STARTING UP

FIGURES

FACING IMPORTANT LEGAL ISSUES

by John Sare

nce you decide to create a family foundation, you will face
important legal issues, especially:

- Defining your foundation's charitable purposes;
- Obtaining recognition of tax-exempt status;
- Selecting the assets that will fund the foundation; and
- Staying out of trouble.

You may decide to tackle the legal issues on your own, drawing on the excellent resources cited in the bibliography for this chapter in Resources for Your Library, p. 248. Or you may inquire whether your own lawyer or accountant has had significant experience in this area or can refer you to someone who has. Friends who have created foundations may direct you to advisors who have been helpful to them. In addition, the National Center for Family Philanthropy and the Council on Foundations may have names of professional advisors in your community who have experience with the creation of family foundations.

---

fig. 1

What Is a "Family Foundation?"

The term "family foundation" is a colloquial expression. The technical term under the Internal Revenue Code is "private foundation" — a concept that entered the tax laws in 1969 to refer to those charitable trusts and nonprofit corporations that are endowed by an individual, a family, or a company for the purpose of making grants to other charitable organizations. Then as now, private foundations (like all other charities) enjoyed a variety of state and federal tax subsidies — namely, exemption from income tax and an ability to receive tax-deductible contributions.

Critics contended in the late 1960s that private foundations abused their special status by (among other things) (1) amassing great wealth without making distributions in support of real charitable causes, (2) retaining unwise investments in family companies in order to prop up the stock price or preserve family control, and (3) paying over-generous compensation to friends and family or making travel and study grants on a discriminatory basis.

Congress eventually concluded that these abuses, perceived and real, warranted special federal regulation, and in 1969 the term "private foundation" took on its distinct legal meaning.

The law now draws a line between "private" and "public" charities and imposes more restrictive rules (described in the section on Staying Out of Trouble, p. 67) on those that are classified as "private." Furthermore, contributions to private foundations qualify for less favorable deductibility treatment than contributions to public charities.

Although there are "private operating foundations" that carry on active charitable or educational programs, most private foundations are grantmaking organizations, technically known as "private nonoperating foundations." Foundations of this type are the focus of this guidebook. Materials cited in the bibliography may be helpful to you if you are still trying to decide whether a grantmaking foundation is an appropriate vehicle for you.

Defining Your Foundation's Charitable Purposes

A family foundation must be "organized" exclusively for tax-exempt purposes recognized by the Internal Revenue Code. The foundation's governing instrument must limit its activities to one or more of the following general purposes: educational, literary, scientific, religious, or charitable.

These purposes (and a handful of others that are rarely relevant) are commonly lumped together under the heading "charitable purposes" or "tax-exempt purposes." The specific purposes you have in mind must fit within one of the recognized tax-exempt categories. If you expect to make grants mainly to well-established charities, such as universities, relief organizations, nonprofit hospitals, arts organizations, religious institutions, and the like, you should have little difficulty specifying suitable purposes in the governing instrument and making grants that will readily qualify under one of the recognized tax-exempt categories.

You may have more novel objectives — such as the woman who wanted to create a foundation to perpetuate her mother's legacy of dressmaking and embroidery, or the man who wanted to provide economic assistance to family farmers to promote the tradition of family farming. If your specific objectives are innovative or even a bit idiosyncratic,

---

fig. 2 — What Do We Mean By...?

GOVERNING INSTRUMENT ➤ The term "governing instrument" refers to the document that contains a foundation's statement of purposes. The governing instrument also specifies whether or not a foundation must be perpetual and may spell out special restrictions on succession or control. If a foundation is structured as a charitable trust, the governing instrument is an Agreement of Trust, sometimes referred to as an "Instrument," "Declaration," or "Indenture" of Trust. If a foundation is structured as a not-for-profit corporation, the governing instrument is called the Articles of Incorporation or the Certificate of Incorporation.

BYLAWS ➤ Although the trustees of a charitable trust occasionally elect to adopt Bylaws, the directors of a not-for-profit corporation almost always do so, and in some states it may be required. Bylaws are typically limited to routine matters of governance and say little or nothing about a foundation's purposes.

TRUSTEE and OFFICER ➤ A not-for-profit corporation ordinarily has a "board of directors" or a "board of trustees," and the board appoints a president, a secretary, a treasurer, or other "officers." A charitable trust usually has "trustees" but no officers, although larger charitable trusts may appoint administrative and program "officers." In this chapter, the term "trustee" is used generically — and can mean the trustee of a charitable trust or a member of the board of a not-for-profit corporation. The term "officer" refers to an officer of a not-for-profit corporation or a charitable trust.

---

your lawyer may be helpful in figuring out whether and how your objectives can be structured to fall within the legal definition of what is "charitable." Fortunately, the legal concept of "charity" is inherently flexible, intended to evolve as the needs of society evolve.

If you wish, you can identify general purposes (educational, charitable, etc.) and then add specific limitations. An "educational" foundation might support

only private colleges and universities in Texas or only museums of Asian art. A "scientific" foundation might support only medical research institutions studying prostate cancer. A "charitable" foundation might support only the relief of poverty and construction of charity hospitals in Peru. There are myriad possibilities. When you define a foundation's charitable purposes, you face an important practical and legal issue: Balancing your desire to achieve specific charitable purposes today, and the virtual certainty that some degree of flexibility will be needed in the future.

To allow yourself flexibility, you may find it helpful if the governing instru-ment gives you the power to change the charitable purposes, without court approval, at any time during your life-time. In some cases, you may wish to empower those who control the foun-dation after your death to amend the charitable purposes — or you may decide that changes of purpose should be prohibited after your death. For an indepth treatment of this subject, see Paul K. Rhoads, "Establishing Your Intent," *Living the Legacy: The Values of a Family's Philanthropy Across Generations.*

Philanthropists often find it appealing to create a foundation that will last in per-petuity. A foundation that pays out the minimum 5 percent a year of its average annual asset value and, net of operating expenses, earns more than that should indeed be able to last forever.

But bear in mind: Forever is a very long time, and the ideas that seem wise at the beginning of the 21st Century may be inappropriate or unworkable a cen-tury, or even a decade, in the future.

A few questions are worth asking before setting up an ostensibly perpet-ual foundation:

- Am I contributing enough money to my foundation to warrant the expense *forever* of the apparatus necessary to manage the assets prudently and give them away responsibly?
- Who is going to run a perpetual foun-dation? For how many generations can I expect volunteers to shoulder the burden of carrying out the philan-thropic objectives I have in mind?
- Is my charitable objective broad enough that I can reasonably expect it to remain viable in perpetuity?
- Should I impose a time limit on my

---

fig. **3** Tips For Crafting Charitable Purposes

- Bear in mind that vague charitable purposes and excessively limited ones routinely yield confusion, discord, and litigation — sometimes during the founder's lifetime, more often in a family foundation's second or third generation.

- Invest ample time and thought in the development of a statement of charita-ble purposes and, if appropriate, a mission statement. Write down your ideas. Let your lawyer convert your concepts into suitable "legalese." Then read the lawyer's draft critically and work with your lawyer to improve it.

- Encourage family, friends, and others whom you trust to ask hard questions about your philanthropic ideas and to participate actively in the process of identifying the right charitable purposes and deciding how they are expressed.

---

fig. **4** Five Key Questions on Charitable Purposes

1. How likely are my charitable objectives to evolve during my lifetime?

2. To what extent are my objectives something that my children or other successors on the board of the foundation will want to pursue?

3. What are the chances that my particular purpose may one day become obsolete or unnecessary?

4. How well have I matched funding with purpose? Too little money? Too much?

5. How can I ensure that later generations won't quarrel over what I mean?

fig.
5

Succession and Changing the Legal Structure of the Foundation

Succession planning is a key aspect of governance. It should be discussed carefully with friends and family and, ultimately, with your legal and financial advisors.

Will the foundation remain in the hands of your family? Will it be placed in the hands of trusted advisors or employees and the people they select? Will it go on perpetually or will it go "out of business" in a generation or two? To what extent, if any, should the governing documents limit eligibility for the governing body or the intended "life" of the foundation? Are your goals for succession best accomplished using a charitable trust or a not-for-profit corporation? Should there be special arrangements if you develop Alzheimer's disease or are otherwise incapacitated for an extended period prior to death?

Many foundations change dramatically after the death or permanent incapacity of the founder. Some divide into multiple foundations, reflecting the geographic dispersion and differences of opinion of the founder's adult children and grandchildren. As a legal matter, the division of a foundation is relatively easy to accomplish, although family discord can complicate the process. The divided foundation enables each branch of the family to pursue its philanthropic goals (and its investment strategies) in the way it sees fit. Such a division

should limit opportunities for internecine conflict. If you create a foundation and sense that its division is inevitable, or even desirable given the family relationships, you might wish to leave a letter of instructions outlining your intentions and hopes for the family's future and the future of the foundation. It may be easier for your heirs to endorse the idea of dividing the foundation if you have endorsed it in advance.

A foundation with close ties to a small group of public charities — a favorite university and a favorite museum, for example — might convert into a "supporting organization" of those charities, and in that way enjoy preferred tax treatment as a public charity. A foundation might even pay out all of its assets directly to favorite charities — on the theory that a "middle man" is no longer necessary or appropriate. A foundation lacking wealth of a magnitude that warrants a staff of investment experts and grants officers might conclude, after the founder's death or permanent incapacity, that it should transfer its assets to a community foundation. A community foundation can hold the foundation's assets in a "field-of-interest" or "donor-advised" fund that furthers the goals of the founder but relieves friends and family of administrative burdens — and should reduce administrative costs as well.

foundation — a fixed number of years after my death or for the lives of my children and grandchildren?
- Should I give the board the flexibility to distribute all of the assets, so that future generations can decide when and if it makes sense for my foundation to go out of business?
- If the assets are large enough and the purpose broad enough to warrant a

perpetual foundation, what kind of staffing and structure do I envision? Should I create that structure during my lifetime?

Crafting a Mission Statement

The governing instruments of many foundations contain extremely broad charitable purposes, often as broad as the law will allow. Then, to provide a

focus for grantmaking, those foundations adopt a mission statement, citing particular charitable causes that will be supported or particular styles of grantmaking that are to be favored (such as challenge grants or venture philanthropy). A mission statement can be a helpful way of achieving disciplined grantmaking today while preserving flexibility over the longer term.

fig. 6 — How Purpose and Mission Interplay

The following example illustrates the interplay of the legally non-binding mission statement and the legally binding statement of purposes contained in a foundation's governing instrument:

Tom Fox (all names are fictional), a 50-year-old investor, forms a foundation to support the preservation of Civil War battlefields and education about the Civil War. Tom accepts the lawyer's recommendation that the foundation have broad charitable purposes in its governing instrument, but a mission statement — freely changeable at any time — that focuses on the Civil War.

In his late 70s, Tom experiences deteriorating health and concludes that the foundation should shift its support to medical research. He tells his lawyer that he wants to leave the bulk of his remaining assets to the foundation and wants those assets forever dedicated to research into cures and treatments for diabetes and arthritis, with a limitation favoring research by public universities. At the same time, Tom is worried that his adult children are not interested in diabetes, arthritis, or any other health-related issues, and he is concerned that they will not take a serious interest in the foundation. He also has told his adult children that he expects them to contribute their own money to the foundation.

Tom and his lawyer agree as follows: The statement of purposes in the foundation's governing instrument will remain broad and unchanged. A new mission statement will be adopted to express the intention that the foundation support research at public universities into diabetes and arthritis and "in the event they are eradicated, other medical conditions affecting the elderly." Tom will sign a new Will, leaving the bulk of his assets to the foundation but on the condition that the assets passing at the time of his death be used exclusively in furtherance of the mission statement in effect at the time of his death.

Tom likes this structure: During his lifetime, the assets of the foundation are spent in furtherance of the mission that is important to him, but he retains the flexibility to change his mind. At his death, his bequest is limited to the specific purposes set forth in a mission statement he approved during his lifetime, but with built-in flexibility in the event diabetes and arthritis are eradicated. Meanwhile, Tom's adult children and other descendants have some flexibility, too. Although the bequest in Tom's Will is limited to the purposes specified in a mission statement he approved during his lifetime, the mission statement can be changed vis à vis all other assets of the foundation. Therefore, assets Tom gave before his death and any assets his descendants contribute to the foundation in the future can be used in support of whatever charitable purposes future generations deem appropriate.

A foundation's trustees can readily revise or replace a properly crafted mission statement, so that the focus of grant-making can change without notice to (or approval by) state charities officials or the Internal Revenue Service (IRS).

Obtaining Recognition of Tax Exempt Status

After your foundation is formed, either as a charitable trust or a not-for-profit corporation, your next order of business is to obtain recognition of its tax-exempt status. This process is initiated by filing Form 1023 with the IRS. This form requires the following information:

- A copy of the governing documents;
- A statement of projected activities (for example, investing donated funds and making grants to other charities);
- A list of trustees and officers, their addresses, and the compensation they will receive for their service to the foundation;
- A projected balance sheet for the last day of the current fiscal year; and
- A budget for 3 or 4 fiscal years, including the current one.

Additional disclosures may be necessary if, for example, the foundation has entered into a lease.

Form 1023 and a filing fee ($500 in 2002) are submitted to the IRS. The IRS typically responds with a letter acknowledging receipt and stating an estimated period of time (customarily about 120 days) within which the IRS expects to issue its determination letter. During the review, the IRS may contact you or your advisors for additional information. Although the IRS query will ordinarily be in writing and will state that the foundation has 2 weeks in which it must respond, extensions are routinely granted, usually by telephone. Written confirmation of these extensions is advisable. The IRS provides a helpful guide to the Form 1023 review process on its website www.irs.ustreas.gov. Nonetheless, completion of Form 1023 by someone who is thoroughly familiar with Form 1023 and with the applicable tax rules can reduce delays.

Once a foundation receives its favorable determination letter from the IRS, the letter should be kept in the foundation's minute book along with its governing instrument, its Bylaws, and a copy of Form 1023. The favorable IRS determination letter — along with the Form 1023, the governing instrument and Bylaws, and minutes of meetings — should be kept permanently in the foundation's minute book. Ordinarily, the determination letter is retroactive to the date the foundation was formed. That means that the foundation is retroactively tax-exempt and that contributions made prior to the issuance of the determination letter are eligible for the charitable deduction. Generally speaking, however, it is not advisable to make a contribution to a foundation until the determination letter has been secured.

States and most local governments recognize the tax-exempt status of foundations that have received favorable IRS determination letters. Additional tax exemptions may be available at the state level — for example, exemption from sales and use tax on goods *purchased* by the foundation or exemption from tax on real property owned by the foundation and used by it to fulfill its charitable purposes.

All states have one or more bureaus with authority to investigate and regulate charities. In most states, those bureaus are part of the Office of the Attorney General or the Office of the Secretary of State. Most states impose registration and annual reporting requirements on charities. Lawyers or accountants thoroughly familiar with local rules and practice may be able to guide you through the state-law requirements. Alternatively, you may wish to speak directly with the charities officials in your state. The staff of the state charities bureau should be thoroughly familiar with the requirements and can send you the necessary forms and instructions. It is increasingly popular to "download" this material from the websites maintained by most state charities officials. The AAFRC Trust for Philanthropy (www.aafrc.org) provides its members with an annual summary of the various states' registration and reporting requirements.

Selecting the Assets That Will Fund the Foundation

Many factors are relevant to the choice of donated assets and the timing of donations to a family foundation. The advice of your lawyer and/or accountant can be particularly valuable in threading through these complicated rules. The bibliography contains citations to several excellent resources on this topic. (See especially, the section of this guide entitled Funding Your Family Foundation, p. 76.) A few examples illuminate the major issues:

Janet Ford creates a foundation in early December. She wants an income tax deduction in the current tax year, so she makes her first contribution the day after the foundation is formed, even though the foundation does not yet have a *favorable IRS determination letter*. She stipulates that the foundation must return her gift if it fails to obtain a favorable IRS determination letter. That is a mistake. Under IRS rules, conditioning a gift to charity on the charity's receiving tax-exempt status makes the gift nondeductible. Janet is better off to wait until a favorable IRS determination letter is safely in hand.

Frank Bass, a filmmaker with a successful production company and a sizeable stock portfolio, is trying to decide which assets he will contribute to a new foundation. He learns from his accountant that the issues are surprisingly intricate:

- A gift of **cash** is the simplest gift. Valuation is not an issue, and in the year of the gift Frank can deduct an amount up to 30 percent of his adjusted gross income if his gift consists exclusively of cash and he makes no other gifts to charity.
- A gift of **publicly traded securities** with built-in capital gain may be the most economically beneficial gift for Frank. He should be able to deduct the fair market value of the contributed securities, and the foundation will be able to sell the securities without incurring the capital gains tax that Frank would have incurred if he had sold the securities himself. However, he can deduct only up to 20 percent of his adjusted gross income in the year of the gift if his gift consists exclusively of publicly traded securities.
- A donation of **real property, artwork or other tangible personal property, interests in a closely held business, and ordinary income property** (such as a copyright or rights under a contract) would provide very little economic benefit for Frank, because his deduction would be limited to the *lesser* of fair market value or his cost. He also learns that a gift of interests in his closely held business could raise issues under the "excess business holdings" and "self-dealing" rules (discussed later in this chapter). Ultimately, Frank decides his real property, artwork, stock in his closely

held production company, and the copyrights from his films should be retained or given to a public charity.
- Because a donation of **mortgaged property** may raise issues under the "self-dealing" rules and the unrelated-business income tax rules, Frank concludes he should not contribute mortgaged assets.

Alice Brady wishes to fund a foundation with publicly traded stock in the company her father founded. The stock is worth about $8 million, but Alice's annual income from her other assets and her job rarely exceeds $300,000. Because of the **deductibility limitations** — primarily, the fact that she cannot deduct more than 20 percent of her adjusted gross income in a given year for a donation of publicly traded stock to a foundation — she discovers that the most she can deduct in the year of her gift is $60,000. Her accountant tells her that she can "roll over" the deductions for an additional 5 tax years, meaning that her total deduction on an $8 million gift would be approximately $360,000 ($60,000 per year in each of 6 tax years). Because of these limitations, Alice decides to contribute only $360,000 worth of stock up front, take deductions over a 6-year period, and defer the rest of her philanthropy until a later date.

A "split-interest" charitable vehicle may be appealing for the philanthropist who wants to make a gift to charity while getting something in return. An interest in property is "split" by divid-

ing the property into two interests — present and future. The classic "split-interest" vehicles are the charitable remainder trust and the charitable lead trust. Although these trusts can be structured in many ways, the basic concepts can be illustrated as follows:

Once Alice Brady decides to contribute only $360,000 of stock to a foundation, her financial advisor points out that her remaining $7,640,000 of stock produces very little income for her and that she has a high exposure to market volatility unless she diversifies. She voices her concerns to her lawyer, who recommends that she create a charitable remainder trust. Using this vehicle, she is entitled to a lifetime stream of payments and, upon her death, the trust remainder passes to the foundation. Because the trust is a tax-exempt vehicle, it is able to sell appreciated assets that Alice contributes and to diversify its holdings without incurring any capital gains tax. Alice anticipates that her income will increase because of the distributions she will receive from the trust. Although the distributions will be taxable to her to the extent they consist of income or capital gains earned by the trust, the creation of the trust entitles Alice to a charitable deduction for the value of the foundation's remainder interest — an amount determined actuarially based on Alice's age at the time of the gift and significantly smaller than the amount of the deduction she would have received if she had donated the assets to the foundation outright. She expects that this additional deduction will offset some of the income and capital gains she plans to receive from the trust.

Philip Harmon has managed to shift a significant amount of his wealth into trusts for his adult children and is now concerned about creating a foundation and providing for his grandchildren. His lawyer recommends a charitable lead trust, which is the mirror image of a charitable remainder trust. In this arrangement, Phil Harmon creates a foundation, which is designated to receive a stream of payments from the trust for a specified period of years, and at the end of that period, the trust property passes in further trust for the benefit of his grandchildren and their families. The value of the family's remainder interest is discounted based on the value of the charity's intervening "lead" interest in the trust, so Phil is able to make a transfer to younger generations of his family at a reduced gift, estate, and generation-skipping transfer tax cost and, at the same time, to transfer assets to a foundation. There is a trade-off: To avoid adverse estate tax consequences from this arrangement, Phil must transfer legal control of the foundation to his adult children and grandchildren. Because of the tables used to calculate the value of the family's remainder interest in a charitable lead trust, it is an especially appealing vehicle during periods when interest rates are low.

Staying Out of Trouble

When you create a foundation, you are creating a new business in a regulated industry. You are committing hundreds of thousands, perhaps millions or tens of millions of dollars, to this business. The IRS, state charities officials, countless journalists, and other watchdogs are looking over your shoulder to make sure you run the business legally and ethically. In the age of the Internet, the availability of information about foundations and the degree of public scrutiny are greater than ever.

You owe it to yourself and the foundation to develop at least a basic under-standing of the applicable rules. You may find that a general understanding of these rules will assist you in evaluating the qualifications of prospective advisors. The following summary is aimed at equipping you with a basic understanding of the key rules, but is by no means exhaustive. The bibliography for this chapter, or qualified legal counsel, should be consulted if you wish to pursue these topics in greater detail.

Meeting Annual Reporting Requirements

A private foundation must file an annual report with the IRS, called Form 990-PF. This form is a highly detailed "information return" that

fig. 7 Tips for Staying Out of the Headlines

- Be prepared to commit a small but reasonable portion of the annual budget to good governance and compliance with applicable laws.

- Seek out lawyers, accountants, and financial advisors who are honest, experienced in the foundation area, and willing to commit the time and resources necessary to provide thorough and thoughtful advice to the foundation.

- Don't hesitate to ask prospective advisors how many foundations they have created and how many they advise on an ongoing basis. Ask for client references and try to find out if the clients believe they have been well served.

- Don't assume that the advisors who help you run your business, or the advisors who handle your estate planning or prepare your tax returns, are necessarily well versed in the intricate rules that govern private foundations.

- Consider including your professional advisors at all board meetings, perhaps even as members of the board, so they can serve as ready resources to help the family solve legal, ethical, and practical issues.

includes information on assets, investment income, donations, salaries and other expenses, and grants and other expenditures for charitable purposes. If a foundation has violated any of the so-called "private foundation rules" (discussed below), that information must be disclosed in Form 990-PF. Many states also require an annual report, the bulk of which is often a copy of Form 990-PF. Both the IRS and state charities officials typically make these documents available for public inspection, and much of this information is now available on the Internet — for example, at www.guidestar.org.

A foundation is required to provide a copy of its three most recent Forms 990-PF as well as its Form 1023 to any individual who requests a copy. If the request is made in person at a foundation office, the request must be honored immediately. If the request is made by mail, the request must be honored within 30 days. A reasonable fee may be charged to cover photocopying and postage. In lieu of providing a copy, a foundation may post its three most recent Forms 990-PF and its Form 1023 on the Internet. The Form 990-PF and the Form 1023 also must be available for public inspection at the foundation's principal office. Although foundations no longer are required to publish notice of the availability of their annual returns for public inspection, at least one state — New York — has imposed its own obligation to publish this notice.

Form 1023 requires the names and addresses of trustees and officers, plus a phone number for somebody — usually the lawyer filing the application. Form 990-PF requires a list of the names and addresses of trustees and officer, but not telephone numbers. To insulate your home address from the disclosure requirements, you may prefer to use an address "in care of" your office or the office of a lawyer, accountant, or other advisor.

Avoiding Self-Dealing

With narrow exceptions, a foundation's transactions (direct and indirect) with "disqualified persons" will be treated as taxable "acts of self-dealing." That is true even if the transactions are on fair and reasonable terms and are approved by disinterested trustees or officers. Such transactions would include sales, loans, or leases between a foundation and a "disqualified person" and arrangements that result in the use of foundation assets by a "disqualified person."

There are some useful exceptions to the self-dealing rules. For example, a foundation may pay compensation to a disqualified person for services rendered, provided the compensation is not excessive and provided state law does not prohibit the arrangement. The IRS takes the position that the only personal services for which a disqualified person may receive compensation are services as a trustee, officer, or staff member and legal, investment, and banking services. Before a disqualified person is paid for services that fall outside those narrow categories, it is advisable to consult with legal counsel about the implications. A foundation also may reimburse reasonable expenses

---

> *fig.*
> **8**   **What in the World is a "Disqualified Person?"**
>
> You become a "disqualified person" as soon as you create a family foundation. So do your spouse, your children, grandchildren, great-grandchildren, and their spouses. Your parents and other ancestors are "disqualified persons," but your brothers, sisters, and their descendants are not.
>
> But that is only the beginning! The trustees of a foundation are "disqualified persons," even if they have made no donations to it. For purposes of the "self-dealing" rules, government officials are "disqualified persons," regardless of their connection — or lack of a connection — to the family. And finally, family businesses, trusts, and estates also can be "disqualified persons," depending on the percentage owned or controlled by individuals who are "disqualified persons."

incurred by a disqualified person in connection with foundation activities.

The penalty tax is imposed both on the "disqualified persons" who participate in the act of self-dealing and on those trustees and officers who knowingly participate in that act by approving it. This tax (like all of the foundation excise taxes except the tax on net investment income) is imposed at rates high enough that foundations and those associated with them cannot treat the tax as an acceptable cost of doing business.

Holding On to the Family Business

A foundation and its "disqualified persons," in the aggregate, may not ordinarily hold more than 20 percent of the voting equity of a business enterprise, and if they do the foundation is subject to an excise tax. This tax is of great concern to Bill Reed, because he plans to create a foundation by donating to it 80 percent of his family company. He discusses the issue with his lawyer, who explains that there is a special "grace period" for gifts and bequests.

For donated assets, a foundation has 5 years from the date of the gift to divest itself of the excess and, if it fails in that effort but can demonstrate sufficiently diligent efforts to divest itself, it might qualify for a 5-year extension from the IRS. The lawyer points out, too, that the 5-year grace period can be extended if Bill delays his gift and

fig. 9 — A Cautionary Tale

Margery and Steve Wilks create a foundation and decide it needs office space. They speak with their son, Bob, and daughter-in-law, Susan, and decide to rent space in an office building owned by a corporation. Although Susan is on the board of the corporation, she receives no compensation for that work, and she is not an officer. Susan owns no stock in the corporation, but she and her children are the sole life beneficiaries of a trust (created by Susan's father) that owns 36 percent of the voting stock of the corporation. The other 64 percent of the voting shares are owned by a group of unrelated investors. The sole trustee of the trust for Susan and her children is a large bank. Susan has no authority to decide whether the trust will retain or sell its stake in the corporation.

The Wilks conclude that the rental fee is fair and that the transaction should be fine because family members own no direct interest in the corporation and because the terms have been negotiated at "arm's length" with a corporation that no family member controls and from which no family member receives compensation.

The Wilks take the lease to their lawyer for review, and the lawyer informs them that there is a tax problem: The corporation that will be leasing space to the foundation is a "disqualified person," she says, and the lease would result in an "act of self-dealing" under the tax laws. She explains the analysis as follows:

1. The trust is a "disqualified person" because more than 35 percent of the beneficial interests in the trust are held for the benefit of individuals (Susan and her children) who are "disqualified persons" because of their family relationship to the Wilks.
2. The corporation is a "disqualified person" because more than 35 percent of the voting power is owned by a "disqualified person" — that is, by the trust described above.

The Wilks' lawyer explains that it is irrelevant for tax purposes whether Susan and her children control the trust or the corporation — and whether the rental fee is fair. The only acceptable solution, from a tax standpoint, is for the foundation to use the space for free. That solution is not financially acceptable to anyone. The Wilks then propose to lease office space from Steve's brother. Their lawyer advises them that siblings are not "disqualified persons," so the lease should be fine. But the lawyer cautions that Steve's brother would become a "disqualified person" if he joined the foundation's board or became a substantial contributor. The Wilks agree that they will not permit Steve's brother to join the board and that the foundation won't accept any contributions from Steve's brother, as long as he is the foundation's landlord.

fig. 10 — When Self-Dealing May Occur

- A foundation buys a table at a benefit dinner and distributes the benefit tickets to family members or other "disqualified persons."

- A foundation owns works of art and permits the founder or other "disqualified persons" to exhibit the works of art at home.

- A foundation pays an honorarium to a government official for giving a speech or participating in a seminar.

- A foundation and "disqualified persons" are investors in the same company, and the foundation holds onto an investment in order to "prop up" the stock price.

- A foundation buys an asset from a "disqualified person," even if the terms are economically advantageous to the foundation.

- A foundation invests in a partnership in which other "disqualified persons" are partners.

- A foundation pays excessive compensation to a "disqualified person" for his or her services to the foundation.

makes a bequest instead. In that case, the 5-year grace period ordinarily would not start to run until the shares of the company are actually distributed to the foundation by Bill's estate. Bill's lawyer cautions Bill that he probably should not give a large percentage of his company to the foundation unless he is certain that there will be a public market for it. If the only prospective buyers are members of Bill's family, or trusts for their benefit, their purchase of shares (from the foundation or from Bill's estate) could easily be "acts of self dealing."

Anticipating Taxable Expenditures

Without exception, grants to political campaigns are "taxable expenditures" and as such can result in substantial

fig. 11 — "Penalty" Taxes Aren't the Only Weapon of the IRS

Technical compliance with the private foundation rules is a necessary condition of Staying Out of Trouble, but it is not sufficient. As a more general matter, a foundation must be operated prudently and for exclusively charitable purposes. A poorly run foundation risks not only imposition of the excise taxes described in this chapter, but also the loss of its tax-exempt status. The IRS has the power to revoke tax-exempt status if:

- A foundation engages in any political campaign activity (Venturing Into Public Advocacy Is OK...Up to a Point, p.189);
- Any part of a foundation's net profits "inures" to the benefit of insiders;
- More than an "insubstantial part" of the activities of a foundation consists of legislative lobbying or confers a private, rather than public, benefit; or
- A foundation engages in repeated or flagrant violations of the private foundation tax rules.

In the final analysis, a foundation jeopardizes its tax-exempt status whenever the totality of its operations suggests that it no longer deserves the benefit of tax exemption. Furthermore, any amount of political campaign activity or lobbying activity may result in hefty excise taxes under the "taxable expenditure" rules described below — sometimes in tandem with the revocation of a foundation's tax-exempt status.

If state charities officials investigate a foundation and find abuses (for example, improper benefits flowing to insiders or a lack of sound financial management), the trustees and officers risk removal and may even be forced to pay monetary damages for any financial harm they do to the foundation.

Some states have specific laws about the role of family members in a foundation. For example, if even one family member is being paid by a California foundation that is structured as a corporation, California's corporate statute requires that at least 51 percent of the seats on the board be held by "disinterested" individuals — i.e., people who are not members of the family.

The rule in New York is more typical: If the board is told the "material facts" about a potential conflict of interest — a category that could include not only compensation to a board member but also business transactions with a board member or an affiliated business — and the arrangement is approved by a disinterested majority of the board, the arrangement ordinarily is permissible. New York permits an "interested" director or officer to be present for the vote on such questions, but some states require that the "interested" director or officer exit the meeting before the vote occurs.

The rules noted above apply to not-for-profit corporations. Even more stringent concepts of the "duty of loyalty" may apply if a foundation is created as a charitable trust, unless the governing instrument expressly says otherwise.

The bottom line is this: The transactions of a foundation can be readily subjected to public scrutiny. If you think a reporter could make a financial arrangement look bad on the front page of the local paper, consult with legal counsel before you do it.

---

charities ordinarily will necessitate the exercise of "expenditure responsibility." Some of the requirements are:

- A diligent "pre-grant inquiry" about the grant recipient.
- A written agreement requiring, among other things, that the grant recipient:
  1. Provide written reports about its use of the grant money;
  2. Return funds not used for the purpose specified in the grant agreement; and
  3. Not use the funds to engage in political activity, legislative lobbying, or other prohibited activities.

Steering Clear of Jeopardy Investments

Investments by a foundation that "jeopardize" its ability to fulfill its tax-exempt purposes may result in the imposition of an excise tax on the foundation and foundation managers who participate in the investment decision. This rule is analogous to the state-law requirement that a foundation's assets be managed "prudently."

---

excise taxes on the foundation and its managers. The same is true for expenditures to publicize a foundation's support of, or opposition to, a candidate for political office. Such expenditures should be avoided altogether. Lobbying should be undertaken with great care. There are many cases in which lobbying expenses also will be "taxable expenditures." (For more information,

see Venturing Into Public Advocacy Is OK… Up to a Point, p. 189.)

Grants to individuals, foreign charities, other private foundations, non-charities, and organizations whose tax status is unknown may be classified as "taxable expenditures" unless the grants are properly structured. Grants to organizations not classified as U.S. public

According to IRS Regulations, some types of investments will be "closely scrutinized": margin investments, commodity futures, oil and gas wells, "puts," "calls," and "straddles," warrants, and short sales. There are exceptions for donated assets and for investments that are "program-related" — that is, investments made in furtherance of a foundation's charitable purposes.

must meet its 5 percent distribution requirement either in the tax year the requirement arises or by the end of the following tax year. The excise tax for failure to meet the annual distribution requirement is imposed only on the foundation.

Paying Tax on Net Investment Income

A foundation's net investment income is taxed at a rate of 1 percent or 2 percent per year. Qualification for the 1 percent tax rate depends on a somewhat complicated calculation linked to the foundation's qualifying distributions in the current tax year, its average qualifying distributions in prior tax years, and its net investment income. Broadly speaking, a foundation that exceeds its average historical levels for qualifying distributions by at least 1 percent of its net investment income can qualify for a 1 percent, rather than 2 percent, tax on its net investment income. A foundation cannot qualify for the 1 percent tax rate in its first year of operation. Accordingly, it may be advisable to delay sales that will result in a significant capital gain until the foundation's second tax year — and to make grants in the first and second years sufficient to qualify for the 1 percent tax during the second year. In recent years, tax reform packages have routinely sought either the repeal or simplification of this tax, but at press time, neither had occurred.

fig.
13   Obtaining Directors and Officers Liability Insurance

Good governance is a tool for keeping a foundation out of legal trouble. By remaining well-informed, attentive, and honest, foundation trustees should rarely, if ever, be subject to removal or financial sanctions. That is true even if the trustees occasionally, in good faith, make errors of judgment.

Even honest and hardworking foundation leaders can be sued or threatened with suit, however, or can inadvertently violate the private foundation tax rules. For that reason, every foundation should consider obtaining insurance coverage for its trustees and officers. This insurance – commonly known as "directors and officers" or "D&O" insurance — should cover defense costs as well as any damages, taxes, or fines that must be paid.

The component parts of this insurance should be reviewed carefully with counsel, to help the foundation assess whether the insurance is adequate to cover the relevant categories of potential liability.

Some types of insurance may be deemed "non-compensatory" and other types "compensatory," which will affect whether the premium payments must be treated as taxable income by those who are insured. Premiums for "compensatory" insurance — for example, insurance covering liability for the private foundation taxes — must be taken into account when evaluating the over-all reasonableness of the compensation a trustee or officer receives.

Those who receive insurance coverage from a foundation should consult with their own tax advisors about the income tax consequences of the premium payments.

For cases that insurance does not cover or situations in which an advance is needed to cover legal or other expenses, an indemnification from the assets of the foundation also may be appropriate, subject to applicable legal limits.

Ensuring Minimum Distributions

A grantmaking foundation must distribute at least 5 percent of its average annual asset value in furtherance of its charitable purposes. The bulk of these "qualifying distributions" ordinarily consists of grants to appropriate grantees, although the reasonable expenses of administration of the foundation also can be counted toward the minimum distribution requirement. A foundation

Phyllis Landers is committed to disaster relief and education in Latin America. She decides she wants her foundation to make grants to organizations based in Latin America or, in some cases, directly to local governments in areas where hurricanes, floods, or earthquakes have occurred. She also wants to award scholarships to students in Latin America who want to study civil engineering and medicine and express an interest in applying their skills in Latin America.

When Phyllis brings up the idea at a foundation board meeting, her lawyer explains that the foundation should not just "write a check." He offers a daunting array of precautions:

- If the grant recipient is an organization not recognized by the IRS as a public charity, a grant agreement and other special steps are required under U.S. tax law.

- Although the tax law does not mandate a grant agreement when the grantee is a foreign government (or a foreign government's agency or instrumentality), it would be prudent for the foundation to put the terms of the grant in writing anyway.

- A scholarship recipient does not have to sign an agreement, but the foundation must instead adopt an objective and nondiscriminatory procedure for the selection of scholarship recipients. This procedure, at a minimum, must:

  1. Require that scholarship winners be selected from a pool sufficiently large to constitute a charitable class;

  2. Enumerate suitable criteria for selecting scholarship winners (for example, academic performance, performance on tests designed to measure ability, aptitude, and motivation, recommendations from instructors, financial need, and conclusions drawn during an interview process concerning ability, character, etc.);

  3. Require that members of the selection committee not be in position to derive a personal benefit if one prospective scholarship winner is selected rather than another one;

  4. Require that the grant either be in the nature of a prize or an award, or for a scholarship for study at an academic institution, or a grant for the achievement of a specified educational objective (producing a report, enhancing an artistic or musical skill or talent, etc.); and

  5. Impose a reporting system, to allow the foundation to monitor the courses taken by the scholarship winner, grades received, degrees attained, articles written, research completed, music composed, etc.

- Before implementation, the scholarship procedure must be filed with the IRS for approval. The procedure is deemed approved if the IRS raises no objections within 45 days.

- Scholarships must be for study at a college or university and must be structured so that they would be excluded from the recipient's gross income — not under current tax law but under the law as in effect until 1986.

- Other rules apply if individuals receive grants that are not scholarships — for example, grants to enhance a scientific or similar skill, to recognize a specific achievement, or to relieve poverty or distress.

Phyllis and the other members of the board discuss these requirements at length and realize that they cannot, as volunteers, adequately handle the workload. The board votes to begin a program of Latin American grants and scholarships — but only after the foundation hires an administrative assistant who can dedicate 1 to 2 days a week to running the program.

fig.
15

**Other Exceptions to the
Excess Business Holdings Rules**

- The threshold of permitted ownership increases from 20 percent to 35 percent if a foundation can establish to the satisfaction of the IRS that the business enterprise is controlled by persons who are not "disqualified persons."

- If a foundation's holdings are 2 percent or less of a business enterprise, then the aggregate holdings of the foundation and "disqualified persons" may exceed 20 percent.

- If a business enterprise receives at least 95 percent of its income from passive sources (such as interest and dividends earned on investments), then the foundation and "disqualified persons" may own any percentage, even 100 percent, of the business.

Summing Up

For the philanthropist who is in the process of creating and running a foundation, the legal issues outlined in this chapter can be distilled into a few basic questions that bear fundamentally on the long-term success of the foundation:

- Have I provided clear guidance about what I envision?

- Have I provided the flexibility that I will need if my charitable goals change with the passage of time?

- Have I defined a mission that is broad enough so that it will endure as long as there is money to fund it?

- Have I structured my philanthropy in a way that best achieves my tax and other financial objectives for myself and my family?

- Do I understand the "ground rules" well enough to know that I can be comfortable operating within them?

- Have I created a system of checks and balances to ensure that the foundation fulfills its charitable mission and remains in compliance with applicable laws?

Affirmative answers to these questions should result in a solid legal framework for your foundation — an enduring structure that will enable you and your family to accomplish the objectives that inspired your philanthropy in the first place.

Funding Outside the Box II: Program-Related Investments

fig. 16

On one of her frequent visits to Mexico, Phyllis Landers meets a woman in Oaxaca, Juana Lopez, who is trying to revive the local silk-making industry. Juana explains that there was an indigenous silk-making craft in southern Mexico prior to the Spanish Conquest. However, the industry was suppressed in the 16th Century when the Spanish, from their base in the Philippines, began to ship silk from the Far East to Mexico and Spain. Juana is cultivating silk worms on mulberry trees on her farm, but she says that too little silk is being produced for a viable industry to be established. Fifteen to 20 local women, most without jobs or any education, are being trained to cultivate the silk, harvest it, and make cloth. Juana sells the cloth in local shops, mainly to tourists. Juana says that she sees the potential to hire more people and perhaps eventually operate a profitable business.

At a foundation board meeting, Phyllis proposes that the foundation make a grant in support of Juana's silk-making activities. Several trustees express the view that a grant would not be appropriate, because Juana appears to be operating a business with a profit motive. Phyllis argues that Juana's business probably will never make a profit, or at least not a significant one, and that the real objective of the activity is to restore a craft tradition that died out nearly 500 years ago and to provide job training and jobs in an impoverished region.

One trustee asks whether the idea of a "PRI" might be appropriate. The trustee explains that "PRI is foundation lingo for program-related investment — an investment no one would ever make except to do good in the world." On consultation with the foundation's counsel, the board learns that the PRI must be for a purpose that is genuinely charitable and consistent with the foundation's governing instrument. The production of income or gain cannot be a significant motive of a PRI. After a review of the relevant documents and the law, the lawyer concludes that the foundation may make the investment as a charitable undertaking.

After some debate about whether to lend money to the project, in exchange for a promissory note, or to invest in the project, in exchange for a share of the equity, the board selects the second option. The foundation will seek, in exchange, a seat on the board of directors of the new business. The trustees conclude that a seat on the board will enable the foundation to provide ongoing business advice intended to ensure the survival of the new company and will prevent the company from abandoning its initial mandate. Protecting the foundation's investment, the trustees conclude, is not a significant objective of taking a seat on the board.

Although the foundation will own more than 20 percent of the stock in the new business, counsel to the foundation advises the trustees that there should not be any problem with "excess business holdings" so long as the foundation can show that an investment in the business is substantially related to the foundation's performance of its charitable purposes.

FUNDING YOUR FAMILY FOUNDATION

by Antonia M. Grumbach

Founders face choices both in how to fund their family foundation and in what assets to use.

The decisions of when to fund a foundation and how much to fund it with will depend not only on a founder's available assets, but also on how the founder plans to use the foundation. A founder can fund a foundation with one lump-sum contribution and make no further gift. Alternatively, the founder may decide to make periodic contributions to the foundation to build up its assets over a period of years. This approach makes sense for founders who are funding their foundations out of annual income; they contribute more in good years and less in lean years.

Some founders establish a foundation as an estate planning vehicle. They do not wish to use it for grantmaking immediately and so they create it, allow it to lie virtually dormant for years, and then fund it with a large bequest in their will or perhaps when they inherit significant sums. Still other founders establish a "pass-through" foundation to make gifts during their lifetimes. They make (or the family business makes) annual gifts to the foundation that support grantmaking and operations. The idea is to fund the foundation for annual operations, and not to commit large amounts of capital to fund it permanently. (For advantages and disadvantages of different methods of funding, see chart, p. 80.)

A founder must also decide which assets to use to fund the foundation. Federal tax law favors the contribution of cash or appreciated publicly held stock by allowing the founder the maximum deductibility. Tax treatment differs for other assets, such as interests in real estate or real estate trusts, stock in an S corporation, stock in a closely held family or other business, art and other valuable personal property, stock options, interests in protected intellectual property, and so on. Because most founders draw their contributions from cash, publicly held stock, or closely held stock, this discussion focuses on those types of assets. Whatever assets they use, founders are advised to review the matter with their lawyer or accountant. (For a discussion of tax deductibility of various classes of assets, see Facing Important Legal Issues, p. 59.)

Constraints Limit Business Holdings

Families that establish private foundations often also own and operate successful business enterprises that can serve as convenient sources of income for the grantmaking activities of those foundations. Thus, family businesses are likely sources of lifetime gifts or bequests to family foundations. Enter the "excess business holdings" rule.

Congress adopted the 1969 Tax Reform Act to address concerns over the possible abuse of the control of charitable assets. One concern was that a donor or donor's family might receive a charitable deduction while still maintaining control of the donated family business through the founda-

Founders Choose Different Routes to Funding

Arthur and Abigail A. started a business together which was so successful that they took it public. The stock did well. In their mid-50s, they decided to establish a family foundation. They signed the papers of incorporation and the same day contributed $25 million of their stock in the publicly held company to fund the foundation. As trustees of the foundation, they kept grantmaking to the 5 percent minimum payout for 5 years to build assets in the portfolio. Now that the assets have reached $50 million, they have increased the annual payout.

Beatrice B. is an entrepreneur whose income varies widely from year to year. She formed a family foundation with her husband and children as trustees. She contributes to the foundation as little as $10,000 a year and as much as $500,000. As the foundation's assets grow, the trustees adjust grantmaking to meet the 5 percent minimum payout rule. Given the rate of return on the foundation's portfolio, the foundation's assets continue to increase in value.

Lawrence L. worked hard as a lawyer and accumulated a tidy net worth. After talking with his wife and children, he formed a family foundation with zero assets and he, his wife, and their children were trustees. Until his death, he contributed $50,000 a year from current income, which the foundation gave out as grants and used to cover operating costs. In his will, he provided for his surviving wife and his children and grandchildren, and he made bequests to a few close friends, favorite charities, and his law school.

The residue of his estate, about $10 million, went to fund the foundation.

Patricia P. received substantial assets when her highly successful husband died. She established a charitable trust to support certain named charities, one of which was a family foundation that she created. The foundation has no assets; it receives $2 million a year from the charitable trust, which it passes through as grants to nonprofit organizations and also uses for operating expenses.

Seth S. took over a struggling family business and built it into a successful international company. He and his wife formed a family foundation and the same day gifted $10 million in closely held company stock to the foundation. The company immediately bought the stock back from the foundation (complying with the rules regarding purchases of stock from a family foundation), generating $10 million in cash for the foundation.

Wendy W., who lives alone, inherited $5 million on the death of her aunt, as did each of her four sisters and brothers. Wendy convinced her siblings to join her in forming a family foundation, with each contributing $1 million to fund the foundation. Wendy lived comfortably on her earned income, and continued to contribute 10 percent of her inheritance each year to the foundation in order to build its assets. The other siblings also made occasional contributions.

tion. Consequently, the 1969 legislation limits the extent to which a private foundation can own an interest in any business enterprise. This is an arcane and extremely complicated area of tax law.

Specifically, the excess business holdings rule limits the amount of voting interest a private foundation can hold in a business enterprise that is not related to its exempt purposes.

For this purpose, a business enterprise is broadly defined to include almost any trade or business, but excludes:

"Functionally related" businesses. For instance, a foundation dedicated to grantmaking in the field of education that supports innovative teaching techniques in public schools could create, or acquire, a business that develops software for innovative curricula to sell to the school district. Because this business is considered "functionally related" to the foundation's charitable purposes, no restrictions apply to the size of holdings in the software company. The foundation could, in fact, hold 100 percent ownership interest.

- Business enterprises that derive 95 percent of their gross income from passive sources, such as dividends, interest, or rent. It is possible to bequeath to a foundation a large interest in a family-owned real estate company if the company's income consists solely of rent from its properties.
- "Program-related investments." These are investments made by a foundation for a programmatic purpose that relates to its charitable purposes, not primarily for the production of income. An example is a foundation that makes health-related grants and also invests in a startup company that is developing a promising drug to combat a particular disease.

Absent one of these exceptions, the size of the holdings a private foundation can have in a business enterprise — the "permitted holdings" — depends on the amount of voting stock of the business that is held by "disqualified persons." The *de minimus*, or safe harbor, rule establishes an upper limit on holdings, below which excess business holding provisions do not apply. Under this rule, if a foundation (and other related foundations) holds no more than 2 percent of the voting shares and no more than 2 percent of all classes of stock in a business enterprise, the foundation will not be treated as having excess business holdings, even if all remaining shares are held by a disqualified person. (For purposes of the 2 percent de minimis rule, the private foundation must include with its holdings stock held by private foundations that are effectively controlled by the same person or persons who control the private foundations in question; and private foundations to which substantially all contributions were made by the same person or persons, or their families, who made substantially all of the contributions to the private foundation in question. This rule prevents a donor from creating several private foundations, funding them with stock in a particular company and then using the foundations to control the company.)

Beyond the *de minimus* rule, voting stock in a business enterprise held by the foundation and its disqualified persons must be aggregated to determine whether a foundation's ownership position exceeds permitted holdings limitations. (Disqualified persons in this context include the founders of the foundation and their lineal ancestors, children, grandchildren, great grandchildren and spouses of children, grandchildren and great grandchildren.) In general, private foundations may not hold more than 20 percent of the voting stock of a corporation — including the voting stock

The decisions of when to fund a foundation and how much to fund it with will depend not only on a founder's available assets, but also on how the founder plans to use the foundation.

owned by all disqualified persons. The foundation can, however, own any amount of nonvoting stock provided that the aggregate of all voting stock held by disqualified persons does not exceed 20 percent of the corporation's voting stock. (The permissible level of holdings increases to 35 percent if effective control of the enterprise rests with one or more persons who are not disqualified persons with respect to the private foundation, and the foundation and all disqualified persons together do not own more that 35 percent of the voting stock of the corporation.)

Moreover, direct ownership by a disqualified person is not necessary in computing the holdings of a private foundation or a disqualified person. In general, any stock or other interest owned, directly or indirectly, by or for a corporation, partnership, estate, or trust, is considered owned proportionately by or for its shareholders, partners, or beneficiaries. Thus, if any of those individuals is a disqualified person, the stock owned, for instance, by the estate or trust of which they are

Fortunately, foundations that have acquired interests in a business enterprise by gift or bequest have a grace period of 5 years after the receipt of stock in a business to dispose of excess business holdings before any tax is imposed.

beneficiaries, must be aggregated as stock owned by the foundation when applying excess business holding rules. Thus, the sweep of inclusion and aggregation is broad.

Any foundation found to have exceeded its permitted holdings and, thereby, to have violated the excess business holdings rule, must dispose of its excess business holdings. Failure to do so subjects the foundation to a 5 percent initial tax on the value of its excess business holdings. In addition, if the

fig. 2 Strategies for Timing Contributions		
STRATEGIES FOR TIMING CONTRIBUTIONS	**ADVANTAGES**	**DISADVANTAGES AND OTHER CONSIDERATIONS**
Fund the foundation with one lump-sum gift.	Clearly establishes the scope of grant-making; simplifies transaction costs.	Grantmaking program may not yet be defined; personal circumstances (e.g., recent decline in wealth) may dictate lower amount or funding phased-in over time.
Fund the foundation through a series of periodic contributions.	Allows for unforeseen personal circumstances and the development of a grantmaking program.	Fewer funds may restrict grantmaking; operating costs are generally proportionately higher.
Establish the foundation at a low asset level, and fund it fully through a large bequest.	Allows for changes in personal circumstances; permits donor to have use of assets during his or her lifetime; provides donor with a window on how the foundation will be governed and managed.	Delays philanthropic impact; heirs may have other expectations that could disrupt family unity; after the foundation receives the bequest, the donor's original mission may not be carried out.
Establish a pass-through foundation, with the founder (or family business) making annual gifts that support grantmaking and operations.	Very flexible because specific timing, amount and scope of program are not set; allows foundation to be responsive to unforeseen needs such as funding to assist with needs resulting from the 9/11 tragedy.	Makes the establishment of a philanthropic program more difficult; does not foster partnerships with other foundations as readily; can limit ongoing strategic focus.

Prepared by Kathryn McCarthy, Director of Client Advisory Services, Rockefeller & Co., and Jason Born, Program Director, National Center for Family Philanthropy.

foundation does not dispose of its excess business holdings after payment of the 5 percent tax, it will be subject to a 200 percent tax on its excess business holdings. This is clearly a confiscatory provision. Fortunately, foundations that have acquired interests in a business enterprise by gift or bequest have a grace period of 5 years after the receipt of stock in a business to dispose of excess business holdings before any tax is imposed. Moreover, the Internal Revenue Service may extend that five-year period for another five years if the

foundation shows diligent efforts to dispose of the holdings and a plan to do so.

Because of the complexity of the rules regarding excess business, advice from expert legal counsel should be sought by any donor considering giving or bequeathing an interest in a closely held company to a private foundation.

fig. 3 — Alternatives for Assets to Fund the Foundation

ALTERNATIVES/OPTIONS FOR ASSETS TO FUND THE FOUNDATION	ADVANTAGES	DISADVANTAGES AND OTHER CONSIDERATIONS
Cash or publicly held stock	Liquid and no valuation problems; cash gifts allow for deductions of up to 30% of adjusted gross income, stock gifts allow for deductions of value of the stock at the time of the gift of up to 20% of adjusted gross income.	Can be a problem if donor is left with non-income-producing, illiquid assets.
Real estate	May be good income producer; could be used by certain charities in their operations; can diversify a portfolio of securities; allows for deduction of up to 20% of adjusted gross income.	Difficult to value and requires day- to-day management. Potential self dealing issues may be raised for certain uses by a related entity.
Closely held stock, including an interest in a family enterprise, or stock in S corporations	Can enhance a family's wealth transfer plan; may produce good income if cash is distributed regularly.	Difficult to value; closely held stock valued at cost basis only; can involve self-dealing issues and concentration problems.
Art and other valuable personal property	Generally do not affect donor's financial well being directly; may be useful in the work of the foundation.	Difficult to value and possibly to sell; deduction generally limited to cost basis.

Prepared by Kathryn McCarthy, Director of Client Advisory Services, Rockefeller & Co., and Jason Born, Program Director, National Center for Family Philanthropy.

SOURCE: Adapted from Antonia M. Grumbach, "Funding a Foundation: What Assets to Use," *Investment Issues for Family Funds: Managing and Maximizing Your Philanthropic Dollars*. Washington, DC: National Center for Family Philanthropy, 1999.

ESTABLISHING A STRUCTURE

GOVERNANCE
Vision, Trust, and Moral Imagination in Trusteeship

by Jason C. Born, Deborah A. Brody, Virginia M. Esposito, and Tory Dietel Hopps

There are those who will come to their family foundation trustee role with the experience of having served on countless nonprofit boards. For them, trustee life is expected to be pretty much a matter of course. Been there, done that, will do it here. Others will have waited years (some might say, years and years) for their turn to serve. Their service may mean validation, trepidation; even "it's finally my turn."

Most boards will have family members of the founder. Those family members may wonder if foundation trustee life is different from other family life. Do I still defer to Dad as a good and dutiful daughter should? Many boards will include trustees who are not members of the family. They may be trusted advisors, friends, or those new to the "family circle" — those selected for their expertise or perspective. They may wonder how they are expected to relate to this family enterprise. Do I get in the middle of a family fracas? What is my responsibility to this donor and to this family?

In creating this family foundation, everyone is — in a sense — new. Even family foundations that are decades old are constantly renewing the process of trusteeship, reflecting the dynamism of families and participation by new members. Regardless of the circumstances and experiences that bring you to the table of a family foundation boardroom, take a moment to consider the complexity in your role. As a trustee of a foundation, you have both a special privilege and an awesome obligation.

Just consider: you have taken on both duty and opportunity; you will be encouraged to be expansively creative while exercising prudent due diligence; you will have the remarkable good fortune to meet and support remarkable people doing astonishing work and you will not be able to support nearly as many as are deserving. As the late Paul Ylvisaker noted in his 1990 essay on family foundations, you have been offered "a free-wheeling opportunity to be socially and publicly influential. Without having to meet the tests either of the market or the ballot box, private persons can independently determine what the needs of society are and how best to go about meeting them."

As a trustee, you will be taking the private charitable legacy of a philanthropic family into the community (even the world). Trusteeship is — first and foremost — a very personal commitment to a public trust.

In this chapter, you will learn the variety of governance structures that other family foundations have used to bring focus and coherence to their policies and procedures. You will have the opportunity to explore the roles and responsibilities of trusteeship. You will be invited to step back and think about trusteeship: what it means to you and others, including your fellow trustees, and — unknown to you now — those who may one day take a role as a trustee of your foundation.

The words of two prominent foundation trustees will take you through your brief introduction to governance and grantmaking. By interweaving their wonderful presentations on trusteeship, you have the chance to think about your commitment as a trustee to ensure that vision, moral imagination, and trust are the hallmarks of your service.

The Founding Vision

Most of those who set up foundations are innovative builders who decide to assign their business gains to philanthropic purposes. This inspired act is, like patriotism, an expression of concern about others. Honoring that benevolent intent is not just honoring a donor's name; it is honoring a donor's overarching original vision. But merely honoring the past does not inspire; reflecting on roots and origins can.

SOURCE: Margaret E. Mahoney, "Trustees" (The President's Essay). *1994 Annual Report of The Commonwealth Fund.*

In her essay on trusteeship, Margaret Mahoney eloquently expresses her belief that the governance of private foundations begins with the founder's vision. Having guided The Commonwealth Fund to reflect the vision of founder Anna Harkness and her son, Edward, Mahoney well understands that trustees are likely to find both the source of their private compact and public stewardship roles by exploring that vision.

David Dodson has worked closely with three very different philanthropic families and serves as a trustee of the Mary Reynolds Babcock Foundation, a family foundation in North Carolina. His insights into the personal dynamics and higher purpose of family philanthropy are captured in an inspiring presentation on trusteeship. Elaborating on the themes of "holding trust" presented by authors Richard Broholm and Douglas Johnson in their monograph, *A Balcony Perspective: Clarifying the Trustee Role* (The Robert K. Greenleaf Center, 1993), Dodson explained:

As trustees, it's clear that we hold in trust the material assets of our foundation. But I believe strongly that we also hold in trust certain intangible assets that are equally valuable currency of our foundations: the history, the traditions, the values of the donors, the institutional principles that have accrued over time and that give our foundations their character and their sense of purpose. ... We have a moral responsibility to see that successive generations of trustees and staff understand the convictions and impulses that brought our particular foundations into being in the first place."

SOURCE: David Dodson, "Personal Responsibility, Public Trust." Presentation to the 1996 Council on Foundations Trustee Workshop.

The Trust in Trusteeship

But if Mahoney and Dodson understand well the legacy of values and vision left to family foundation trustees by their founders, they understand equally well the privilege of the public responsibility of the trustee role.

The legal presumption that exempts nonprofit institutions from taxation is that those institutions are operating exclusively for the public good, that they are private institutions serving a public trust. …Foundation trustees act for the benefit of the public at large — that ultimate but nebulous body of individuals that may or may not stand to benefit directly from the good work of foundations. Some years ago Thornton F. Bradshaw, then chairman of the John D. and Catherine T. MacArthur Foundation, noted that not having to answer directly to any constituency increases the "extraordinary" power foundations hold. "It means," he said, "that organized philanthropy is restricted in its actions only by the intelligence and conscience of those who run foundations."

SOURCE: Mahoney Essay.

Dodson echoes that sentiment by explaining Broholm and Johnson's second principle of trusteeship: building trust — "with the board itself, between board and staff, and between the foundation and the external publics that it serves."

To build trust suggests that we need to live out our ethic of integrity and consistent relationships … doing what you say and doing what you mean. This is how trust is built. This is how trust is earned. No institution, particularly foundations, can be considered trustworthy unless the communities and stakeholders with whom it interacts view it as honorable, honest, and faithful to its own stated values.

SOURCE: Dodson Presentation.

Moral Imagination

Paul Ylvisaker once cautioned that, while "healthily disciplining," the term stewardship might be too passive. There will be nothing passive about your stewardship of a family foundation. But it is very likely that the lively, dynamic process of what Mahoney calls "setting the course" will be a most energizing, occasionally frustrating, but always fulfilling experience.

Responsible boards are not born. They are composed carefully. A board must be large enough to be diverse, yet small enough to be deliberate. Certain personal characteristics of board members are essential — competence, integrity, intelligence, judgment, and empathy. …A foundation needs trustees who can work together productively, but it does not require that they be unanimous in their opinions or uniform in their outlook. … A foundation's extraordinary potential for good springs from its board's ability to act as a collective, to be cohesive in fulfilling its public trust. As Alfred North Whitehead remarked, "No member of a crew is praised for the rugged individuality of his rowing." Success in fulfilling their collective responsibility lies with trustees recognizing that the act of giving is secondary to the importance of the work supported.

As Erik Erikson believed, "Caring is the virtue that is born from the struggle to take responsibility." …Demonstrating that a foundation deserves trust begins with its board of directors consciously taking on the job of trusteeship, refining the habit of reasoned reflection, and keeping the institution faithful to the basic vision, while responding to the times. "None of us knows the single way to the greatest good," social scientist Gilbert Brim reminds us. But the justification for foundations existing at all is that that private wealth can risk the search for ways to enhance the broader good.

SOURCE: Mahoney Essay.

And, as the first two principles of *A Balcony Perspective* are holding trust and building trust, the last is logical as a conclusion and magical as a result: fulfilling trust. As Dodson explains, "that simply has to do with trying to live out the values that we say we live by and fulfilling the sense of promise and responsibility that is conferred upon us by society as foundations."

Fulfilling the trust society places on us calls on trustees to exercise what a former colleague called "moral imagination" — the ability to push ourselves beyond the moral minimum, to listen closely to the world around us and respond based on our highest and best institutional values. If we as trustees can pay attention to holding in trust history and values over time, building trust internally and in our external relationships, and fulfilling trust through exercising moral imagination, fitting our values to changing circumstances, and then rigorously assessing with the help of others whether or not we are living up to our potential, then we begin to create a culture of responsibility that is consistent over place, over time, and over generations.

SOURCE: Dodson Presentation.

Inspired, effective trusteeship of family foundations is rooted in the stewardship of both the founder's vision and in the concept of the public trust. It will never be either/or and there will likely never be a perfect balance. It may well be that dynamism that offers the greatest challenge, excitement, and opportunity of the family foundation trustee.

Structuring Your Board

The governance structure of your foundation determines who makes decisions, how these decisions are made, and how you and your board will act as stewards of the foundation's assets. This structure also determines how key stakeholders who do not serve on the board — family members, outside experts, nonprofit practitioners, and the constituencies you serve — can play an important and ongoing role in the life of the foundation.

From your initial choice of board members to your decisions about how best to orient and select future trustees, it is important that you spend sufficient time thinking about your options for effective governance structures. Although it may be hard to imagine now, if you plan for your foundation to continue more than one or two generations into the future, there are likely to be many situations in which clear guidelines regarding board structure will make all the difference between a smoothly functioning philanthropic institution, and one where perceptions of unfairness and uncertainty abound.

Assessing Your Family Structure and Goals

Prior to developing the governance structure for your foundation, consider the current structure and dynamics of your family and how these relate to your goals for the family's role in the foundation. Questions to address with your spouse and other family members include:

- What is your vision for your family foundation?
- Are you committed to working collaboratively to develop and govern the foundation?
- How many children do you have? How many children do they have?
- Do your children expect to be involved in the foundation? Do they expect their own children to participate in the foundation, either now or at some point in the future?
- Do you plan to involve several branches of the family in the governance of the foundation? Are the branches "spread" equally in terms of number and relative age of family members?
- Is the foundation expected to last in perpetuity? Do you have firm ideas about the mission of the foundation? Do you expect this mission to change over time, or to essentially stay the same? Do your children (or others you plan to involve) agree with and support this mission?

---

fig. **1**   **Structuring a Family-Inclusive Board**

The Surdna Foundation is one of the oldest family foundations in the United States. Founded in 1917 by John Emory Andrus I, it recently embarked on a bold new program to engage the extended family in the family's philanthropic activities. The trustees' task was formidable. At last count, the eight branches of the Andrus family, including spouses, numbered 343 and ranged in age from infancy to 92. Some 200 members of the fourth and fifth generations are over age 25. The sixth generation will be even larger. Working out an equitable and practical system for engaging so many family members requires the Surdna trustees to rethink the foundation's notions about inclusion and succession.

Broader family involvement had not been in the minds of those who led the Surdna Foundation during most of its history. In fact, only a select few in each generation were tapped to serve not on one, but on several of the family's charitable boards simultaneously. To the rest of the extended family, the activities of the Andrus' charities were a mystery. They knew that some relatives in New York gave away money but the family's philanthropies were far removed from their lives and thoughts. The current Surdna board wanted to change that. They believed that the time to open the philanthropies to the extended family was long overdue… .

EXCERPTED FROM *Sustaining Tradition: The Andrus Family Philanthropy Program.* Washington, DC: National Center for Family Philanthropy, 2001.

- How large a board do you want?
- What other opportunities are there to involve family members (or others) who do not officially serve on the board of the foundation?
- Are there family members or colleagues that are interested in serving on the board? Are there family members or colleagues who may be interested in participating in other ways?

Devoting time to these questions will be one of the biggest contributions you can make to the establishment of your foundation. The governance structure you develop will be greatly influenced by your answers. This assessment of your family's structure and dynamics is essential to the creation of a positive culture for the governance and management of a family foundation.

At the same time, you do not need to answer all of these questions up front. The foundation's board will be revis-iting some of these from time-to-time over the life of the foundation. Having some idea of the answers to these questions will help you build in guidelines for the initial board structure, however, and will make many of these questions much easier to answer down the road.

Talking with other families and advisors as you move forward can be one of the most helpful methods for learning about how family structure and board structure are likely to intersect. Remember, many other families have been down this path before. "Part of our learning process was to meet with other families as a family and go over in detail how they structured themselves," says John Abele, trustee of the Argosy Foundation. "It is enormously helpful and valuable to meet with other intelligent people and bare all and listen to what they have to say." For suggestions of families to talk with, contact the National Center for Family Philanthropy, your local regional association of grantmakers, or other support organizations you may know.

Choosing an Initial Board Structure

Foundations established as corporations can change the articles of incorporation by filing papers with the appropriate state agency; the board of a trust

> **fig. 2**
>
> ## Membership System Includes Family Over the Long Run
>
> The Taylor family (fictional name) created a structure where all family members above the age of 21 were given membership status within the foundation. The original members were also members of the third generation of the descendants of the founder of the family, Joseph Flagler.
>
> At the first meeting of the members, the 16 eligible family members elected seven trustees of the foundation. The trustees of the foundation were given the authority to make decisions about grants and investments of the foundation. Other members are expected to play a supportive role, both by providing funds to the foundation and by providing ongoing feedback to updates on its programs. The members meet each year to formally elect the trustees and to hear updates on the foundation's activities. The members are also asked to contribute personally to the foundation through a letter that goes out annually from the foundation chair. This membership structure has allowed dozens of non-trustee family members to be involved in the foundation, as it has grown over the 51 years since it was initially established.

is bound by the trust indenture, which can be changed only by court order. Starting with simple but clearly defined policies is the most straightforward path to take in either form.

It is important to remember that each of these structures can be tweaked to the specifics of your situation — for instance, you may decide to go with a membership-based system, but reserve the right for you and/or your spouse to always have the option to serve on the board, regardless of the family vote.

Some families find that they are comfortable having a majority of nonfamily members on the board, as long as they retain long-term control over the foundation. One well-known family foundation uses a membership system whereby all family members above the age of 18 serve as corporate "members." Each year the members as a group elect five foundation trustees out of 12 total. Currently all five of these member-elected trustees are family members, although this may not always be the case. The remaining seven trustees are elected using a nominating committee process. To ensure that the family retains some degree of ongoing control over the board's membership, the members by majority vote can remove a trustee at any time for no specific reason. See the box at left for an example of another family that has chosen this basic structure.

Choosing Initial Board Members

Your initial choice of board members can have long-term effects on the direction of the foundation. Some founder couples start out with only themselves and a trusted advisor serving on the board. Others involve their children, siblings, or favorite nieces and nephews. Additional potential sources of founding board members include:

- Experts in a particular cause or field (scientists, artists, futurists, etc.);
- Spokespersons or authors about a particular cause or field;
- Local community foundation or private foundation trustees;
- Politicians and other community leaders; and
- Representatives from the constituencies you seek to serve.

It is important to identify initial board members who will help you develop the culture you seek to develop for your board. Key aspects of this culture may be that board members participate regularly, are engaged and knowledgeable about a broad range of issues, and are able to bring a variety of perspectives to the foundation's long-term strategies.

Founders and their families may wish to develop a board profile to help them think about potential candidates based on the attributes and skills that these individuals bring to the board. This "profile" may be useful both for the choice of initial board members, as well as for identifying and selecting future

trustees. Key categories to consider in such a profile might be:

- Areas of specific expertise (legal, financial, marketing, administrative, etc.);
- Areas of program expertise (can be of direct or indirect relevance to foundation's mission);
- Age (do you want multiple generations represented);
- Gender and Race/Ethnic Background;
- Geographic location (particularly if the foundation has a specific focus in one town, community, or region);
- Past board experience (nonprofit, foundation, and corporate); and
- Other skills and attributes that may be important to the founder or the family.

Another approach is to develop a short "job description" or a statement concerning the standards and values that you expect your board members to uphold. "Qualities of a Good Trustee," from *Foundation Trusteeship* by John Nason describes one set of desired qualifications and background (see next page).

Whatever your choice of initial trustees, it is important that you balance your desire for privacy and flexibility, with your potential need for outside guidance and experience.

Electing Board Members and Officers

This statement describes the process by which trustees are elected, including timing, training requirements, attendance requirements, and term limits. Officers typically include the president,

In *Foundation Trusteeship: Service in the Public Interest,* John Nason revisited his exploration of the role of philanthropic governance that he began in his 1977 landmark book, *Trustees and the Future of Foundations.* In his second volume, Nason offered a list of the ten qualities of a good trustee.

1. Interest in and concern for the foundation and its field or fields of operation. The job is too demanding for anyone who lacks a fair degree of enthusiasm for the task.

2. Some understanding of the area of the special purpose foundation and some broad perspective on the problems of society for the general-purpose foundation. Eleanor Elliott of the Foundation for Child Development suggests that every trustee should be able to answer the question: "Namely: in 50 words or less, what is this place all about?" (From: "On Being a Trustee," *Foundation News & Commentary*, May/June 1984.)

3. Objectivity and impartiality are a *sine qua non*. The board table is no place for special pleading, for temperamental bias, for personal whim. The trustee is judge, not advocate, save with respect to donor's priorities.

4. Special skills. The board will need certain special forms of competence among its members — management, investment experience, familiarity with budgets, and knowledge of the law. Not all trustees need possess all these attributes. The value of planning and ...analysis of current membership lies in making certain that some trustees will possess some of these special kinds of expertise.

5. A capacity for teamwork, for arriving at and accepting group decisions. Irresolvable differences, the tactics of confrontation, *ad hominem* arguments, and lack of respect for one's fellow trustees are destructive of intelligent group decisions. These qualities demonstrate the danger of diversity carried to an extreme. Collegiality in the form of uniform outlook is stultifying; collegiality as a way of disagreeing, yet working harmoniously together is essential.

6. Willingness to work. This means a willingness to give time and thought to the affairs of the foundation, to arrange one's personal schedule so as to be available to attend meetings, to serve on committees, to undertake special assignments, and to wrestle with the problems of the foundation.

7. Practical wisdom. This is more easily recognized than described. It involves the capacity to see the whole picture, to recognize the validity of opposing arguments, to distinguish principle from expediency, and to temper the ideal with what is realistically possible.

8. Commitment to the foundation as a whole and not to special interests or constituencies. The trustee's responsibility is to the foundation.

9. Commitment to the idea of philanthropic foundations. No foundation is an island unto itself. Every trustee, even in small family foundations, has a responsibility to act in such a way that the foundation world is strengthened and not weakened.

10. Moral sensitivity to the act of giving and to the need for giving. Paul Ylvisaker called the latter a "sense of outrage"--outrage over people dying of cancer or of AIDS, over children born to poverty and deprivation, over the destruction of the environment, over the threat of nuclear annihilation. Merrimon Cuninggim [a former college president and foundation trustee] described the former as "the potential immorality of giving," the ego satisfaction of the giver, the corrupting influence of the sense of power.

(One family foundation found this list so compelling that the board drafted a Trustee Qualification and Values Statement based on it. For this statement, see p. 241.)

vice president, secretary, and treasurer, each with defined duties with respect to the board and the foundation

Setting the Number of Board Members
Some foundations choose to allow a broad range in the number of trustees that may govern the foundation, while others stick to a specific number. If the foundation has been established in the corporate form, you may state a range of acceptable sizes. In these cases, the minimum/ maximum may be changed by resolution of the full board. *Family Foundations: A Profile of Funders and Trends*, a report developed by the National Center for Family Philanthropy and the Foundation Center, states that the median board size for family foundations is between three and eight members, depending on varying levels of assets. Please note that — depending on the purpose of your foundation and how you have decided to govern its work — you may have significantly more or less board members than these averages.

Establishing a Committee Structure
Many family foundations (more than 50 percent, according to the Council on Foundations) establish one or more board committees to help govern and manage their work. Board committees can help accomplish several objectives, including:
- Distributing the administrative and management workload of the foundation, particularly when there are no staff;
- Dividing key work of the foundation into well-defined categories;
- Involving trustees (and in some cases outside experts and family members not serving as official trustees) in key activities of the foundation; and
- Introducing younger family members to the work of the foundation at their own pace.

The following committee names and descriptions are adapted from the bylaws of the Baltimore-based Marion I. and Henry J. Knott Foundation.

- *Executive Committee:* May exercise the administrative powers and authority of the full board, except the power to amend the bylaws or charter or approve any action not permitted by law.

- *Grant Committee:* Reviews grant requests and reports recommendation to the full board prior to a regular meeting. Recommends grantmaking policies and guidelines for approval by the board.

- *Nominating Committee:* Creates and establishes criteria for new trustees. Prepares a slate of nominees for trustees, officers, and committee members to be voted on at the annual meeting (sometimes called the "Membership Committee"). Some families also ask this committee to develop guidelines for board orientation and ongoing training.

- *Investment and Finance Committee:* Supervises the management of the foundation's assets and investments, develops guidelines and objectives for outside advisors, reports to the full board on foundation's finances, and approves annual budget for foundation activities.

Methods for Engaging Family Members and Other Individuals
One or more of the following options may be used to enhance the basic structure that you choose to establish. Each of these methods serves different purposes, and one or another may not be appropriate at all stages of the foundation's existence.

Setting Up a Board
Membership Rotation System

Family foundations sometimes set up board rotation systems when there are now — or may be one day — a large number of eligible family members seeking to become involved in the governance of the foundation. Typically, representatives from specific generations or individual branches of the family will rotate membership on an annual or semi-annual basis. Founders may choose to "exempt" themselves from the rotation system, or to retain the option in any given year of rejoining the board. Families that use rotation systems commonly set up a staggered rotation, so that when new trustees rotate onto the board, there are still several board members left to ensure continuity and organizational memory to the board.

While it is unlikely that such a system will be appropriate at the founding stage of the foundation's existence — unless the founders have a large number of children or adult grandchildren — board rotation policies can be effective at specific points in a family foundation's existence.

Families that establish board rotation systems — as well as those who wish to engage the broader family on an ongoing basis — are encouraged to find effective techniques for keeping all family members updated on the work of the foundation. This may be through occasional email announcements; distributing copies of meeting minutes and major grant reports; occasional briefings about the work of the foundation; a special page on the foundation's website or occasional newsletter; and other possibilities.

Deciding on Membership
Procedures and Criteria

These procedures describe how families identify, select, and orient new board members.

fig. 4

Sample Board Rotation Policy

The Board of Directors shall consist of seven members. Five of these will be family, defined as direct descendants of the Foundation's original donor. Three of these will be children and two will be the grandchildren of the donor. The grandchildren will serve two-year terms on a rotating basis. Two of the board members will be from the community, not direct descendants of the donor, and will serve a maximum of two consecutive three-year terms.

The rotation of grandchildren serving on the board is determined by age beginning with the oldest grandchild. Each grandchild must be 21 before he or she is elected to the board. Minor children will enter the rotation on their 21st birthday.

SOURCE: Anonymous Foundation, from *Family Advisor* packet on Board Composition, Council on Foundations, 1996.

Family foundations sometimes set up board rotation systems when there are now — or may be one day — a large number of eligible family members seeking to become involved in the governance of the foundation.

They should be designed to:
- Help potential new trustees understand what is expected of them,
- Allow current trustees to gauge the interests and experiences of potential new trustees, and
- Establish the process by which new trustees are added to the board

Some families require potential board members to fill out an application form or take part in a formal training process. Others ask that they serve on an adjunct board or meet specific qualifications or attributes.

"In some families, members of the second, third, and even fourth generations are eager to serve as foundation trustees," writes Michael Rion, author of *Responsible Family Philanthropy* (Council on Foundations, 1997). "In these cases, responsible philanthropy and ethical treatment of family members means developing specific criteria for trustees and applying these criteria objectively in inviting new trustees."

The Emily Hall Tremaine Foundation, a family foundation with more than 30 family members forming the pool from which the board is formed, strives for the following. The board should:
- Reflect the seven branches of the family's second generation;
- Not be dominated by any one branch;
- Reflect at least two generations; and
- Reflect diverse experience, skills and perspectives.

Selection of board members is based on core selection criteria, including energy and commitment to Emily Hall Tremaine Foundation's values and mission. Full board membership is preceded by a period of training and development.

Establishing Adjunct, Associate, or Next Generation Boards

Adjunct or next generation boards may be appropriate for situations where there are a large or growing number of younger family members who may want to become involved in the work of the foundation, but who do not yet have the available time or expertise required to serve as full board members.

Examples of adjunct/next generation boards abound. The Frees Family Foundation has created a "junior advisory board" for direct descendants of the Frees family who are aged 10–21 years. The foundation believes the adjunct board:
- Allows for a smoother inter-generational transfer of power and responsibility;
- Increases the likelihood of future interest and active participation in foundation endeavors;
- Provides training for foundation management;
- Provides an experience of the "reality" of involvement;
- Promotes the creation of new ideas, directions, and issues; and
- Helps internalize the values of philanthropy and volunteerism.

The Frees Foundation requires that grants recommended by its Advisory Board follow the overall Foundation guidelines, and places several other limitations designed to ensure that the Advisory Board members work together and consider the outcomes of their grantmaking. It is important to recognize that all grants made by adjunct boards must be formally approved or ratified by the formal board, and that board members are responsible for developing a process that ensures that these grants are made to eligible organizations.

The Self Family Foundation of Greenwood, South Carolina has also established a Next Generation Adjunct Board, made up of members of the next generation 18 years of age or older. Bubba Self, former chair of the Self Foundation's adjunct board and great-grandson of the founder, notes of his adjunct board experience that, "Being a successful steward and advocate for positive change is much more involved than just writing a check. It takes a proactive effort and much diligence along with careful, calculated decisions as to what programs and ideas are worthy of support and might become catalysts for other resources in the area. It's a constant learning process."

Alice Buhl, consultant to a number of family foundations, cautions that prior to involving the next generation in such a manner, it is important to accurately gauge the level of interest that exists. "Interest can be encouraged, but not forced," says Buhl. "There needs to be a genuine motivation to participate." In addition, it is important that you are clear about your expectations for younger family member's eligibility and expected length of service on such a board. If you set up an adjunct board for your grandchildren, and ask them to put in a great deal of time, energy, and commitment to this activity, at what point should they be formally considered for full board

fig.
5

Model for Foundations with Many Eligible Trustee Candidates

The Harris and Eliza Kempner Fund is a family foundation focusing its grant-making efforts on the greater Galveston, Texas, area. Board and family members reside in locations throughout the country. The Fund has developed the following model for involving current and future generations of family members in the work of the foundation.

The Harris and Eliza Kempner Fund has a professional staff of one (plus 1 1/2 support) and 43 family members of the third and fourth generation who are eligible to be trustees. There are nine trustees on the board, seven of whom are family. Up until 1988 trustees served for life. Two changes approved that year allow more rotation on the board: a mandatory retirement age (75) and nine-year terms (three family trustees were grandfathered and are exempt from the nine-year term limitation). Even with these changes, opportunities to serve are few and far between.

In 1990 the trustees approved Chairman Nonie Thompson's plan to establish advisory committees to provide opportunities for nontrustee family members to experience the grant process. Once a year three committees meet: one to select candidates for the Fund's student loan program and two to review grant requests related to environmental protection, population control, and third world development. There are 12-15 participants each year. They receive 4-6 grant requests to review and recommend. Their packets include suggestions for grant evaluation and information on how to review financial statements. Their committee's allocation is always less than the total being requested, so the members discuss, debate, and make the difficult allocation decisions. When time allows at their meeting, a workshop is provided on a subject relevant to foundation/philanthropic issues.

The value of this program is that the participants have an opportunity to find out if they have any interest in foundation matters. Those who do are easily identified: they sign up year after year, arrive with their homework done, take seriously the deliberation process, and understand the implications of their decisions. The advisory committee meetings usually occur in the same time frame as family business meetings and other family gatherings, allowing them to visit with trustees and other family members, many of whom have their own foundations. The executive director has frequent opportunities to interact with them.

When the time comes to consider a replacement trustee, the trustees have a short list, with all the candidates having a proven interest in and aptitude for trusteeship.

membership? Establishing clarity around expectations will help make this a positive learning experience, and one that does not result in feelings of undue entitlement or frustration.

Considering Community Advisory Boards

Another option used by many family foundations is an outside advisory board made up of community representatives, experts, or other individuals that may have a particularly valuable perspective to lend the foundation. *(Note: although some refer to advisory boards in the same way as adjunct or associate boards, in this chapter we refer to adjunct/associate boards as a specific type of advisory board in which younger family members are involved.)*

Advisory boards allow family foundations to be more directly connected and accountable to the communities they serve, and to have additional perspective on the latest trends and developments in a particular issue area.

The Springs Foundation of Fort Mill, South Carolina, recognized the potential for a community advisory board to inform family decisionmaking, and in the early 1990s established a Community Advisory Committee that they use to this day. To create the initial committee, the Springs board asked for nominations of community leaders in each of their three geographic target areas — Lancaster County and the towns of Fort Mill and Chester. Citizen advisors are limited to three-year terms, and the Springs Foundation chose to create staggered durations to encourage continuity. Francie Close, family member and trustee of the foundation, notes that, "Even those who were very apprehensive about having outsiders involved now acknowledge it's the best thing going for us. We value their opinions enormously. It's how we make sure real needs and community voices drive the agenda."

Other useful strategies exist for families seeking to include the viewpoints of others without asking them to serve on the board or an advisory board. Some of these include:

- Inviting speakers to board meetings or luncheons;
- Meeting with representatives of the local community foundation, Jewish Federation, or United Way to learn about key projects and programs they are involved in;
- Holding a focus group on a specific program area;
- Commissioning or participating in a community needs assessment; and
- Developing a survey of grantees or community leaders about the strengths, weaknesses, and overall effectiveness of the foundation.

Regardless of the strategy chosen, finding ways to include outside perspectives is a proven means of informing family discussions and long-term foundation strategies.

Involving Nonfamily Members and Considering Diversity

While some families choose to include community representatives and other individuals outside the family on one or more advisory committees, a growing number include nonfamily members as official board members of the foundation. According to *Trends in Family Foundations Governance, Staffing, and Management* from the Council on Foundations, nearly three of five respondents had boards that included nonfamily members (community representatives and/or family or business associates). One family foundation board member explains: "The board members believe that outsiders can make a good situation better by bringing management experience and knowledge of community needs to the foundation."

There are many well-documented reasons for including individuals from outside the family and from a variety of backgrounds on the board. Nonfamily board members can enhance the work of the foundation by:

- Bringing specific expertise or experience that is missing from a board;
- Serving as a neutral moderator for family disagreements and discussions;
- Evaluating staff performance when the staff person is a family member;
- Providing an outside perspective, and an intellectual curiosity to the board, expanding the family's vision for the foundation; and
- Increasing the diversity of the board, and allowing the foundation to be more accountable to society at large.

How comfortable will you and your family be with nonfamily members in the boardroom? What level of confi-

---

fig. 6 | **A Statement of Inclusiveness**

One foundation that has actively reflected on the value and importance of diversity is the Z. Smith Reynolds Foundation, based in Winston-Salem, North Carolina. The foundation's board formally approved the adoption of a Statement on Inclusiveness, which reads in part:

The Foundation has the conviction that inclusiveness benefits everyone and is not only compatible with but also promotes excellence. The Z. Smith Reynolds Foundation's grantmaking policies reflect the belief that organizational performance is greatly enhanced when people with different backgrounds and perspectives are engaged in an organization's activities and decision-making process.

dentiality do you require? Are there individuals who you can trust to respect that confidentiality? Can you find nonfamily trustees who understand and respect the goals of the donor and the family, and who will be willing to help pass this legacy along to future board members?

It is perfectly reasonable to have separate selection criteria and board terms for nonfamily trustees, and/or other safeguards that give you and your family the authority to retain control of the foundation's long-term direction. As Deborah Brody, author and senior program director for the National Center for Family Philanthropy, once wrote, "While families can't choose their relatives, they do choose nonfamily trustees. And they must decide how to involve them."

Over time, you may wish to develop a short history of the foundation's goals and activities, key accomplishments, and model projects.

Governing the Board

A first order of business for any governing board is, of course, to adopt policies and procedures for governing and managing itself. Following are suggestions on several subjects of importance in board governance and management.

Setting Board Terms and Limits

Thirty-five percent of family foundation respondents to a survey by the Council on Foundations indicated that they limit board service in one way or another for some or all board members. Of these, 73 percent limit the number of years per term that a board member can serve (median of 3 years), and 30 percent limit the number of consecutive terms that a board member can serve. Another common limit on board service for those responding to the Council's survey were minimum and maximum age limits. 37 percent of respondents reported a minimum age limit (median age limit of 21), while only 17 percent defined a maximum age limit (median of 70).

Board terms can serve many useful purposes, including:
- Developing a shared understanding of the ongoing participation of board members
- Encouraging board members to take a break from the foundation and to step back and view the work of a foundation from a non-board perspective
- Allowing younger and extended family members join the board over time
- Helping board members realize that they have "permission" to step down

Developing a Foundation and Board History

Over time, you may wish to develop a short history of the foundation's goals and activities, key accomplishments, and model projects. This may include a history of the founders and their goals for establishing the foundation (often referred to as the donor legacy statement). Another useful piece of information to include in such a history is a brief overview of who has served on the board, particularly if this includes nonfamily members, or individuals who may not be familiar to future trustees.

Adopting Guidelines for Board Meetings

Some families choose to develop or observe guidelines for how they interact in board meetings and discussions. Robert Hull, author of *The Trustee Notebook*, describes one family's simple but effective ritual of repeating the following pledge together before the start of each board meeting:

In deference to my solemn public trust as a trustee of this foundation I will hereby attempt to put aside my preconceptions, my biases, and any entangling relationships with my fellow trustees that might limit my ability to see things clearly or make rational judgments and decisions of behalf of the public good.

Families take varied approaches. Sarah Cavanaugh, a family trustee and former executive director for the Russell Family Foundation, focuses on the positives of family dynamics and history, and includes time in each board meeting agenda to celebrate and share family stories, photos, and heritage.

Agreeing Upon a Meeting Schedule
An agreed-upon meeting schedule provides guidance around the timing and location for the annual and other meetings of the full board. This helps ensure that trustees and other family members are able to plan for and participate in these meetings on a regular basis. Some families choose to have at least one of the meetings in conjunction with other annual family gatherings — Thanksgiving, Easter, or the annual family reunion — to minimize travel expenses and time, and to add a new level of meaning to these events.

---

fig. 7   Surdna Foundation Statement of Board Culture

- We have respect for one another and for one another's rights as a board member.

- We value honesty and truthfulness. We go beyond niceness, politeness and avoidance to niceness, politeness and directness. We owe each other both negative and positive feedback.

- We value due process. We seek a process on the board that will mirror our intention of personal empowerment. Just as we seek to empower others through our grantmaking, we wish our own process to empower ourselves and serve as a model for foundation governance.

- We acknowledge that differences can be energizing and can lead to learning. Collaboration and conflict go hand-in-hand.

- We seek to align ourselves around a common vision and deepen our conviction that our work together will make a difference.

- We seek to work together as a team, with a shared sense of purpose and inspiration. After bringing our unique insights as individuals to our collective process, we will endeavor to support decisions taken by the whole.

- We will seek consensus first. After airing disagreements, we will use voting as a fallback technique to permit us to move forward.

- We value Board leadership, which facilitates our process, and helps bring us to a consensus.

- We seek innovation and the group's acceptance and encouragement of individual initiative and risk taking.

- We encourage board members to commit fully to making the Foundation the best it can be.

- All board members share responsibility for facilitating our process and resolving conflict. We are committed to improving facilitation skills and sharing leadership roles.

Specifying a Quorum Requirement

This statement specifies the number of trustees required to constitute a quorum, the minimum number of trustees required to amend policy or vote on behalf of the full board. The statement should include a notation as to whether trustees connected to the meeting via conference telephone or similar equipment may be considered as participants in the meeting, and whether they may count to the overall quorum requirement.

Establishing Grounds and Process for Removal

Some families choose to state explicitly the circumstances under which a trustee will be asked to leave the board, and what the process is for doing this. The most likely reason for removal is non-attendance or non-participation. Other possible reasons include refusal to follow stated policies or guidelines of the foundation, divorce, or some other similar circumstance.

Filling Vacancies

It may also be helpful to develop specific guidelines about how to deal with a temporary vacancy on the board, particularly when there are several individuals in line for service, or if there is some form of branch representation in place.

Meeting State Regulations

Are there any state regulations that affect how your board is structured? One important example of such a regulation is the state of California's rules against compensating family members who serve as board members or staff for foundation boards in which more than half of the trustees are family members. Foundations established in the corporate form are typically required to file corporate annual reports with the Secretary of State. State law also establishes the fiduciary duties of board members.

Obtaining Directors and Officers Liability Insurance

Prudent boards may want to ensure that they are protected from a variety of potential lawsuits by arranging for directors and officers liability insurance. While such suits are rare, and successful claims even rarer, you may want to discuss this matter with counsel.

Developing a Board Handbook

This summary notebook should include copies of each of the policies you develop, as well as a history of the foundation, meeting schedule, and other key documents that your board members may need. This handbook should be updated on an annual basis — you may even wish to consider making this an online document, so that trustees can access it wherever they may be, and it can be easily updated.

Going Forward

A basic rule to keep in mind when considering and developing your foundation's structure is as follows: it is always easier to establish a policy regarding a specific situation before it becomes a burning issue. Establishing and amending structure by definition affects one or more of the stakeholders in your foundation. The more you and your founding board are able to anticipate and think through the likely consequences of your policies, the more likely it is that these consequences will be positive and reinforcing to the work of the foundation. Other key thoughts to keep in mind:

Remember the importance of expectations and clarity. Wherever possible, document your basic philosophy and expectations in writing or videotape, and have regular conversations with the board about these areas (some founders even put in their bylaws a requirement that future board members occasionally review the founder's values, philosophies, and particular interests). If your goal is to have future trustees develop their own mission statement and priorities, let them know this as well. You might be surprised at the importance these documents may have… and if you don't explain what your goals are, how can those who follow know?

Decide on which you value more — flexibility or control. Just as you need to check in from time-to-time with your mission and grantmaking guidelines, effective board structures must be able to adapt over time. You — and eventually your future trustees — will need to occasionally ask themselves the following questions:

- Is our current structure working?
- Does it reflect the current priorities of the family and the foundation?
- Have conditions changed either in the family, or in the community?

You can't plan for every eventuality, and you shouldn't try to. Rather, seek to provide overall guidance and understanding about your goals and dreams, and to trust those who follow you with the wisdom and accountability that is required of all successful stewards.

Understanding Board and Trustee Roles and Responsibilities

When a man assumes a public trust, he should consider himself as public property.

— THOMAS JEFFERSON

All boards have some elements in common. For example, they must:

- Support and promote the organization's mission;
- Operate as a productive, decisionmaking group;
- Set up a process for board members' nominations, selection, and succession;
- Secure resources so that the organization can operate efficiently and effectively;
- Ensure that finances are being well spent and well managed;
- Set policy standards and guidelines;

- Hire, support, and evaluate the chief staff officer or determine other administrative and management structures; and
- Assess their own performance and effectiveness as a board.

This section addresses the following questions:

- What is the job of a family foundation trustee;
- How can we operate as a productive, decisionmaking group?
- What does good trusteeship require?

What Is the Job of a Family Foundation Trustee?

Family foundation boards have advantages over other types of boards because families usually have an intimate knowledge of one another and a common ancestry that binds them together. Families can also have strong historical and emotional ties — both positive and negative — that can impede or enhance their decisionmaking.

Many family boards also include nonfamily members. These nonfamily trustees can play an important part in

The more you and your founding board are able to anticipate and think through the likely consequences of your policies, the more likely it is that these consequences will be positive and reinforcing to the work of the foundation.

helping the family broaden its perspective and networks.

Let's assume that you are joining your family foundation's board for the first time. How should you prepare? What do you need to know?

First, you will want to learn as much as you can about the communities your foundation serves. You can gain this knowledge by studying demographic, economic, and social trends, by being aware of issues facing the community, by talking with other community leaders and members of other boards, and by participating in your local regional association of grantmakers seminars and networking events.

In the early years of your foundation, trustees will have to address start-up issues including:

- Defining the mission and goals of the foundation, selecting and training the initial board members;
- Developing policies and procedures for operating as a board; and
- Structuring and then putting in place

the foundation's administrative and grantmaking processes.

Some fundamental responsibilities will be constants throughout the foundation's life. In addition to the governance responsibilities mentioned above, family foundations will need to:

- Approve and oversee the grantmaking strategy and grantmaking process;
- Manage and oversee the foundation's financial assets, budget, and expenses; and
- Ensure that the foundation operates according to the legal and fiduciary requirements of both federal and state governments.

All boards must change as their members change and their organizations evolve; however, a family foundation must be particularly flexible and prepared to deal with the changing nature of its participants. Marriage, divorce, death, and generational transitions all play a part in redefining your particular foundation. Reviewing the responsibilities of trustees on a regular basis is an essential part of the governance journey.

How Can We Operate as a Productive Decisionmaking Group?

A critical early board responsibility is to define and uphold a vision and mission for the foundation. Many new family foundation boards find that it is helpful to take the time for a board retreat and to hire an outside facilita-

---

fig. 8 — Sample Trustee Position Description

1. To evaluate on a regular basis:
   a. The organization's effectiveness in accomplishing its mission;
   b. The role and performance of the Executive Director on an annual basis;
   c. The effectiveness of the allocation of resources;
   d. The effectiveness of individual trustees and of the board of trustees as a whole; and
   e. Whether the foundation should continue as an organization.

2. To establish and oversee:
   a. Institutional policies including but not limited to a policy of non-discrimination;
   b. Personnel policies; and
   c. Systems for fiscal accountability.

3. To take responsibility for planning by:
   a. Ensuring that there is a mission statement;
   b. Ensuring that there is a strategic plan; and
   c. Overseeing the implementation of the strategic plan.

4. To oversee the acquisition and allocation of funds by:
   a. Defining the investment goals;
   b. Monitoring the management of investments; and
   c. Approving the fund's overall program plan.

SOURCE: *The Trustee Notebook*, National Center for Family Philanthropy, 1999.

All boards must change as their members change and their organizations evolve; however, a family foundation must be particularly flexible and prepared to deal with the changing nature of its participants.

tor to interview board members and help you craft the goals and agenda for the meeting.

Following are key subject areas for consideration.

Set Policy Standards and Guidelines

Successful boards of trustees adopt policies that set standards for quality, ethics, and prudence in foundation operations. Your policies should:

- Define expectations for high quality grantmaking programs;
- Define expectations for the foundation's performance; and
- Require wise and prudent use of funds and management of assets.

Since many newly created family foundations do not hire an outside executive director — at least initially — it is doubly important to put policies in place so that trustees performing staff work are both guided and protected from conflicts of interest or other legal or ethical dilemmas. Depending upon how your family foundation is set up, the board itself may be responsible for carrying out these policies, or it may choose to delegate some responsibilities to an executive committee or to an executive director.

Family members often wear multiple hats. For instance, you may have a family member who is the foundation's executive director or administrator. In some cases, it might make sense for this person also to be a trustee; however, you may decide that the clearest route to take to avoid any confusion is to have the family members choose to be either a staff person or a trustee.

Hire, Support, and Evaluate Management

If you choose to appoint an executive director or administrator, either from within or outside your family, successful governance depends on a good relationship between the board and this staff person. In general, your staff person will implement board policies, while the board will depend on the staff for guidance and educational leadership. This relationship works best when there are clear, mutually agreed-on expectations and job descriptions. The partnership thrives on open communication, confidence, trust, and support. To be effective, trustees and boards must:

- Clearly define what characteristics, qualities, and experience they are looking for in an Executive Director;
- Select and retain the best staff or management support possible;
- Define clear parameters and expectations for performance;
- Conduct periodic evaluations for the based on honest and constructive feedback; and
- Support the staff and create an environment for success.

Families that choose to have a family member as staff deal with a special set

of circumstances. First, you must clearly define the job. Then it is essential to make sure that the family member is chosen fairly and has the appropriate skills (management, program, and interpersonal) to adequately perform the job. Perhaps most difficult of all, the family member's performance in this role — whether compensated or volunteer — will also need to be assessed in as unbiased and professional a manner as possible. Families with a paid nonfamily staff member may have an easier time, since the relationship may be conducted strictly on a business basis. Finding and retaining an effective staff person requires constant board diligence and oversight, including written personnel policies, job descriptions, and performance reviews. (See Setting Up Shop, p. 115.)

Evaluate the Board's Performance and Effectiveness

Effective boards engage in a continuing process of self-assessment or evaluation of their performance. They do so in order to identify where they are performing well as a board, and where they might improve. Discussion about board roles and responsibilities can strengthen communication and understanding among board members

Well-conducted board self-assessments lead to better boards. The results of an assessment may include:
- A summary of board accomplishments;
- A better understanding of what it means to be an effective board;

- Clarification of what trustees expect from each other and themselves;
- Improved communications among trustees and between the board and staff;
- Identification of problems, potential issues, and areas to improve;
- Opportunity to discuss and solve problems that may hurt board performance;
- Identification of strategies to enhance board performance;
- Agreement on board roles and trustee responsibilities;
- The setting of board goals and objectives for the coming year; and
- Renewed dedication to the board.

Evaluating the board's performance is not the same as evaluating individual trustee performance. The purpose of a board self-assessment is to look at the board as a whole; although, a side benefit may be that individual board members gain appreciation for the roles and responsibilities of trusteeship.

Many board members are not sure how to evaluate themselves. The process of self-evaluation may be formal or informal. The important thing is that the process provides useful information for the board members. Informal self-evaluations may consist of an open-ended discussion in which board members identify those things that enhance and challenge effective participation and performance. Thus, the board may not need a self-evaluation instrument or survey.

A small committee of the board can be appointed to design and propose the process and criteria. Each and every board member should participate in the self-evaluation by completing a board self-assessment instrument (if used), being interviewed, or being active in the discussion.

If the foundation has an executive director or administrator, he or she is also an important resource. Varying levels of staff involvement in the assessment may be appropriate, from being a full participant in the process, to contributing advice and support for the process, to providing comments on the board/staff relationship. Some boards conduct the board and staff evaluations in tandem, since the success of one entity in the partnership depends on the effectiveness of the other.

fig.
11 Some Ways to Think About Board Effectiveness

Board Organization. Does the board operate as a unit? Does the board meet according to its policies, and engage in orderly meetings? Are officer responsibilities clear and do officers fulfill them? Do committees operate effectively and contribute to board success?

Community Representation. How does the board involve the community it serves? Does the board have strategies for seeking input from diverse interests?

Policy Direction. Do board members understand foundation's mission, policies and programs? What issues have most occupied the board's time and attention during the past year? Were these closely tied to the mission and goals of the institution?

Board–Executive Director Relations. Do the board and executive director/administrator have a respectful partnership and open communication? Are their roles clearly defined?

Foundation Operations. Does the board have clear policies related to fiscal affairs, asset management, and human resources? Does it have clear standards and processes for grantmaking? Does the board have and adhere to clear protocols for communicating with staff?

Board Behavior. Does the board behavior set a positive tone for the institution? Do board members work well together as a team? Are different perspectives encouraged and incorporated into decisionmaking? Does the board have and adhere to a code of ethics?

Advocacy. Do board members help portray the foundation in its best light? Do they attend foundation events? Do they help promote the image of the foundation in the community?

Board Education. Are new board members well oriented? Are all board members encouraged and supported in engaging in ongoing learning?

SOURCE: Adapted from the Association of Governing Boards of Colleges and Universities.

Consultants and facilitators are often helpful to boards in developing and conducting an evaluation. They can provide an independent, non-biased influence to help keep board discussions focused and positive.

Prepare New Trustees for Service

Bringing new trustees onto the board is going to be critical to your foundation's long-term effectiveness. This may include family members from the younger generations, community leaders, or professional experts (e.g., a lawyer, accountant, or financial planner). You might want to design a series of orientation sessions for the new trustees. These might include:

- Scheduling information and discussion sessions with the board chair, other experienced board members, and the staff, if applicable;

- Discussing protocols and guidelines for communicating with other trustees and staff;

- Requiring new trustees to read and discuss the foundation's bylaws, grantmaking guidelines, board policy manual, and other documents critical to the foundation's operations;

- Scheduling site visits to grantees or potential grantees with other trustees or with the staff; and

- Providing new trustees with copies of orientation materials from the family

philanthropy field such as the National Center for Family Philanthropy's *Trustee Notebook and Foundation Trusteeship*, a classic reference book for trustees available from the Foundation Center.

Create an Effective Board Meeting

What are the ingredients of effective board meetings? Board meetings are only as successful as the thought that goes into the planning. As you consider the suggestions presented below, keep in mind that what is an extremely effective board meeting for one family may not work for your family. What is important is to check in with each other about what works and what doesn't. Make sure that meetings remain a good use of people's time, that important issues are getting addressed and that the work between meetings is clearly defined and assigned. You want your board to be engaged and prepared for the next meeting.

Suggestions:

- Have a structured agenda. Provide an opportunity for board members to have input into the creation of the agenda, and send the agenda to the board in advance of the meeting. This helps everyone come prepared to accomplish the items on the agenda.

- Do strategic planning on a regular basis.

- Be sure that staff or the board member responsible prepares good briefing materials and sends them out well in advance of the board meeting.

- Be sure that all board members are kept fully informed between meetings. Whether one family member or a large complement of family members leads your foundation, the entire board is legally responsible for the foundation's activities.

- Board meetings should engage everyone sitting around the table. The most satisfying board meetings are those in which substantive issues are openly and fully discussed.

- Set aside time at least once a year to consider major issues that are likely to effect your foundation and its work in the years ahead.

However you choose to design your meetings, be sure to plan ahead, keep board members well informed between meetings and in advance of meetings, and take time to build board cohesion and have some fun.

GOOD ADVICE> "We meet approximately monthly by phone to decide on grants. And then at the quarterly meetings we are much more likely to review some ongoing projects and at least once a year talk about the overall big picture of where we're going."
PENNY NOYCE, THE NOYCE FOUNDATION

Ensure Good Board Communication

While board meetings are of critical importance, the communication that goes on before, between, and after board meetings is equally important. Your board will need to determine what distinguishes official communications from unofficial communications. Will your board make use of written reports, periodic conference calls, or email? Who will oversee the collection and distribution of relevant material?

Increasingly, boards are making use of email and websites, but not everyone is comfortable with electronic forms of communication. In addition, you will need to find a balance between a sufficiency and an excess of information. This may take some time and need to be revisited over time. (See Communicating: Enhancing Process, Participation, and the Public Face of Your Foundation, p. 191.)

Offer Board Education

Board education comes in a variety of forms and is an on-going ingredient of a successful board. Some boards budget a specified amount of time and money for board activities that include.

- Bringing in outside presenters to board meetings to speak on specific topic (vary the speaker's focus over time to cover both programmatic content and board responsibilities);
- Encouraging trustees to attend professional meetings or conferences;

While board meetings are of critical importance, the communication that goes on before, between, and after board meetings is equally important.

- Using site visits to educate the board on grantee concerns and needs; and
- Creating a bibliography for board members.

GOOD ADVICE ➤ "We have three meetings a year, at least one of those is a day and a half and there is a social aspect to it. We bring in a speaker or a resource at two of the board meetings. We also send out regular news clippings and reports we think might be of interest."
NANCY DOUZINAS, THE RAUCH FOUNDATION

Summary: What Does Good Trusteeship Require?

Good trusteeship requires the ability to function as part of a team, and a team functions best when all members are encouraged to contribute their strengths and are committed to working together. Effective boards are thoughtful and knowledgeable. Trustees on effective boards listen well, ask good questions, analyze options, think critically, and clarify their most important values and priorities. They explore issues thoroughly and make policy decisions based on thorough deliberation and comprehensive understanding.

The best boards are future-oriented. They recognize that today's world requires flexible institutions and leaders who are willing to adapt and grow in response to the changing needs of society. Trustees who act with vision, with intelligence, with curiosity and with enthusiasm create a board that is an agent for positive change. Effective boards and trustees engage in ongoing learning about board roles and responsibilities; are curious and inclusive; are positive and optimistic, and support and respect one another.

While all this may seem a bit daunting, by starting a family foundation you have already become a trustee of the public good. Fortunately, you are in good company. An entire community exists to help you find your way consisting of fellow trustees of family foundations, organizations that offer support and services, and resource materials.

WHEN A CONSULTANT CAN HELP

by Barbara D. Kibbe

An important characteristic of most respected — and successful — grantmakers is self-reflection. They plan, they assess, they evaluate, and they communicate. And, sooner or later, many look to outside experts or consultants for help with specific tasks.

When starting your family foundation, an outside expert or consultant might be able to help — but help with what?

When a Consultant Can be Useful

Typical projects a family foundation might employ a consultant to undertake include:

- **Family Matters.** As families work out relationship issues, they must also develop (or follow) a vision, start the grants process going, and manage foundation's assets. With such a complex array of relationships and responsibilities, a consultant's experience in similar situations — as well as his or her essential neutrality — can break down barriers to consensus and make the business of the family foundation more manageable.
- **Management and Structure.** Family foundations often must deal with internal challenges about grantmaking. A consultant can help sort out family members' roles, the decisionmaking process, and issues of power and money.
- **Needs Assessment.** You may know the mission but not the grantee community. A consultant can define and quantify the needs, research existing programs, identify gaps in the system of services, and make recommendations about where to invest foundation dollars to make the greatest impact.
- **Preparing RFPs and Assessing Proposals.** Your foundation has decided to launch its first new initiative aimed at bringing high-quality science education to middle school children.

If it seems that the best means for selecting an appropriate grantee is by asking for proposals, a consultant might help prepare a Request for Proposal (RFP), draft and help circulate the document, and even help design a proposal review process that helps ensure the best projects are considered for funding.

- **Evaluation.** More and more family foundation boards want to know if the grants they make are effective. The objectivity, as well as the technical expertise, of an outside evaluator can be helpful in setting up an evaluation process.
- **Dissemination and Communication.** A communications consultant can help a founder and family talk though a communications strategy.

Locating the Right Consultant

In many ways, finding a qualified consultant is more difficult than finding a doctor. At least with physicians you have a reasonable assurance than anyone who has graduated from a bona fide medical school and has a license to practice medicine has studied — and hopefully learned — something about how to safeguard and improve peoples' health. Physicians are often certified in specialties. Consultants have no required course of study, no certification, no continuing education requirements, not even a required apprenticeship.

Usually, the best way to identify good consultants is to network with colleagues from other foundations. Even with a strong recommendation, however, it is imperative to interview more than one consultant. Some useful questions to ask consultant candidates might include:

■ Whom have you worked for in the past, and what did you accomplish for them?

■ Have you ever consulted on the same issue that our foundation now faces?

■ What led you to consulting as a career?

■ What is your work process? How would you work with our board and family members?

If the consultant seems promising after the personal interview, follow up by checking references. Ask for a client list, not the consultant's handpicked batch of satisfied customers.

Look for three main qualities in a consultant — *skill*, *sensitivity*, and *experience*. Direct your inquiry to determine whether your candidates possess them.

Good choices are usually the result of clarity about the aims and limitations of the consulting process, combined with agreeable personal chemistry between the consultant and client. So, give equal time to gut feelings and to matching the skills of the consultant with the project and the precise needs of your family and foundation.

What to Expect from Consultants

Once the consultant has been selected, the amount of care taken in defining the assignment can mean the difference between a successful endeavor and one that goes awry. One way to ensure that the relationship and work product stay on track is to have the consultant prepare a workplan for the foundation project manager review.

The agreed-on Scope of Work serves as a blueprint for the consulting process. It should spell out both the problems to be addressed and the goals of the collaboration,

---

fig.
1

Traits of a Good Consultant

Because of the immense variation in the consulting role and lack of licensing or other widely accepted standards of qualification, specifying precise, objective standards of competence is difficult. Although no two consultants work in exactly the same way, all capable professionals will demonstrate three essential qualities.

SKILL ➤ Most consultants develop specialties — such as meeting facilitation and planning, assessment and evaluation, or board development and staff training. They keep up with developments in the field by studying the new literature, staying in touch with colleagues, and reexamining their own theories, biases, and experience. Their professional credibility is based on their consistent ability to perform at an exceptionally high level in the areas they have embraced as their own.

SENSITIVITY ➤ Consulting is very often group work, including families. Some consultants relish the complexity of family behavior. They anticipate the problems that inevitably crop up during any kind of collective endeavor. And they know how to harness the energy of the family, without turning the process into a therapy session or allowing it to disintegrate.

EXPERIENCE ➤ Good consultants have track records. They won't be using your project as a highly paid internship to learn the fundamentals of grantmaker management. Your foundation's goals and problems will neither surprise nor confound the seasoned consultant.

roundly sketching activities that will be pursued over a defined period.

The consultant should be provided with basic information about the foundation and the family before being asked to prepare this workplan. Some foundations actually disseminate an RFP as a means for locating consultants interested in working on their project or problem. Such an RFP should offer information about the organization, as well as background on the project or problem the consultant is being asked to address. It also can be quite specific about the kind of written response the foundation expects — e.g., qualifications, experience with similar projects and organizations, proposed workplan, timeline, and budget. Whether the foundation chooses to issue an RFP or simply call a number of consultants for interviews, a detailed workplan should be prepared by the consultant before work commences, and it should be done free of charge. The proposal and workplan should include:

- Statement of the problem to be solved or the objectives to be achieved;
- Approach and methods to be used in reaching the goal;
- Tasks to be undertaken, including details of each step;
- Personnel responsible for accomplishing the tasks;
- Costs for the entire project, broken down into logical categories; and
- A timeline showing key milestones.

Evaluating a Consultant's Work Product

A successful collaboration with a consultant depends on determining whether expected goals have been met. Thus, goals must be carefully established from the beginning. It is sometimes difficult to evaluate fully the performance of even the best consultants. Try to keep the following in mind:

- Evaluation is a continuing process. Quality must be tracked from the beginning of the consulting relationship, with sufficient opportunities for adjusting the process if it runs off course. The consultant should be available to discuss progress during regularly scheduled meetings or on an ad hoc basis.
- Interim reports are necessary. Any project that lasts more than 8 weeks probably requires a brief, written progress report by the midway point. That report can serve as the basis for a more detailed discussion with the consultant during which you make certain that everybody involved is holding up his or her end of the job. (i.e., it shouldn't significantly increase the cost of services). It is an informal document, serving as an indicator of the project's general health, making explicit much of what you've probably already seen or intuited, and ensuring that the overall focus remains steady. The report will not cap or complete discussion on the project but rather open it up.

Remember, nothing turns out as planned. The consulting process usually produces both delightful new information and unwelcome revelations. As a result, some changes in strategy may be necessary. Still, it is important to resist the temptation to respond to each layer of discovery with a new policy or revised workplan. Hold steady until the whole picture emerges.

SOURCE: Adapted from Barbara D. Kibbe, "Working with Consultants," *Resources for Family Philanthropy: Finding the Best People, Advice, and Support*. Washington, DC: National Center for Family Philanthropy, 1999. An additional source is Barbara Kibbe and Fred Setterberg, *Succeeding with Consultants*. Washington, DC: The Foundation Center, 1992.

SETTING UP SHOP
Ways to Manage Your Family Foundation

by Deborah A. Brody

You are at the beginning of one of the most challenging and rewarding endeavors a family can undertake. Sound management is key to success in this endeavor.

Establishing good management processes and procedures for your family foundation at the outset supports the program goals and content of your philanthropy. Like many founders, your experience in managing ventures — perhaps you have run a family business, chaired a civic organization, or reared a family, for that matter — will put you in good stead for managing a family foundation.

Experienced family grantmakers advocate an integrated approach to management, an approach that links the seemingly mundane activities of daily operations directly to charitable mission, legal requirements, and the founder and other board and family members.

A way to look at management as you launch your family foundation might include:
- Managing in support of the charitable mission;
- Assessing what work must be done;
- Deciding how the work can be done;
- Determining where the work will be done;
- Identifying and securing the tools you will need;

- Considering administrative expenses; and, most importantly,
- Realizing your great expectations.

Office management and operations are tools to allow you and your family to accomplish something important. The late Paul Ylvisaker — a family foundation trustee — once said:

Foundations are a remarkable human invention. They provide private persons a freewheeling opportunity to be socially and publicly influential. Without having to meet the tests either of the market or the ballot box, private persons can independently determine what the needs of society are and how best to go about meeting them.

By starting and running a family foundation, you have chosen to place your personal funds in a public trust. That decision gives you the potential to have a tremendous influence in your community — to affect the lives and livelihoods of people on the front lines of nonprofit agencies and the constituents they serve. As a foundation founder, your job is to make the fundraising process a productive experience for grantees. Even if grantee proposals do not result in immediate funding, they can lead to acquiring new information, meeting new people, and establishing a collegial relationship with your foundation. Strong management can support this entire enterprise.

Managing in Support of the Charitable Mission

This above all: to thine own self be true,
And it must follow, as the night the day,
Thou canst not then be false to any man.
— HAMLET. ACT I. SC. 3.

A mission statement represents a family foundation's values, goals, and purpose. In addition to defining the foundation's overarching goals, it can provide a framework for managing the foundation. According to management guru Peter Drucker, "Understanding one's mission is the essence of effective strategy, for the small nonprofit enterprise or the Fortune 500." Drucker recommends asking, "What is our business/mission? Who is our customer? What does the customer value?" Your customers are your grantees, your community, and, in the broadest sense, society.

If you are not already deeply involved in your area's nonprofit community, you will want to learn as much as possible about it. You might want to set up individual meetings with local government, business, and nonprofit leaders. Invite a group of them to lunch, or even conduct formal focus groups. This will help guide and inform you as you rise to the challenge of setting up an efficient management structure that takes the foundation's mission, family dynamics, and grantees into account.

For example:

- If you want your foundation and family to be visible in the community, consider renting an office with a conference room in the downtown area of your city and hire a friendly, outgoing staff person to manage that office.
- If you want family members to conduct meetings or do work at the foundation, you will need extra office space for their use.
- If your family prefers to remain behind-the-scenes and give as much as possible of the foundation's assets to charity, you may be able to set up shop in a family member's home or business.
- If your foundation's mission is to protect the environment, you might want to have your foundation's office in an environmentally sound building, print foundation documents on recycled paper, and use other recycled office materials.
- If your foundation funds the arts, you might want to support local artists by hanging their artwork in your offices or by providing them with free or low-cost studio space.

These are just a few examples of how family structure and foundation mission might affect management and operational decisions. There are as many permutations of these as there are families and organizations.

Assessing What Work Must Be Done

Work, and thou wilt bless the day
Ere the toil be done.
— JOHN SULLIVAN DWIGHT (1813-1893)

Setting up the foundation office and putting management systems in place will take a fair amount of time initially. Once set up, however, the office should run smoothly, freeing you and your family to focus on foundation mission. Questions to consider include:

- How will we manage the board?
- Will we accept unsolicited proposals?
- If so, how and when will we accept and review proposals?
- How many grants and what types of grants will the foundation make?
- What kinds of follow up will the foundation undertake after a grant is awarded?
- What records should we keep?
- How should bookkeeping and accounting be handled?
- How will we let people know about the foundation?

Some of the day-to-day tasks involved in managing a family foundation include:

- Answering mail, email, and telephone calls;
- Writing materials for the foundation, if needed, such as a brochure, a web page, a fact sheet, grant summaries, and board and committee minutes;
- Coordinating meetings, distributing minutes, and preparing briefing

materials for the board;

- Soliciting and screening grant proposals;
- Identifying and conducting due diligence on grantees;
- Scheduling and keeping records on site visits to potential grantees;
- Attending or organizing networking meetings;
- Issuing and mailing checks to grantees;
- Following up with grantees by answering their questions, monitoring grant expenditures, and managing grant evaluations, if the foundation chooses to do them.

While some of these tasks are basic to running any office, family foundations have one task that most other organizations do not — determining how best to involve and work with other members of the family. This responsibility generally influences many management decisions.

Deciding How the Work Can be Done

One summer day the Little Red Hen found a grain of wheat.

"A grain of wheat!" said the Little Red Hen to herself. "I will plant it."

She asked the duck, "Will you help me plant this grain of wheat?"

"Not I," said the duck ….

When the wheat was ready to harvest, the Little Red Hen said to herself, "I will harvest the wheat and make bread out of the flour …."

"And now," said the Little Red Hen, "who will help me to eat the bread?"

"I will!" said the duck.

— THE LITTLE RED HEN

A basic truth often underlies a children's story. As with the Little Red Hen, in many families, the day-to-day work of running a foundation falls to one individual. To avoid this, try to involve other family members in whatever way possible — site visits to grantees, editing board books, identifying projects to fund, or anything else that engages them. Every family seems to have someone who is a good writer, a computer whiz, a networker, etc. Be sure to take the time to tap into those

---

fig. 1

Help Is On the Way

A number of organizations exist to serve grantmakers. You may consider joining or using the services of one of these organizations. Start by asking questions about the programs and services the various groups offer and how best to tap into them. National membership organizations include the Council on Foundations, BoardSource, the Association for Small Foundations, and Independent Sector. Another genre of national membership groups, known as "affinity" groups of grantmakers, provide networking and education around issue areas such as health, the arts, refugees, and children, youth, and families, to name a few. In addition, there are many local membership groups such as regional associations of grantmakers (or RAGs). The Forum of RAGs (www.rag.org) can put you in touch with the association nearest you.

The National Center for Family Philanthropy and several university centers on philanthropy can provide you with information and resource materials on just about any topic related to family giving.

Many of these groups hold meetings, conferences, workshops, seminars, and the like. Some new foundation trustees burn themselves out on the conference circuit because — not knowing what to attend — they attend everything!

A better suggestion is to start slowly, attend one or two national and local meetings, and then take it from there. Keep in mind that most family foundations exist for a very long time, so you may be involved in your family foundation for the rest of your life. Pace yourself.

skills and interests. Ask family members what skills and time commitments they can offer, and what kind (if any) of outside help they are most comfortable with. It may be more work up front, but in the long run the foundation — and often the family — will be stronger. Family members will feel more invested in the enterprise, and bonded to the family team.

Recruiting Family Volunteer Staff

Many families choose to operate their foundations, especially early on, with volunteer staff from the family. Some, like Charlie Kettering who runs the Kettering Family Foundation, believe that having a family member staff the foundation "ensures that the family will stay involved and that the foundation will fund projects that are meaningful to the family and adhere to the donor's intent." Sometimes a family member takes on the responsibilities for the foundation's day-to-day work by default, but in the long run it is far better to think staffing through systematically.

Whether staff is paid or volunteer — family or nonfamily — it is a good idea for board members to discuss what qualities, skills, and experience they are seeking. Other steps include writing a description of what the job responsibilities might be, deciding who is ultimately responsible for hiring and overseeing the staff, conducting interviews, and finally, identifying candidates.

When I retired from the business world in late 1992, it was the first time in over two decades that I could concentrate on my dream of giving something back to society and helping others. It was then that I launched the Morino Foundation.

Previously, the hectic pace of the computer software industry had all but monopolized my attention, especially during the late 1980s and early 1990s, when my associates and I brought our company through a series of complicated acquisitions and mergers that resulted in one of the world's largest software companies, Legent Corporation. In 1992, the company was in both a solid financial state and a strong market position, and was under the leadership of a strong management team, so I was able to step down and begin a new journey in the nonprofit realm.

My early vision for the Morino Foundation was simple: I wanted to play a supportive but active role in the grant projects we would support. This role — what I call a "passive activist" — would mean assisting grantees not only financially, but also by serving as an advisor to them. It would entail providing appropriate contacts who could help them financially or otherwise, and in some cases, even rolling up my sleeves and working alongside them on planning, developing, and marketing their projects. The idea was not to take control of the projects but mainly to help the grantseekers succeed by providing the expertise, assistance, and resources to which they might not otherwise have ready access.

Much of this activist philosophy stems from my business roots. I had an active management style, a desire to be involved in day-to-day work operations, and a commitment to build and cultivate relationships with my co-workers. Over the years, I was blessed with many close friendships and relationships with people at Legent, its customers, and even its competitors.

This personal approach is crucial to the Morino Foundation's success. Our role is to be involved and supportive, but not controlling. Take the process of awarding a grant. The key is to look at the potential award from both a business perspective and a personal one. Business sense helps me determine whether a project is technically or financially feasible. My personal involvement enables me to judge whether the potential grantee is committed to his or her mission, has the skills to accomplish his or her goals, and whether the right chemistry exists for successful cooperation between us.

EXCERPTED FROM *The Genesis of the Morino Foundation*, 1995, The Morino Institute.

fig. 3 Staffing Your Family Foundation

When family members find a true fit between the foundation's mission and their career goals and skills, having a family member as a family foundation staff can be ideal. Still, some of the biggest challenges may include:
- Learning how to run an office;
- Working alone or with a very small staff;
- Reporting to a member of your own family;
- Setting work/family boundaries with family members; and
- Hearing criticism from other family members.

Family members who run their family's foundation advise:
- Stay neutral;
- Err on the side of over communicating and being overly accountable for your work;
- Obtain consensus from the family whenever possible; and
- Hire an outside facilitator to help with board meetings.

Be sure to take into account family dynamics when assessing staffing options. First, what type of skills, interests, and time do board members have? Each family member brings different skills and professional experiences and has different levels of time and interest in the foundation. Some trustees might enjoy reading proposals and making site visits. Others might have credentials in financial and asset management. If there is a lawyer on the board, he or she might be able to provide pro bono legal counsel or at least oversee the work of outside counsel.

Think about how different family members can complement one another.

fig. 4 Management and Marriage

For many years, the husband and wife team of John and Geri Kunstadter have been the staff and board of the Kunstadter Family Foundation. Founded with profits made in the ladies "foundation" (undergarment) business, John's grandfather ran the Kunstadter Foundation from his business office. Later, John's father managed the foundation, also out of his business office, with help from a secretary. When John's father died, John and Geri took over day-to-day operations of the foundation.

John and Geri were both at a point in life where they had the time, interest, and financial wherewithal to run the foundation, and they believe in keeping foundation administrative expenses as low as possible. Thus, they became unpaid foundation staff. They also had room in their New York City apartment to set up an office. John recalls, "Gradually the time and space required to run the foundation expanded. With such limited space, we are disciplined about throwing away things we no longer need." Now, their older daughter comes into the city and spends about 10 hours a month cleaning out the files for them.

John and Geri are frugal with the foundation's dollars. Not only are they not paid, but also they pay for most travel and expenses out of their own personal funds. Even postage is charged to their personal account. John states fervently, "This is money in trust for the public and not for our own personal use."

The computer age has been a godsend for small family foundations like the Kunstadter Foundation. Email, Internet, and faxes make it possible for the couple to do most of the foundation's secretarial work. They spend about $500 a year for help, if needed, with mailing their annual report, word processing, data entry, and answering mail. They keep the foundation's finances on the computer and sometimes get help with bookkeeping, which amounts to less than $1,000 per year (also paid out of their personal funds). An accountant completes the tax return with information the Kunstadters keep in the computer in Excel or Word.

For example, Uncle Harry, a retired CPA, might oversee the foundation's accounting. Cousin Carol, just out of the Kennedy School with an MPA, might handle daily operations. Bill, an attorney and longtime family friend, might serve as General Counsel. Aunt Lydia, the socialite and volunteer extraordinaire, might manage public relations.

Be careful, however, not to pigeonhole family members. One of the many joys of having a family foundation is that you get to see family members in different lights. For instance, you might have a stern actuary in the family who relishes interpretive dance in his free time. He could head up the arts grantmaking program. Or your nephew, the economics professor at Stanford, might be willing to review your investments and help grantees with their finances. Many professional development opportunities, such as investment and grantmaking workshops sponsored by national and local groups, are available to help trustees bone up on rusty skills or cultivate new areas of expertise.

According to the Council on Foundations, more than half of the family foundations that responded to its most recent *Management Survey* employ a family member as their foundation staff. In some cases, these family members are also board members. Some forfeit their seats on the board; others do not, and must be extremely careful to avoid real or perceived conflicts of interest. For most families, selecting a family member (or members) to be the foundation's staff may not be as easy as it was for the Kunstadters. Still, some families feel more comfortable — at least initially — having a family member at the helm.

Deciding to Hire Paid Staff

What prompts a family foundation board to hire paid staff? Some donors decide they need more time to pursue other interests. Some find that other family members are not in a financial position to volunteer. Still others find that family members are either not qualified or are not interested.

In its *2001 Member Survey*, the Association of Small Foundations found that 54 percent of its respondent members employed paid staff. That percentage ranged from 14 percent (for foundations with assets of less than $500,000) to 29 percent (assets of $2 million or more), 67 percent (assets of $5 million or more), and 95 percent ($50 million or more).

The first step toward hiring paid staff is to write a job description for the prospective employee. It is also a good idea to have written personnel policies and to set salary and benefits based on objective measures. Find out what similarly sized family foundations pay and what their employee policies and practices are. Keep these documents short and simple, and adjust and supplement them as the foundation evolves. Sample job descriptions, personnel policies, and information on family foundation staff salaries and benefits are available from organizations such as the National Center for Family Philanthropy, your regional association of grantmakers, the Council on Foundations, and the Association for Small Foundations. In budgeting for personnel, you may also wish to budget time and money for staff to attend the Council on Foundations or the regional association of grantmakers' Institute for New Staff and family foundation conferences as orientations. Also, the Society for Human Resource Management, www.srhm.org, can provide more generic sample documents and advice.

Kathy Good, of Good Management Associates, advises organizations on human resources issues. She believes that: "It is important that someone hiring staff for the first time understand what an employment relationship involves from a legal perspective. This may vary from state to state, but reference materials are easily found on the Internet and in popular bookstores." Good also advises that organizations that only intend to hire one or two employees not spend too much time developing written policies and job descriptions from scratch.

Although many families find their staff person through word of mouth, you might also want to advertise. Again, the groups mentioned above are good places to send your position announcement.

Should the Foundation Pay Compensation or Reimbursement?

Compensation generally refers to fees paid to an individual for service on the board, as well as fees that board members may receive in exchange for providing professional services to the foundation — including legal, accounting, and other necessary activities for accomplishing the foundation's mission.

Reimbursement refers to payment for expenses that board members or staff incur while attending foundation meetings, site visits, and other activities. Depending on where a trustee or staff member lives and what other responsibilities they are asked to take on, these expenses can range from a small amount to thousands of dollars per year.

What the Law Says

Family foundation members and trustees are classified as disqualified persons, and as such are subject to special rules regulating self-dealing and "conflicts of interest" in private foundations. For purposes of this essay, we refer to the governing boards of foundations as "trustees." Please note, however, that there are different legal responsibilities imposed upon governing boards depending on whether they are formed as a corporation or a charitable trust.

Anyone related to the founder of the foundation is almost assured of being considered a disqualified person. (For more information, see Facing Important Legal Issues, p. 59.) Compensating, paying, or reimbursing the expenses of a disqualified person is viewed as self-dealing, and may be subject to significant fines for both the foundation and the individual trustees.

However, the law contains an important exception to this self-dealing rule. This exception allows payments to disqualified persons (other than payments to a government official), provided that these payments are for personal services that are *reasonable* and *necessary* to carrying out the exempt purposes of the foundation.

---

fig. 5 — Using a Search Firm

Some families choose to retain a professional search firm when hiring their executive director — most often when the staff person will be a nonfamily member. Others, such as the Meadows Foundation, which had a large extended family to choose from in selecting a new president, chose to use a search firm for the family to ensure that the process was objective.

Family foundations may want to use a search firm if:
- The job market is tight;
- The board does not have time to handle all of the tasks involved in the hiring process;
- The foundation wishes to tap into a national pool of candidates;
- The foundation wants to keep the search — and the foundation's name — confidential;
- The foundation board is not experienced at vetting resumes and interviewing candidates; and
- The foundation board wants expert advice throughout the process.

Executive search professionals usually charge a substantial fee; however, the work they do in helping you get clear about what type of person you are looking for and in helping to identify appropriate candidates can save thousands of dollars in the long run.

To find a reputable search firm, check with your national and local networking groups. Ask colleagues what firms they have used and about their experiences with these firms. Call the National Center for Family Philanthropy for information on search firms that have experience working with family foundations. Supplement this with research on the Internet including a visit to the Association of Executive Search Consultants' (www.aesc.org) website.

What the Law Means

The law's basic intent is to keep family foundation donors and boards from compensating family members and other disqualified persons at levels that are higher than appropriate for the services they provide. The law does not specify what "reasonable and necessary" services and compensation may be, but there are a number of considerations and sources to refer to when thinking about these issues.

Many foundations and trustees, reflecting upon the nature of foundation board service more generally, follow a strict interpretation of the law's intent. This view holds that private foundations exist in order to fund nonprofits. Ensuring that funds are used primarily for this purpose is the law's clear intent. Thus, only in very special cases should a foundation consider compensation or reimbursement.

Questions for the Board

- Do we as trustees, in addition to governance roles, also perform services that are commonly considered "professional" or "managerial" positions — such as managing investments, providing legal or accounting services, supervising staff, sending out regular mailings, and other activities? Is this spread equally among all of the trustees, or the responsibility of one or two of the trustees?
- Is philosophy on the issue of compensation consistent with expectations of trustees in terms of their board service

— do we take into account the time associated with site visits, meetings, and other board activities when deciding on what level of commitment is appropriate and necessary for continued board membership?
- Have we kept accurate and complete records regarding the amount of time

---

fig. 6

Family as Staff: The Greenlee Story

Hiring a family member as a paid staff person proved to be an excellent move for the Greenlee Family Foundation of Boulder, Colorado. Anne Kemp is executive director and daughter of the founders. Like the Kunstadter Family Foundation, the Greenlee Family Foundation's assets are about $2 million.

Anne left a full-time job as a development officer at a university to run the foundation. As a paid family executive director, she works out of her home. The board consists of her father, mother, and a brother. The board sets her salary by looking at the Council on Foundations *Grantmakers Salary Report*. Her family conducts her annual performance evaluation, but no longer tries to do so with a formal written document. "At first," according to Anne, "it was awful. My brother lost the form. Mom filled it out in crayon. And my father sent me flowers, and told me I was doing a wonderful job." She adds that, no matter how professional they try to be, "The one thing you cannot factor out of family foundations is family."

Anne loves her job and hopes one day to turn the foundation's mantle over to her brother so that he can share in the fun. She is, however, careful to point out that much of the work is not very glamorous. The administrative work is boring and perfunctory. She answers the telephone, responds to the mail, crafts budgets, and prepares materials for the board. Anne also enjoys being active in the Colorado Association of Grantmakers, saying, "It helps me to keep in touch. I spend several hours a day working alone in my basement or at my office and need to schedule time to interact with people from nonprofits and other foundations."

There are pros and cons to hiring family members to staff the foundation. On the plus side, family members understand the family history, dynamics, goals, and issues. They are likely to be more invested in the foundation's success. Their presence might promote more family connection and involvement. On the negative side, they may be too intimately connected to the family to be impartial. They may not be the most qualified candidates. Other family members may be jealous of not having what they perceive as a "cushy foundation job." And it may be difficult for one family member to evaluate objectively another member's job performance.

The law's basic intent is to keep family foundation donors and boards from compensating family members and other disqualified persons at levels that are higher than appropriate for the services they provide.

contributed by board members in the past? Do we wish to keep these records in the future?

- How many proposals received each year are not funded due to a lack of grantmaking funds available? Would significantly more grantmaking funds be available if trustees were not compensated/reimbursed?

Family Participation

- Is payment of compensation for service necessary for an individual trustee's continued participation? Will this have an impact on family branch participation in the foundation?
- If there are younger family members on the board, should they be treated differently? Should there be compensation for these individuals while they are in school? Should this end or be phased out once they get jobs?
- Is paying compensation to some trustees but not others likely to cause divisiveness within the family?
- Is there a tradition or system within the family regarding family branch participation in the foundation? Is membership on the board viewed as a privilege in and of itself, and might providing compensation raise issues of fairness within the family?

- What are the family's values regarding voluntary boards? How can these be best reflected in a compensation policy?

EXCERPTED FROM Jason Born, *Board Compensation: Reasonable and Necessary?* Passages. (Washington, DC: National Center for Family Philanthropy, 2001) available at www.ncfp.org.

Developing a Compensation and Reimbursement Policy

If your board decides to offer trustee compensation or reimbursement, you can develop a policy for this. Although such a policy does not guarantee that you have complied with the IRS's "reasonable and necessary" guidelines, it provides your board members with a clear understanding of when they will be compensated or reimbursed, and when they will not.

How was the policy developed? Include a short description of the rationale for your policy:

- Review printed materials and surveys on the subject;
- Conduct a survey of similar organizations;
- Contact associations of foundations or nonprofits for information on this issue;
- Review actual out-of-pocket expenses of trustees; and

- Review fees paid for similar services for other similar organizations.

Is there a position description for staff? Having a position description for family staff that specifies the duties and skills needed to perform the functions of the position will help the family justify the compensation level they set.

What will compensation be based upon? If compensation is to be provided, state clearly whether it will be paid on an annual or some other basis, and on what basis the amount was determined. The policy should state that each staff member is responsible for submitting a report documenting time spent on foundation activities (although not legally required, such a report could prove very helpful for audit purposes). The policy should also state specifically that this compensation must be reasonable for the services provided and necessary for the effective operation of the foundation.

What expenses will be reimbursed, and what are the limits on these expenses? Being specific about these limits will minimize misunderstandings and disagreements.

What expenses will not be reimbursed by the foundation? Reimbursable expenses might include transportation to meetings or site visits, foundation business entertainment, and other expenses. You may also agree to cover some but not other expenses.

Who decides what level of compensation to provide and approves requests for reimbursement? The policy should identify who will make these decisions. Using outside advisors may help to avoid family resentments in situations where family staff members are compensated differently. This person or committee can also ensure that compensation and reimbursement are budgeted and tracked appropriately.

Finding an Alternative to Compensation

If your board decides that providing direct compensation for family staff service is not appropriate or desired, you may still want to consider instituting one or more of the following options to honor and encourage their ongoing service:

- *Discretionary grants:* Some foundations allow their family staff to make a small number of discretionary grants to nonprofits of their choice, most often within the foundation's stated guidelines (another option is to provide a small discretionary grants budget to each trustee). (See the section on Discretionary Grants in Establishing Grantmaking Interests and Priorities, p. 185.)
- *Matching grants:* These grants are usually made in recognition of an individual staff member's personal gift to a nonprofit, where the foundation matches the gift according to some predetermined formula (often one-to-one) up to a certain amount each year.

fig. **7**	**Can the Foundation Pay for Spousal Travel? For the Travel of Other Family Members?**

Generally, no. The assets of the foundation cannot be used to finance family reunions. Spouses and children of board members are disqualified persons. If foundation assets are paid to them for travel or related expenses, such payment is an act of self-dealing. Obviously, if the spouse or child is also a board member (or staff), the reimbursement of reasonable expenses for necessary foundation activities is not a violation. But assuming the spouse or child has no official duties, such reimbursement is self-dealing.

There are two methods for making such reimbursement payments that satisfy the legal concerns. First, treat the reimbursement as part of the reasonable compensation paid to the board member or staff member whose spouse or child is being reimbursed. The amount of reimbursement must show up as reportable income to the board or staff member on a form 1099 or W-2.

Example: A board member takes his or her spouse to a Council on Foundations conference for family foundations. If the expenses paid by the foundation for the spouse are counted as compensation to the board member — and the board member's total compensation is reasonable — there is no self-dealing. Why? Reasonable compensation for personal services is the main exception to the self-dealing rules.

Second, develop legitimate and meaningful duties for the spouse and/or children that further the charitable purposes of the foundation. Providing companionship and attending social receptions with a board member would not be considered meaningful foundation duties.

Example: To train the next family generation in the traditions and operations of the foundation, the foundation approves an advisory committee composed of children of the donor. This committee will review all applications for grants in a particular subject area and make final recommendations to the governing board. Reimbursing these children for reasonable expenses of attending an appropriate board meeting or a training conference would be legitimate foundation expenses.

SOURCE: John A. Edie. *Family Foundations & the Law: What You Need to Know.* 3rd ed. Washington, DC: Council on Foundations, 2002.

- *Supporting outside voluntary board service:* Some foundations encourage the service of their family staff members on other voluntary boards by agreeing to make an annual gift (perhaps $500 or $1,000) in honor of that service.
- *Supporting outside family members' involvement:* Consider reimbursing the travel of a spouse or children of the family staff member to attend board meetings or educational conferences. This type of benefit must be treated as compensation, but again can be a nice way of encouraging participation by the extended family in the activities of the foundation.

When hiring a staff person from outside the family, again, you will need to define the job, salary range, and reporting relationships.

Please note that, in each of the above instances, the full board is legally responsible for approving the grants and ensuring that recipients are eligible grantees. Still, these options encourage foundation trustees to continue to develop and support their own causes and interests, and send a clear message that the foundation values highly the individual's time and commitment to the nonprofit sector at large. (Laws on trustee compensation vary by state. In California, for example, family board members can be paid for service only if the governing board consists of 49 percent family members or fewer. Check with your state Attorney General's office on this point.)

On the Outside Looking In

If the potential pitfalls of hiring a family member concern you, you might want to explore hiring someone who is not a family member. A family foundation is a work in progress. Many families have family members as staff initially and then replace them with nonfamily staff or vice versa.

When hiring a staff person from outside the family, again, you will need to define the job, salary range, and reporting relationships. You can identify candidates either informally through professional networks, or more formally through the regional association of grantmakers and other nonprofit associations and periodicals such as the *Chronicle of Philanthropy*. If you feel more comfortable having professional help conduct the search and are prepared to pay for it, you might want to hire an executive search firm or an individual consultant to guide the search.

Sharing Staff

Many small family foundations share staff as a way of maximizing efficiency and saving costs. Employees can be shared in many ways. A community foundation, a nonprofit organization, or a for-profit company that specializes in managing small foundations could manage the foundation. A number of these opportunities are available around the country, often with different emphases. For example, some manage family foundations that have what they consider to be a social change or progressive agenda. Others manage family foundations that want to pursue what they call a "strategic grantmaking agenda." That is, they help donors who want to fund in very specific, targeted areas. Others may have been started as vehicles to manage the philanthropy of individual family members and now takes on other families as clients. Some of the services these organizations can perform include identifying and screening potential grantees, working with families to clarify their goals and interests, and managing the day-to-day administrative details of small and large giving programs.

Philanthropic collaborative groups can be powerful tools for families to use to gain prompt, affordable access to expertise and a network of like-minded givers. Families that opt for this type of shared arrangement also have the benefit of having access to high-level consulting staff and expert administrative staff on an as-needed basis. They benefit from sharing a central office to hold meetings and are in an ideal position to collaborate with other funders and grantees. In much the same way, some community foundations or religious organizations, such as Jewish

Family foundations generally use a variation of four models in planning the management of their organization — the administrator consultant, director, or family staff model or some combination. All of these models are effective, depending on what is important to the family. The two major considerations in selecting a model are: how much time family members want to devote to the foundation; and how much control over foundation activities the family wants to maintain. Geographic location and the expertise and experience of trustees will also have a bearing.

ADMINISTRATOR MODEL

This model requires a staff person who works part or full time and deals primarily with administrative issues. This person might handle correspondence and telephone calls, log in grant requests, track the grant process, arrange for meetings, send letters and grant approvals, make bank deposits, and reconcile financial records. When the administrator model is employed, the foundation is generally housed in a specific office, although the administrator may work for more than one foundation or may handle other work for a trustee, lawyer, or financial advisor who is related to the foundation. Sometimes administrative staff time is provided on a pro bono publico basis by one of the trustees.

Strengths of this model include:
- Foundation trustees are freed from routine administrative tasks.
- Trustees maintain hands on direction of the foundation.

Possible problems are:
- The administrator needs a clear supervisor and may need help in adjusting to differing board chairs.
- The model assumes that trustees have the time to provide grant review and leadership.

CONSULTANT MODEL

In this structure, an individual is hired to do specific tasks that recur regularly but are not necessarily ongoing. For instance, a consultant might receive grant requests and prepare recommendations for the trustees. Or an individual might be asked to manage financial resources. The consultant is usually paid an hourly or daily rate and may spend extensive time on the foundation during a grant review process twice a year, for instance. In some foundations, the consultant acts as an executive director, assisting the board in developing grant focus areas and requests for proposals.

Strengths of this model include:
- The cost of ongoing staff and office space is not necessary.
- It is possible to hire specific expertise on a part-time basis that the foundation could not afford full time.

Possible problems are:
- The consultant needs to maintain close contact with the trustees and reflect their values and interest in his or her recommendations.

- The foundation may be less visible without a specific office and as staff member who is easily accessible.
- Response time to applicants may be delayed because the consultant works for the foundation only sporadically.

DIRECTOR MODEL

According to this scenario, the foundation hires an executive-level staff person to provide recommendations and oversight for most of the foundation's activities. This staff person is usually — but not necessarily — full-time and may be called the executive director. The executive director oversees any other staff, manages the office, makes grant and program recommendations to the board, works with the chair to develop the board agenda, and provides recommendations for financial management.

Strengths of this model include:
- Trustees can provide leadership without spending large amounts of time.
- A professional staff person has time to follow opportunities and developments in the community.
- A nonfamily executive director may act as a calming influence if there are volatile family dynamics.

Possible problems are:
- This staffing model is the most costly.
- The staff person might not accurately reflect the values and interests of the trustees.

FAMILY STAFF

A family member serves in a specific staff role on a part — or full-time basis. The family member may receive a salary and function in the same way a staff person might.

Strengths of this model include:
- A family member knows the family and its values and concerns.
- A family member may have a longer-term commitment to the foundation.

Possible problems are:
- A family member can be more easily caught up in the family issues or dynamics and may be seen as having a point of view or position.
- It may be harder to implement appropriate accountability measures for trustee staff because of family relationships.

SOURCE: Adapted from a presentation made at the Council on Foundations 1997 Family Foundations Conference by Alice C. Buhl and Judith K. Healey.

Philanthropic collaborative groups can be powerful tools for families to use to gain prompt, affordable access to expertise and a network of like-minded givers.

Federations, manage family foundations for an administrative fee.

Using Consultants

Another option is for an independent consultant to manage one or more family foundations. An experienced consultant can easily manage several small family foundations from a home or office. In this case, it is important for the founder — and possibly the entire family — to have strong rapport with the consultant — especially if it is your first foray into involving a nonfamily member in the foundation.

This is how one consultant who manages two different family foundations describes her job:

The families live all over the country, so much of my work is accomplished via phone, email, or fax. I also make some site visits to grantees. These boards meet two to four times a year with interim meetings conducted via conference calls. My responsibilities include analyzing proposals that come in, preparing board dockets, and making recommendations on funding based on the foundation's guidelines. I also decline requests outside the guidelines and oversee the preparation of follow-up reports to the board. I have also helped the foundations to develop and modify grant guidelines.

One consultant helped his foundation's trustees to realize that they could accomplish better and more satisfactory grantmaking if they did not accept unsolicited proposals as the family had a clear vision and direction for its grantmaking. Sometimes the voice of an outsider can help the family see a solution that may not be apparent to them. Another important function of a staff person is to provide coaching, advice, and technical assistance to grantees.

Be sure to issue a formal contract or at least a letter of agreement with your consultant. Some boards prefer to have a retainer agreement with their consultant for a fixed number of hours per week. The consultant can bill at an agreed-on hourly rate if the board needs extra hours of work at busy times, such as the week before a board meeting or the end of a grant cycle. This system works well because it guarantees the consultant will be available for an agreed upon amount of time. At the same time, it allows for the foundation board to request more work when needed while not paying for it on an ongoing basis. One trustee, usually the board chair or another officer, can be designated to oversee the consultant's work and review and submit invoices to the accountant. The founda-

tion should also be prepared to reimburse consultants for expenses incurred while conducting foundation business.

Such a professional staff person may introduce the family to new options. For example, before one small family foundation hired a consultant, the trustees awarded only direct-service grants. Now they are making their first program-related investment for low-income housing.

Judith Healey, a consultant to the Weyerhaeuser Family and the Laura Jane Musser Foundations, has been working with family foundations for more than 25 years. In her experience, "For many family foundations, hiring a consultant is a stage or a phase. They are easing into a more permanent relationship with a nonfamily staff person." Her trustees believe that most family foundations require someone who can guide their grantmaking strategically rather than a pure administrator.

Administrative work is the easiest to hire out," according to one trustee. Another trustee cautions that "The best consultants don't get involved in family dynamics." In addition, consultants should be held to a strict conflict-of-interest agreement that is included in their original contract with the foundation. If the foundation is considering funding a nonprofit that the consultant has a relationship with, the consultant should inform the board of the relationship and offer to pass the work to another professional. Also, if the trustees feel that a consultant is aligning him or herself with family factions, they should address this with the consultant right away.

Moving to a Full-Time Paid Executive Director

Sometimes a family foundation evolves into the director model after a number of years of operating with part-time family or consultants as staff. For example, the Jones Family Fund is a 50-year-old foundation. When the foundation was begun, it was run out of the family business office. When the son of the founder became the staff, he leased a small office and hired a part-time secretary. Eventually, he also hired a full-time assistant.

Four years ago, the fund reached a turning point. It had grown from $20 million to more than $100 million in assets. The board decided to hire its first nonfamily executive director. They retained a search firm known for finding nonprofit leadership to identify an executive director. The board was looking for someone with expertise both in philanthropy and in their funding areas: the sciences and education. They also wanted someone with administrative experience.

After a careful search, they hired an executive director. The individual they chose is highly qualified and also has good chemistry with the family, which is critically important.

Determining Where the Work Will be Done

Regardless of the management model you choose, the business of running the foundation has inevitabilities. Once you decide what work needs to be done and who will do it, you must decide where the work will be done. Here again, family foundations face choices.

Using a Home Office

Many small family foundations use a home office because it saves on administrative costs and is convenient for their staff, particularly if the staff is part-time. Some family foundation staff use a spare bedroom with a computer, desk, and filing cabinets for documents they are currently using, while securing space in their basement for longer-term filing and storage. Consultants who are juggling several clients may have a separate dedicated office, business phone, fax, computer, printer, and filing cabinets that may be in their home or in a leased office space. When using a home office, it is important to have a professional place for meetings with grantees, foundation board and committee meetings, and community meetings that the foun-

dation may host. Family foundations are often creative about borrowing or renting space from other foundations or nonprofits, their regional association of grantmakers, or even the public library, for these purposes.

Kim Dennis, executive director of the D&D Foundation, worked for several years part-time from a home office. She liked the flexibility of getting up at 4:00 in the morning to get work done:

"For many family foundations, hiring a consultant is a stage or a phase. They are easing into a more permanent relationship with a nonfamily staff person."

I was often talking on the phone while cooking dinner, sorting laundry, etc. It would have been easy to shut work out, but I didn't want to. I occasionally gave people my home phone number but only in those instances where I knew the person well enough that I didn't worry if they heard kids screaming in the background or knew I was washing dishes while we talked. I guess what it comes down to is that my work has always been very much a part of my life. Most of my friends are people I've gotten to know through work, so it's a bit of a seamless web.

Kim now runs the foundation out of an office leased from a larger organization and has taken on another part-time job in addition to running the foundation. She now enjoys being downtown and easily available for meetings, which points out some of the trade offs for both options.

Part of the beauty of working for a family foundation is that the staff is often given the flexibility to craft an arrangement that fits their lifestyle. Jane Leighty Justis, a family foundation trustee and staff person with a home office, cautions that, for many people, separating their home and work lives is very important. Running a family foundation from home makes this an even steeper challenge. When working with a staff person — whether a family member or outsider — it is important to be respectful of their work preferences while being very clear about what type of work style and environment the board expects.

Using the Family Office

According to the Family Office Exchange, an organization that advises wealthy families:

A family office is the organization that is created, often after the sale of family business or realization of significant liquidity, to support the financial needs (ranging from strategic asset allocation to recordkeeping and reporting) for a specific family group.

If your family has such an office or is considering starting one, running the family foundation from the family office is a viable, cost-effective model. Many family offices are prepared to provide staffing for:

- Trustee responsibilities;
- Grantmaking services;
- Program assessment;
- Investment management; and
- Administration and compliance.

The family can hire a dedicated staff person to handle family foundation responsibilities or can build them into the job descriptions of existing staff. According to Mariann Mihailidis, membership manager for the Family Office Exchange, about half of family offices have a philanthropic component. Some family offices handle administrative, financial, recordkeeping, and investment responsibilities for the family foundation, which frees the foundation's trustees to focus on the grants.

For example, the Russell Family Foundation in Gig Harbor, Washington, is run alongside a family office, with a separate foundation staff. The foundation contracts with the family office staff at fair market rates to handle bill paying, budgeting, financial reporting, and cash flow operations. This arrangement allows the foundation professionals to focus exclusively on board development, strategic planning, grantmaking, and public affairs.

The Randall L. Tobias Foundation in Indiana also enjoys this arrangement, sharing one support staff and two financial advisors with the family office. According to Executive Director Suzanne Hazelett, the foundation does not pay overhead expenses and uses all of the family-office-owned equipment for free. But the foundation pays for anything above and beyond the daily operations of the family office, such as large foundation mailings or printing. What is the biggest advantage of sharing with a family office? "Financial expertise at your fingertips," says Hazelett. The foundation receives the benefit of an in-house financial advisor and a controller.

Relying on the Family Business

Many family foundations operate out of the family's business office, which can be a blessing for a new foundation. The foundation can use the business's office space, secretarial support, equipment, and sometimes even professional staff. For example, the first Lawrence Welk Foundation executive director was a vice president from the family business, and the foundation was used as a pass-through vehicle for charitable funds from the business. When Lawrence Welk's son succeeded him as head of the family business, his daughter, Shirley Fredricks became the foundation's executive director.

According to Fredricks, running a family foundation as part of a family business means the foundation will depend on the personalities in the company. She recommends that the corporate board be separate from the family board to ensure the foundation gets the attention it deserves and that the company avoids conflicts of interest. This model works well for families that might want to set up the foundation as a pass-through because they will not have to come up with the funds up front to endow the foundation. Plus, they can use the company's management resources to run the foundation. For example, a secretary from within the corporation handled the administrative work for the foundation and a financial officer handled the asset management and financial functions. Also, Fredricks was originally an employee of the corporation. She later became a foundation employee when its bylaws were changed.

Because family foundations are often one-person operations, working out of a family business office can provide the stimulation of other professionals. For example, when starting out, Emily Tow Jackson operated her family foundation, the Tow Foundation, as the sole staff person, and worked from her family's business office, which had 130 employees. Now, her foundation's activities have grown to the point where it has its own office and a separate staff.

Sharing Space

If your family does not have a family business or a family office, and you would still like to share space, many options for doing this are available in the nonprofit world. According to the Council on Foundation's *Trends in Family Foundation Governance, Staffing, and Management*, 43 percent of the family foundation respondents share office space. Of those, almost half share with a family business. One-fifth-shared space with another foundation, and one-fourth shared staff either with a family business or with another foundation.

Establishing a Foundation Office

Many family foundations choose to set up an independent office, especially when they have more than one staff person. They may also have extra offices available for trustees and consultants as well as a conference room for board and committee meetings. Having an office can give the foundation a presence in the community. Many leased office suites allow the lessee to share a receptionist, copier, fax, computer equipment, and furniture.

Identifying and Securing the Tools You Will Need

It may be best to think about your office equipment holistically. Things to consider include selecting, installing, and maintaining office furniture and filing cabinets, phones and voice mail, a fax machine, and computer hardware and software.

An easy approach to setting up an office is to hire a specialist to locate furniture, equipment, and office space. You can specify if you would like to have new or used equipment and furniture, office

Ways to Share Space

fig. 9

The Consumer Health Foundation and Trellis Fund, both located in Washington, DC, share space, equipment, ideas, and friendship. On a practical level, the relationship saves on overhead costs. The two foundations split the rent and allocate use of the equipment. They also share the expenses of publications and periodicals. "You can spend thousands of dollars on journals and library materials," says Hope Gleicher, executive director of a family foundation called the Trellis Fund. "So, we share subscriptions. We also route materials that one foundation, but not the other, receives."

Bruce Hirsch, executive director of one of four family foundations in San Francisco that has shared office space says: "It allows you to be with people who are doing similar work to yours and to learn from each other. If there is any challenge, it is in making joint decisions and in ensuring that everyone is getting a fair shake cost wise." He stresses the importance of monitoring costs, engaging in open discussions, and making joint decisions.

EXCERPTED FROM the Council on Foundations, *Family Matters* newsletter (Vol. 6, No. 2, Spring, 2001).

space in a high-rent or lower cost area, and on and on. If costs are a concern, you may want to explore purchasing used office furniture and computers from auctions of recently defunct businesses or even through the Internet.

A computer can handle many administrative functions. Depending on your in-house computer skills, you may need outside technical support to help set up your office and troubleshoot when problems arise.

Should You Have a Website?

Websites are essential tools for many organizations today. In addition to functioning as communications and public awareness tools for family foundations, they can also be helpful for management purposes. They allow you to post your foundation's mission and guidelines so that you do not have to print and mail numerous copies. You can also accept letters of inquiry and grant applications online, which saves time and resources for you and for applicants.

At first, you may want a site hosted for little or no cost by another organization. There are groups that develop websites for nonprofit organizations and handle hosting, site maintenance, updates, and technical support. The Foundation Center (www.fdncenter.org) offers free of charge, a basic web design service and web presence to grantmaking foundations (more than 100 to date) interested in providing their program descriptions

and guidelines, application information, grants lists, requests for proposals, newsletters, tax returns, or other information online. In addition to — or as a precursor to — a website, you might want to consider an "intranet." This website is password protected and can be made available exclusively to family members. It can keep board members in touch with one another and enable you to share information easily but privately.

Choosing Technology for Grants Management

Computer software is an essential tool for grants management. A handful of companies specialize in grants management software for foundations. The Council on Foundations' magazine, *Foundation News & Commentary*, frequently publishes articles about technology for foundations, as well as a vendors' directory, as does the *Chronicle of Philanthropy*. Still, for small foundations sometimes the basic tools are the best — at least initially.

Jane Leighty Justis of the Leighty Foundation recommends, "Start with a simple system like Excel. Then figure out what information you want to know as you go along. If you think you

---

fig. 10 The Paperless Office

Remember the claims that the Internet would usher in the paperless office? It's not as far away as you may think. Nate Berry, program director and sole staff member of the Sandy River Charitable Foundation, says that in the fall he will have a comprehensive on-line grants review system in place, contributing to a significant reduction of paper. What led to this decision? "I have a very small office," says Berry, whose background in computer engineering also was a factor. Board members "are fitting the foundation into a corner of their homes."

"The choice was either volumes of paper or to make use of electronic media," says Berry. The foundation receives proposals by invitation only. Accompanying each invitation is a full Adobe Desktop package, suggesting that applications and reports be returned by email in PDF format. Where necessary, proposals are scanned and converted to the PDF format. All are then posted on the foundation's board member-only website. For convenience of use, the board book on CD-ROM in PDF format is also mailed to all board members, who may call or email Berry with questions or comments. Some paper still goes out to board members — 30 pages or so for meeting, a "significant reduction" from the 370 pages that went out in the last shipment before conversion to CD-ROM, Berry says.

will need a fancier system, consider packages and systems that will allow you to record, manipulate, and report that information."

Once you are ready to consider some off-the-shelf grants management software packages, a useful resource is the Grants Managers Network (www.gmnetwork.org), a membership group of more than 300 staff from foundations who are responsible for the policies, procedures, technology, and administration of their organization's grantmaking. This group provides a forum to exchange information about grants management and its relevance to efficient and effective grantmaking through a newsletter, list server, website, annual meeting, and regional programs.

How to Handle Accounting and Recordkeeping

In setting up and managing your foundation's accounting, bookkeeping, and other recordkeeping systems, you may feel like old Polonius in Hamlet: "Though this be madness, yet there is method in't." Many small foundations hire an outside accountant or accounting firm to handle their day-to-day bookkeeping and accounts payable. The foundation treasurer or board chair usually supervises this function in tandem with the foundation's executive director.

Every private foundation (which includes family foundations) must file an annual tax return, Form 990-PF. To facilitate this

fig. 11 Technology Help for Your Foundation

Some excellent resources for help with technology needs exist on the Internet for nonprofits. These include:

- Techsoup (www.techsoup.org). This site provides recommendations for nonprofits' technology needs and advice on how to make the best use of technology.
- Technology Works for Good (www.technologyworks.org). TWFG connects nonprofits, funders, tech assistance providers, and technologists into a living, growing solutions network.
- Fund for the City of New York (www.fcny.org). The Nonprofit Computer Exchange and Internet Academy of the Fund for the City of New York helps organizations make the best uses of technology through: computer/Internet classes, technology seminars and conferences and technology consulting.

Email and the Internet have truly revolutionized grantmaking. Foundations can have their grantmaking guidelines available on their website and can receive letters of inquiry and grant requests electronically. Some opt to have electronic forms on their websites, while others prefer to receive emails or emails with MS Word or Excel attachments. Your foundation can also acknowledge the receipt of letters of inquiry or grant applications electronically. Moreover, sharing proposals with trustees via email can be a huge time and money saver!

In setting up and managing your foundation's accounting, bookkeeping, and other recordkeeping systems, you may feel like old Polonius in Hamlet: "Though this be madness, yet there is method in't."

form filling, the foundation must keep accurate and complete records of its investments, expenses, and grants. In addition, the foundation must list the trustees and staff and their compensation, if any. According to the IRS, the 990-PF is the most complicated tax

form there is. Thus, having an accountant who works for other foundations and has an expertise in working with tax-exempt organizations is essential.

Whether a family foundation operates out of a home or in an office and is managed by volunteers or paid staff, recordkeeping remains an essential function. Records and files can be organized in many ways, and foundation administrators can come up with a system that makes sense for their foundation. If you are uncertain about how to get started, visit other local family foundations and ask how they organize their records and what they like or dislike about their systems. Ask what they would do differently if they were starting from scratch. Again, your regional association of grantmakers can be helpful to you in identifying and meeting colleagues.

Considering Administrative Expenses

Every family wants to run its foundation as efficiently as possible. But how do you determine what administrative expenses are reasonable?

Administrative expenses for foundations typically include salaries and benefits, legal and professional fees, rent, travel, printing, and similar expenses. Administrative expenses are affected by many factors including:

- The purpose of the foundation;
- Activities other than grantmaking;
- Whether grantmaking is local, regional, or national;
- The size and number of grant recipients;
- The size and number of grants; and
- The number of staff and consultants.

fig.
12
What Records Should My Foundation Keep?

RETAIN PERMANENTLY:
- Articles of incorporation or instrument of trust and Bylaws;
- Minutes of trustee meetings and committee actions;
- Form 1023, the application for tax-exempt organizations filed with the IRS;
- The IRS's favorable determination letter;
- Any correspondence from the IRS approving the foundation's grantmaking procedures; and
- Ruling from state authorities granting tax exemption.

GRANTEE RECORDS (KEEP FOR AT LEAST 6 YEARS):
- Initial grant requests and subsequent correspondence;
- Grant agreements;
- Letters of tax-exemption;
- Financial reports;
- Grant progress reports; and
- Cancelled checks.

FINANCIAL DOCUMENTS (KEEP FOR 6 YEARS):
- Form 990-PF;
- Financial statements; and
- Contracts.

Materials related to unsuccessful grant applications can be discarded or returned to the applicants. Some foundations keep a log of rejected proposals with notes on the reasons for not funding the proposal.

SOURCE: Martha Cooley and the Council on Foundations, *Management*. Family Foundation Library. Washington, DC: Council on Foundations, 1997. See also Chapter 3, Facing Important Legal Issues

Keep in mind that higher administrative expenses are not necessarily a bad thing. Some small foundations decide that it is important that they have a visible role in the community. It requires time and money to hire and retain staff, join local and national associations, convene community meetings, visit grantees, and become involved in local causes. Jane

Leighty Justis advises, "The more active a foundation wants its grantmaking to be, the more expenses it is likely to incur." Administrative costs are best thought of in relation to what you want to accomplish — either with your grantees or within the philanthropic field (attending conferences, volunteering for committees, etc.). Often it is necessary for a start-up family foundation to pay extra administrative expenses to hire and train staff, secure office space, purchase office equipment, and conduct special outreach into the community.

Realizing Your Great Expectations

Great Expectations, written by Charles Dickens in 1860-61, is the story of orphan Pip and of his encounter with Magwich, the convict on the Kent Marshes, of his love for the beautiful and heartless Estella, and of the mysterious fortune that falls into his lap . . . .

Like Pip, perhaps a mysterious fortune has fallen into your lap, and now you are ready to begin your great adventure and realize your great expectations. Good management is about putting systems and processes into place that will help advance your philanthropic vision and will keep your foundation operating smoothly and in good stead for years to come. Shirley Fredricks, trustee and former president of the Lawrence Welk Foundation, believes that running a foundation is an iterative process. Her advice is: "Take things one step at a time. Try out different ideas. And, most importantly, don't be afraid to make changes — even if something *is working*, it might still be a good idea to try something different!"

FASHIONING an INVESTMENT STRATEGY

by Jason C. Born

The highest use of capital is not to make more money,
but to make money do more for the betterment of life.

———HENRY FORD———

The returns on a family investment in philanthropy are —
or can be — extremely high, both internally and externally. When such
an investment is well executed, a family can achieve the cohesion that
comes with a sense of higher purpose and cooperative effort.

———PAUL YLVISAKER———

Although Henry Ford and Paul Ylvisaker were not talking specifically about the investments that a family foundation's endowment makes, their comments are equally appropriate to this process. Investing the assets of a family philanthropy is — or can be — both a challenging and rewarding experience, and is probably best thought of not only in terms of assets, but also of what those increased assets can accomplish.

As someone who has established or is about to establish a family foundation, you may be familiar with and skilled at thinking about your own investment goals and strategies. If you have served on boards of other nonprofits or corporations, you may also know what it takes to oversee management of an institution's portfolio and assets.

As the founder and a trustee of your family's foundation, however, you will encounter very special circumstances related to your investments. You and your board will make important investment strategy decisions about funding a legal entity that is regulated by the Internal Revenue Service (IRS) and state agencies. You and your board will assume legal and ethical duties of obedience, loyalty, and care to the foundation. Those duties require you to adhere to the foundation's charter and mission, avoid self-dealing and conflicts of interest, keep the foundation's best interests in mind, and act as a "prudent investor" on behalf of the foundation.

You will also be acting within an environment of your family: siblings, children, in-laws, and next generations. You may want to train family members who may not be knowledgeable about their fiduciary responsibilities with regard to the foundation.

Most important, you will need a strategy that allows you to carry out your hopes and dreams for the foundation. A thoughtfully fashioned investment strategy, implemented with discipline and flexibility, seems all the more important in today's world. The first year of the 21st century brought extraordinary levels of volatility to the financial markets. Concerns about terrorism, the collapse of Enron, and the bursting of the dot com bubble created a new set of conditions for investment managers. Although there will always be uncertainties about the future, founders of family foundations today may face an especially challenging task in developing their investment strategy.

This chapter contains background, ideas, and suggestions to help you and your board think about how to develop investment policies and practices that meet all legal requirements and are consistent with the goals and mission of your philanthropy. Sections in the chapter aim to help you in:

- Linking resources to philanthropic purposes;
- Establishing the spending policy;
- Overseeing the investment strategy;
- Determining the family's role;
- Reducing investment costs;
- Revisiting goals and objectives; and
- A final word: reviewing the checklist.

Linking Resources to Philanthropic Purposes

Some founders plan their philanthropic purposes well ahead of time, while others are more given to let those purposes evolve over time. In either case, it is helpful for you and your board to have a clear, shared understanding about investment goals and strategies. It's desirable to agree on policies and practices regarding the management of money: bookkeeping, reports, audits, archival records, etc.

Your philanthropic goals will drive both the spending policy of the foundation and the investment strategy designed to support that spending policy.

Many founders spend considerable time in the first few years of their foundation's life exploring these issues. You may want to discuss your thoughts on these matters with other members of your family before passing the reins of the foundation to the next generation.

Considering Perpetuity

Consider perpetuity. Simply put: will your foundation last for a specific term of years, cease to exist when it achieves a specific goal, or exist in perpetuity? Depending on the answer to this question, your investment strategy will be very different.

If your main goal is to support an issue that requires urgent attention, you may choose to focus your foundation's grant-making activities over a short and concentrated period of time. One foundation that took this approach is the Aaron Diamond Foundation. In the late 1980s, foundation president Irene Diamond and the rest of the trustees recognized that they had an opportunity to make a real difference in AIDS research, an area that at the time was sorely lacking funding. With this in mind, the foundation increased its annual grantmaking to a level that allowed it to become a key supporter in AIDS research. Despite the fact that this decision resulted in the

foundation spending itself out over the next decade, the board felt that the subject was important enough to warrant such an approach.

An equally compelling case can be made for creating philanthropic funds that build resources now and for the future. This approach guided the Harris and Eliza Kempner Fund in Galveston, Texas. Started in 1946 by five members of the Kempner family, the fund has grown from an initial asset value of $38,500 to almost $50 million today. The original donors, as well as the current trustees, recognized the value of a perpetual foundation, as described in the fund's 1996-1997 biennial report:

> The impetus for starting a foundation in 1946 came from the family's concern for the many local charities it supported. They realized that conditions that typically follow economic depressions and wars could affect their ability to support charities in times of greatest need. A philanthropic philosophy thus evolved: "Allow the more prosperous years to provide for the lean ones."

Many good reasons support either spending out a foundation's assets or establishing a foundation in perpetuity. Key reasons for the former approach include:

- The founders want to work with

fig. 1 Glossary of Key Investment Terms for Family Foundations

ASSET ALLOCATION. The practice of spreading risk across a range of investment assets and management styles to balance the effect of market forces and volatility in relationship to the risk level that is acceptable to the investor. According to modern portfolio theory, as much as 95 percent of the return of a diversified portfolio of assets is attributable to the distribution (allocation) and regular rebalancing of a range of investment classes and styles within those classes.

EXCISE TAX. The tax on the net investment income of private foundations of 2 percent per year. This tax may be reduced to 1 percent under certain circumstances.

FIDUCIARY RESPONSIBILITY. The task of investing money or acting wisely on behalf of a beneficiary. In the foundation field, such responsibility is exercised on behalf of the donors and the grantees.

LIQUIDITY. The ease with which a financial asset can be converted to cash.

PAYOUT REQUIREMENT. The Internal Revenue Service requirement that private foundations must distribute 5 percent of the value of their net investment assets annually in the form of grants or eligible administrative expenses.

REBALANCING. A common strategy used to ensure that asset allocation guidelines are met over time, as changes in the portfolio occur due to changes in the values of individual assets. There are two primary rebalancing strategies: calendar and threshold. Calendar rebalancing is typically done on a quarterly or annual basis. Threshold rebalancing is done whenever guideline ranges are exceeded. Under either method, trustees can choose to rebalance back to the endpoints of the asset allocation guideline ranges or back to the target or "normal" allocation. Many consultants favor rebalancing back to the target on an annual basis because it results in lower transaction costs than other approaches.

RATE OF RETURN. A measure of investment performance for a specified pool of assets. The rate is determined on a total return basis, including realized and unrealized changes in market value in addition to earned income (i.e., dividends and interest income). Managers may report returns before or after management advisory fees, but returns are always reported after brokerage and trading costs.

RETURN REQUIREMENT. The rate of return on investment needed by a private foundation to meet its spending goals. For example, for a foundation that intends to exist in perpetuity, the return requirement is that its investment returns be equal to (or greater than) the total of (1) its grants spending objective, (2) the expected average annual inflation rate over the investment time horizon, (3) its estimated annual operating expenses, and (4) its estimated investment fees and expenses.

RISK. The measurable possibility of losing or not gaining value.

SOCIALLY RESPONSIBLE INVESTING. A style of investment decision making that takes into account social and environmental, as well as financial, concerns. One form of this is known as "mission-related investing," which attempts to align an institution's mission with its investment strategies.

SPENDING POLICY. An agreed-upon policy that determines what percentage of a foundation's endowment will be spent to cover both the operating costs and grants of an institution. Typical spending rules combine calculations based on previous years' spending, the current year's income and investment return rates, and the policy of the foundation for covering grant commitments.

VOLATILITY. A measure of the degree to which the price of a security goes up or down over a specified period. Highly volatile stocks tend to move up or down more than the market as a whole, while those with low volatility move up or down less than the market as a whole.

other family members to see their philanthropic assets at work during their lifetimes.

- The founders want to commit the full resources of the foundation to address a specific problem now, in the hopes that more resources in the short term will help solve it.
- The founders expect others (including heirs) to engage in their own personal philanthropic efforts and to address the problems of future generations.
- The founders are concerned that the foundation may lose the family's involvement over time, and/or may lose touch with their original purposes in establishing the foundation.

Key reasons for establishing a foundation in perpetuity include:

- A foundation established in perpetuity can grow its endowment to become larger and potentially more effective in bringing about lasting improvements in society.
- The founder can empower the trustees to alter the foundation's mission, thus ensuring that its grantmaking will be directed to relevant social needs over time.
- Many social problems are deeply seated, and only a foundation with a perpetual endowment can press reforms for many years in its effort to make a difference.
- Many founders feel that a foundation is an important part of their legacy — to the family, to the community, and to society at large.

The spending policy of a family foundation determines what percentage of a foundation's endowment will be spent annually to cover both operating costs and grants.

Trustees of a foundation destined to spend out by a certain date will want to emphasize current income and liquidity in their investment strategy. Those governing a perpetual foundation will likely want to develop a strategy designed for long-term income growth in principal.

However you may feel about the question of perpetuity, consider carefully what you want to accomplish — and what you want your family to accomplish — prior to committing to a long-term investment strategy or spending policy.

Establishing the Spending Policy

The spending policy of a family foundation determines what percentage of a foundation's endowment will be spent annually to cover both operating costs and grants. Internal Revenue Service (IRS) regulations require that private foundations spend at least 5 percent of their net investment assets as "qualifying distributions" each year. Qualifying distributions — also referred to as "payout" — of a foundation generally include:

- Grants to public charities, nonprofit organizations, and individuals (includ-

ing scholarships or aid to those in distress);
- Administrative and programmatic expenses associated with grantmaking; and
- Amounts paid to acquire assets used directly in carrying out the charitable purposes of the foundation.

Bottom Line: You Must Meet Payout Requirements. Your family foundation must meet federal annual minimum payout requirements (5 percent of net investment assets), as well as current costs of grantmaking and administration.

Expenses incurred in managing the endowment of a family foundation do not count toward the 5 percent distribution. These expenses include:

- Investment management fees;
- Brokerage fees;
- Custodial fees; and
- Salaries or board meeting expenses to oversee investments.

Families must address a number of important questions when setting — or evaluating — the spending policy of their foundation, including:

- Is the foundation fully funded or will additional assets be received?

- Does the foundation board want to exceed annual, minimum payout requirements? If so, by how much? In every year or only in years in which the foundation's investments do well?
- Does the board want to grow the foundation's endowment or is it satisfied maintaining the value of the endowment on an inflation-adjusted ("real") basis?
- How can program objectives best be achieved: By spending more now? By constant and sustained effort over time? Or by growing the endowment so that more can be spent in the future?

A spending policy often includes guidelines and conditions for investment and portfolio growth. When establishing the spending policy, you and your board must also determine whether the return requirement implied by the policy is realistic and achievable over time.

Examples of the primary goals for spending policies adopted by foundations include suggestions to:
- Meet the minimum distribution requirement (5 percent annually);
- Distribute 5 percent of assets in grants, plus administrative expenses;
- Spend 5 to 6 percent of the average value of the endowment over the previous 12 quarters, making additional grants toward the end of the year as needed to fulfill the distribution requirement;

---

fig. **2** | **Example of a Family Foundation Spending Policy**

INTRODUCTION:

The foundation is adopting the following spending policy in order to:

- Provide a more predictable and stable stream of revenue for its grantmaking and other activities; and
- Maintain the purchasing power of this revenue stream and the foundation's assets over the long term.

To achieve these goals, over a multiple-year period the trustees will take actions that will result in total spending equaling no more than 5.3 percent of a 3-year average of the market values of the foundation's assets at the beginning of the fourth quarter.

SPENDING RULE:

In calendar year 2002, the foundation will set its annual spending at the 2001 spending level, plus funding needed for one-time capital expenses of the _____ project.

In calendar year 2003, spending will be set at the 2002 spending level or 5.3 percent of the average of the market values of the foundation's assets on October 1, 2001, and October 1, 2002, whichever is greater.

In subsequent calendar years, spending will be set at the previous year's spending level or 5.3 percent of the average of the market value of the foundation's assets at the beginning of the fourth quarters of the preceding 3 calendar years, whichever is greater. In no case will spending exceed 6 percent of the previous year's market value (as determined as of the beginning of the previous year's fourth quarter).

The trustees will undertake a formal review of the spending rule at least once every 5 years. Should future market values either increase or decrease dramatically, the trustees will reconsider the spending rule, and either adjust spending or make changes in the spending rule as appropriate, keeping in mind the above stated goals.

- Spend 5 to 5.5 percent, while focusing on qualifying for the reduced excise tax rate of 1 percent;
- Meet the 5 percent distribution requirement but consider paying out a bit more, depending on program objectives and current investment returns;
- Maintain or moderately increase the value of the endowment and distribute the remainder of the investment return; and/or
- If the foundation is considering spending out, pay out 10 percent per year, with the expectation that all assets will be paid out within a predetermined horizon;

As these examples show, foundation spending policies usually begin with grants payout requirements and then include other factors such as administrative expenses, past grantmaking by the foundation, grantee needs, and the status of current market returns. Whatever the criteria, the 5 percent minimum mandate set by the IRS must always be met.

Developing an Investment Strategy and Policies

Once you have established an initial spending policy for your foundation, you are ready to develop an investment strategy to help meet requirements of that policy. Several important steps are involved in developing an investment strategy. These include:

fig. 3 — Calculating the Return Requirement

RETURN COMPONENT	PERCENT OF AVERAGE ASSETS
Spending objective	5.50
Expected rate of inflation over investment time horizon	3.50
Estimated investment-related fees and expenses	0.75
Average annual investment return required	**9.75**

- Calculating the return requirement;
- Developing an overall asset allocation strategy;
- Considering foundation-specific factors; and
- Developing the strategy and a written investment policy for the foundation.

Calculating the Return Requirement

The return requirement for most foundations (those not planning to spend out) is the amount needed to maintain the value of the endowment while also meeting the spending objectives of the foundation. One return requirement calculation is illustrated in the sidebar.

Thus, to maintain the real value of its endowment, a foundation with a 5.5 percent spending policy (and with these expectations for inflation and fees) needs to achieve an annual investment return of 9.75 percent.

Creating an Overall Asset Allocation Strategy

The asset allocation strategy is the primary determinant of your investment returns. This strategy is the key investment focus of your board (and/or investment committee), and is far more important than individual security or manager selection. Some observers estimate that as much as 95 percent of a foundation's investment returns result from the asset allocation decision. (This estimate comes from Gary P. Brinson, L. Randolph Hood, and Gilbert L. Beebower, in their "Determinants of Portfolio Performance," *Financial Analysts Journal*, July-August 1986, pp. 39-44. While some practitioners dispute this exact figure, the fact that asset allocation is the single most important determinant of portfolio performance is almost universally accepted.)

Diversification among asset classes reduces risk because each type of asset responds differently to changes in the market. Because asset classes perform differently under different time periods and conditions, foundation rates of return can be stabilized and/or improved by mixing asset classes that have different characteristics and patterns of return.

The average annual return on domestic stocks was approximately 13.5 percent from 1926 through 1998. Over that same period the return for bonds was 5.8 percent. Thus, to achieve a rate of return that allows your foundation to maintain or grow the real value of its endowment, you will almost certainly need to invest a substantial percentage of the foundation's assets in stocks or other assets with the potential for high rates of return (real estate, venture capital, hedge funds, etc.).

Still, private foundations have significant cash flow requirements, and bonds are often used to provide a steady stream of income over time. Therefore, some mixture of stocks, bonds, alternative investments, and cash equivalents is usually necessary for a family foundation. See the profile of the Sample Family Foundation in the sidebar for more information about how one (fictitious) family foundation decided on its own asset allocation.

Considering Foundation-Specific Factors

A number of foundation-specific factors influence a foundation's asset

fig. 4 The Sample Family Foundation Asset Allocation Decision

The fictional Sample Family Foundation in the table below has assets of $20 million and has identified its asset allocation strategy as follows:

ASSET CLASS	ESTIMATED ASSET CLASS RETURNS (%)	TARGET ALLOCATION (%)	EXPECTED RETURN (%)	ALLOCATION RANGE MINIMUM (%)	MAXIMUM (%)
Cash and T-Bills	5.0	5	0.3	5	10
U.S. Stock	10.5	55	5.8	40	60
Foreign Stocks	12.0	15	1.8	10	20
U.S. Bonds	6.5	25	1.6	20	40
		100	9.5		

The Sample Family Foundation first determined that it needed a return of 9.5 percent to achieve its spending objectives. It then considered the asset classes in which it was willing to invest. The board decided to invest in cash equivalent investments (this asset class includes money market funds, Treasury bills, and commercial paper), domestic stocks, foreign stocks, and U.S. bonds. The board decided not to allocate any part of the portfolio to alternative investments or real estate. It determined that it preferred more liquid investments and was concerned about the level of expertise, due diligence work, and management time that would be needed properly to manage those asset classes. The Sample Family Foundation also decided to focus on investing in domestic stocks, foreign stocks, and U.S. bonds, as it had been advised that the benefits of diversifying beyond these types of standard asset classes would be more than offset by the significant additional costs that this would entail.

The Sample Family Foundation then estimated the returns that it could expect from the included asset classes over a 5-year time horizon. The estimated asset class returns were based on both historic returns and the board's view of likely future returns. In developing the return estimates, the board considered political, economic, demographic, and business factors as well as trends with implications for the future.

The next step was to determine a target or normal allocation for each asset class. Developing the target allocation for the included asset classes was an iterative exercise. The 5 percent allocation to cash equivalents was based on the amount the Sample Family Foundation thought it would need to pay grants and expenses, plus the average uninvested cash balances that it estimated its investment managers would be holding. The 25 percent allocation to bonds was the amount considered necessary to provide diversification and income flow in the form of the regular interest payments that bonds provide. After allocating a total of 30 percent of the portfolio to cash equivalents and bonds, 70 percent remained for allocation to stocks. A higher allocation to foreign equities was initially considered because of the higher level of estimated future returns. After giving consideration to the greater volatility of foreign stocks and board member preferences, however, it settled on a 15 percent foreign stock allocation. The remainder of the portfolio was allocated to domestic equities.

The Sample Family Foundation then calculated the expected return for this asset strategy. The expected return was calculated by multiplying the target allocation percentage by the expected asset class return. The total expected return turned out to be 9.5 percent, which met the Sample Family Foundation's return requirement.

The final step in the asset allocation process was to establish range minimums and maximums for each asset class. The ranges were determined primarily on the basis of the board's preferences and comfort levels with respect to the various asset classes. The board determined that cash equivalent balances in excess of 10 percent would be excessive. It also determined that the allocation to U.S. bonds should not fall below 20 percent or exceed 40 percent. The board then made similar judgments in establishing allocation range guidelines for domestic and foreign stocks. The Sample Family Foundation plans to adopt a rebalancing policy that will require that an asset class be rebalanced back to the target allocation at the end of any year in which the minimum or maximum is exceeded.

The Sample Family Foundation is currently formulating its plans for asset management. It plans to index some portion of the domestic equity and U.S. bond portfolio because it believes that these markets are so efficient that few active managers can consistently outperform the indexes on an after-fee basis. It plans to hire investment managers to manage its foreign and small domestic company stocks because it believes that skilled managers can generate excess returns for these asset classes. The Sample Family Foundation is also developing investment management policies to guide its board, investment managers, and employees.

SOURCE: Jeffrey R. Leighton. "Developing and Overseeing an Investment Strategy," *Investment Issues for Family Funds: Managing and Maximizing Your Philanthropic Dollars*. Washington, DC: National Center for Family Philanthropy, 1999.

allocation decision. The question of perpetuity and the return requirement of the foundation have been discussed. Other important factors include the board's risk tolerance and the foundation's investment time horizon.

Risk tolerance refers to the board's concern regarding the likelihood and frequency of realized investment returns falling below expected returns. Riskier asset classes have greater potential payoff, but a higher likelihood of falling outside of expected returns (sometimes above, sometimes below). Some board members are uncomfortable with highly volatile asset classes, and choose to steer clear of them in the asset allocation decision. By definition, riskier investments can also result in significantly lower returns in some years, potentially making it difficult to meet multiyear grant commitments and future cash flow requirements. Used in moderation, however, riskier asset classes can actually lower the overall risk of the total portfolio.

The time horizon of a foundation's investment strategy also relates directly to the asset allocation decision. The longer your foundation's time horizon — which reflects its willingness to ride out declines in the value of individual assets, as well as its ability to meet short-term payout commitments — the more you will be able to use diversification and other strategies to take advantage of high-risk (and potentially higher return) asset classes. If your time horizon is short, as is the case if you are spending out the foundation or if your board has a high level of risk aversion and is not willing to sustain short-term losses, your asset allocation decision will want to steer clear of more volatile asset classes. The illustration in the sidebar clearly shows how volatility and risk of loss decrease as the time horizon lengthens.

Adopting the Strategy and a Written Investment Policy

The foundation's investment strategy and policy helps guide the board, the investment committee, and managers and consultants who manage portions of the foundation's portfolio. This policy addresses the following:

- **Statement of objectives:** ties the investment policy to the mission and goals of the foundation (may include the specific return requirement, description of time horizon, diversification, and target risk levels, etc.).
- **Oversight of the policy:** describes who will be responsible for various investment-related tasks (the investment committee, key staff person, outside investment managers, etc.).
- **Asset allocation:** provides guidelines for the acceptable range for each asset class as a percentage of the overall portfolio (see sidebar).
- **Rebalancing procedures:** describes how and when the portfolio is rebalanced (usually either on an annual basis, or if one of the asset classes reaches the threshold of its acceptable range).

fig. 5 — Average Annual Returns on U.S. Stocks
Rolling Time Periods from 1925 to 1998

	1-YEAR PERIODS (%)	5-YEAR PERIODS (%)	10-YEAR PERIODS (%)
Best Period	54.0	23.9	20.00
Worst Period	-43.3	-12.4	-0.90

This table shows the best and worst returns for large company U.S. stocks for 1-year time periods as well as over rolling 5- and 10-year time periods. Single-year returns were as low as negative 43 percent and as high as +54 percent between 1925 and 1998. A foundation that evaluated its returns over a 5-year time period would have had annual average returns as low as -12.9 percent for the worst 5-year period or as high as +23.9 percent over the best 5-year period. If the time horizon is further extended, the average annual return over the worst 10-year period would be -0.9 percent and the average annual return over the best 10-year period would be 20 percent.

SOURCE: Toni Brown, Callan Associates, in Jeffrey R. Leighton. "Developing and Overseeing an Investment Strategy," *Investment Issues for Family Funds: Managing and Maximizing Your Philanthropic Dollars.*

- **Performance benchmarks:** include any of a number of possible common indexes and measures to help review ongoing performance (examples include the S&P 500, the Russell 2000, and the Lehman Aggregate Bond Index). Benchmarks are chosen based on their relevance to each asset class.

Jeffrey Leighton, former chief financial officer for the David and Lucile Packard Foundation and an experienced foundation investment consultant, summarizes the key points for developing an investment strategy as follows:

- **The best investment strategy focuses on the investment process and policies, not the details.**
- **The single most important strategy decision is the asset allocation policy.** Manage risk by diversifying and investing to meet return objectives, not to maximize returns.
- **Give policies and strategies time to work and stay the course through market upswings and downswings.** Don't abandon a new strategy too soon. Investors who chase after the best returns end up doing just that — chasing after the best returns.

fig.
6   Example of an Investment Policy for a Family Foundation

The purpose of this statement is to establish the investment policy for the management of the assets of the _____ Foundation.

OBJECTIVES: The goals for the foundation's investment program are (1) to earn sufficient investment returns to provide for a 5 percent level of annual charitable distribution plus operation expenses, (2) to earn an additional return to maintain the purchasing power of the foundation's invested assets after distributions and expenses, and (3) to enhance the purchasing power of the invested assets, if possible. These goals will be pursued without incurring undue risk relative to the practices of comparable charitable foundations.

DISTINCTIONS OF RESPONSIBILITIES: The Investment/ Finance Committee is responsible for establishing the investment policy that is to guide the investment of the foundation's assets. The investment policy describes the degree of overall investment risk that the Committee deems appropriate, given prudent investment principles and the basic objective of the preservation of the purchasing power of the foundation's assets.

Investment managers appointed to execute the policy will invest foundation assets in accordance with the policy and assigned policy guidelines, but will apply their own judgment concerning relative investment values. In particular, investment managers are accorded full discretion, within policy limits, to (1) select individual investments and (2) diversify assets.

ASSET ALLOCATION: It is the policy of the Investment/Finance Committee to invest the foundation's assets as follows:

ASSET CLASS	TARGET ALLOCATION (%)	ALLOWABLE RANGE (%)
Domestic Stock	55	51 – 59
Non-domestic Stock	15	11 – 19
Total Stock	70	67.5 – 75
Bonds*	30	26 – 34

Bonds will have a minimum rating of BBB or its equivalent.

REBALANCING PROCEDURES : Normal cash flows will be used to maintain actual allocations as close to the target allocations as is practical. At times, markets may move in such a way that normal cash flows will be insufficient to maintain the actual allocation within the permissible ranges. In these cases, balances will be transferred as necessary between the asset types to bring the allocation back within the permissible ranges, as described above. Rebalancing shall take place no less than once, and no more than twice, per year.

DIVERSIFICATION: The investment program shall be broadly diversified in a manner that is in keeping with fiduciary standards to limit the impact of large losses in individual securities on the total invested assets of the foundation.

LIQUIDITY: The foundation will advise investment managers of any anticipated needs for liquidity as such needs becomes known. Investment managers are to presume no need to maintain cash reserves other than those identified by the foundation.

PROXY VOTING: The Investment/Finance Committee delegates the responsibility for proxies to the individual investment managers. The Committee will vote proxies consistently and in the best interest of the foundation.

PERFORMANCE BENCHMARK: The foundation's investment objectives are to achieve a rate of return consistent with the asset allocation policy stated earlier. Over reasonable measurement periods, the rate of return earned by the foundation's assets should match or exceed that of a policy benchmark comprised of the following broad market indices and weights:

	POLICY BENCHMARK
Wilshire 5000 Stock Index (%)	55
MSCI All Country Ex-U.S. Index (%)	15
Lehman Brothers Aggregate Bond Index (%)	30

The individual managers' returns will be compared with appropriate market indices. For performance evaluation purposes, all rates of return will be examined after the deduction of investment management fees.

- **Don't try to time or outguess the market.** William Sharpe, a recent winner of the Nobel Prize in Economics, noted that the markets, on the whole, are likely to do just as well when an investor is out as when the investor is in.
- **Avoid fads.** David Salem, president of The Investment Fund for Foundations, has noted that, by the time a new asset class has proven worthwhile, the big bucks have already been earned.
- **Review manager and total portfolio performance at least annually.** Make sure that investment guidelines are being followed.
- **Control costs.** The best way for many organizations to improve overall returns is by exercising better cost control over fees and transaction costs.
- **Rebalance the portfolio when asset allocation guideline ranges are exceeded.** Failure to rebalance the portfolio is tantamount to a decision to change the asset allocation strategy.

SOURCE: Jeffrey R. Leighton. "Developing and Overseeing an Investment Strategy," *Investment Issues for Family Funds: Managing and Maximizing Your Philanthropic Dollars.*

An example of one investment policy, with descriptions of each of these components, is presented in Figure 6 (on p. 147).

Overseeing the Investment Strategy

Many family foundations oversee their investment strategy through the establishment of an investment committee. Ideally, this committee is comprised of individuals with broad and diversified knowledge of investments. Members of the committee will be able to articulate the policies, actions, and results of the investment strategy to all current and prospective board members (whose understanding and experience in investments may be quite varied).

Some foundations work with investment consultants to develop their investment strategy and policies, and to select individuals to manage aspects of the portfolio.

Determining Investment Committee Responsibilities

The investment committee generally assumes some or all of the following responsibilities:

- Ensures that the foundation's investment goals and objectives are in line with its grantmaking goals and objectives;
- Determines long-term allocation among asset classes;
- Determines choice of preferred investment manager styles;
- Determines whether to use separate accounts or mutual funds;
- Selects individual managers, consultants, and advisors (if necessary);
- Reviews the performance of individual managers and asset classes; and
- Reports to the full board on the endowment's recent and long-term performance.

Depending on the complexity of these decisions, the committee may engage investment consultants to help them think through these responsibilities. In addition, a number of endowment management tasks must be undertaken regularly by committee members, foundation staff (if they exist), or an outside professional (accountant, lawyer, etc.). These activities typically include:

- Managing endowment cash flow;
- Monitoring asset allocation;
- Ensuring accurately reported quarterly and cumulative investment performance for individual managers and the endowment as a whole;
- Ensuring proper custody of endowment holdings and necessary record-keeping on investment transactions;
- Preparing agreements with managers, mutual funds, brokers, and securities custodians;
- Ensuring that shareholder proxies are voted;
- Managing the investment consultant (if present); and
- Providing necessary staff support for the investment committee (scheduling meetings, distributing reports for discussion in advance, as well as providing advance reports on the endowment for board of trustees meetings).

SOURCE: John E. Craig, Jr. "Understanding Trustee Responsibilities and Duties," *Investment Issues for Family Funds: Managing and Maximizing Your Philanthropic Dollars.*

Finding Investment Advisors

Many family foundations work with outside investment managers for some

tasks. Steps to consider when looking for outside assistance include:
- Determine what types of assistance you are looking for (see sidebar);
- Develop a position description that lists the attributes you are looking for, including educational, experience, and performance requirements, as well as personality requirements and investment style;
- Talk with foundations, institutions, and individuals you know to get sug-gestions for prospective managers and consultants;
- Send a request for proposal (RFP) to those individuals/firms you would like to meet. This RFP will help your foundation determine each firm's experience, performance, fee struc-ture, and staffing, as well as its research policy and practices, reporting pro-cedures, and client service proce-dures; and
- Set up interviews with those candi-dates who meet your qualifications and requirements.

Selecting Investment Advisors

Any investment firm or individual you approach will have tailored information on its performance over specific time periods. To ensure that you get helpful performance figures, make sure that those you meet with calculate performance in accordance with the guidelines of the Association for Investment Management and Research, and that they give you returns for 3-, 5-, and 10- year periods. Questions you may wish to consider when interviewing managers include:
- What is their general approach to investing?
- What is the succession plan if they retire, become ill, or leave the firm?
- What other foundation clients do they work with? May you talk with them?
- What type of reporting and evaluation arrangement do they typically follow?
- What questions do they have about the position?

Questions you may want to ask your-self include:
- Am I comfortable working with this manager? Does his or her style match my own?
- Am I confident that the foundation will receive significant added benefit for the fee dollars I am spending?
- Are there other options (index funds, mutual funds, etc.) I may wish to explore as an alternative to hiring an investment manager at this time?

Working with Investment Advisors

If you decide to hire advisors, you will want to establish reporting arrangements that make sense for both of you. Identify and agree on the performance benchmarks you would like to use, and establish reporting schedules for each of your managers. Investment managers should be expected to outperform their benchmarks on a net-of-fee basis, and if they fail to do so over an extended period (a couple of years or more), inquire as to the reasons why. Remember that even the best managers will have periods where they underperform in relation to their peers or benchmarks.

Determine how often you would like the manager to report to the board, and in what form these reports are presented (for instance, quarterly written reports and annual board presentations). Evaluations should also take into account the manager's investment style, and how this style may have affected recent performance. Ensure that the manager continues to follow the specific guidelines he or she has been given.

Determining the Family's Role

Because you have set up your foundation as a family foundation, you and your board may want to consider issues with implications for individual family members. Which family members show interest in serving on the investment committee? Must they be board members to do so? Which bring special knowledge or skills to the work at hand. To what extent should branches of the family, or generations, be represented? Also important, of course, are the personalities and interpersonal skills of family members who are called upon to serve in a group environment.

Members of the family who are selected to serve on the investment committee must be prepared to spend additional time on foundation-related activities. Determining who serves on the investment committee can be a difficult task. Traditionally, these committees have been made up of the founder and those trustees with the most experience in this area. Because all members of the board are considered fiduciaries of the foundation, however, it is important that each current and future trustee has a general understanding of investments activities.

Family foundations employ a wide variety of methods to teach younger and/or less experienced family members about financial stewardship. Common practices — both informal and more structured — include:

- Placing next-generation and less-experienced trustees on the investment committee with more experienced board members/advisors;
- Spending a day with foundation money managers at their offices;
- Requiring money managers to conduct a 2- to 4-hour instructional seminar for new/future board members;
- Making occasional educational seminars part of the investment counselor's job description;
- Incorporating at least one learning segment related to finances at every board meeting;
- Developing a formal orientation-training program of from 1 to 3 days for next-generation members (a significant portion of which covers financial management);
- Sending trustees to professional conferences, seminars, and workshops on investment-related topics; and
- Establishing a separate Next Generation Advisory Board that includes a small fund to manage and a requirement that the advisory board report on its activities at every full board meeting.

SOURCE: Lester A. Picker. "Training the Next Generation," *Investment Issues for Family Funds: Managing and Maximizing Your Philanthropic Dollars.*

Reviewing Disqualified Persons Requirements

Family members sometimes find themselves playing a direct role in managing one or more of the asset classes or individual funds in the foundation's portfolio. This practice may be illegal under certain circumstances. It is very important, therefore, that you and the rest of the board be familiar with the self-dealing rules. Situations to keep a close eye on include:

- **Compensating investment managers who are disqualified persons.** All family members are disqualified persons.

The general rule here is that the amount of the compensation must be reasonable, where reasonable means that a similar organization would pay such an amount for similar services under similar circumstances.

- **Compensating property managers who are disqualified persons.** This act is defined by the IRS as self-dealing and is, therefore, not permissible.
- **Lending money or extending credit to a disqualified person.** This act is defined as self-dealing and is not permissible.
- **Benefiting from joint investments.** Disqualified persons are generally not allowed to make investments in the same investment partnership.

---

fig.
8   **Roadblocks and Bumps in the Road**

Family foundation boards may experience challenging situations while overseeing the investments of the foundation, including:

- **Family members as paid investment managers:** Prudent boards will be wary of arrangements in which a family member is paid to manage the investments of the foundation. Reviewing the performance of a family member is not always easy, and trying to remove a family member as manager can be even more difficult. Combined with the need to ensure that the compensation arrangement is within the self-dealing rules, this practice may not be one that you will want to tangle with.

- **Liquidity considerations:** Foundations have annual payout responsibilities and, in most cases, ongoing operations costs. As such, you need to ensure that an adequate amount is kept in cash or some other easily converted investment type for annual (or more frequent) grant payments and other expenses.

- **Over-management of the endowment:** Just as individual investors do, foundation boards have a tendency to over-manage their investments — buying and selling new funds, changing advisors, and even changing investment styles regularly. Because of the high cost of these transactions, and because foundations usually invest for the very long-term, it is important that the board resist these temptations

and, whenever possible, stick to a predetermined strategy through the inevitable ups and downs of the markets.

- **Time lags between meetings:** At the same time, cases arise where individual stocks or classes of stocks experience rapid shifts in price, and action may be needed either to rebalance the portfolio or take other more radical action. Because many foundation boards do not meet more than one or two times per year, it is important to have some system in place to account for these situations — this could be as simple as giving one or more of the trustees discretion to make these decisions.

- **Disparity of interests and abilities:** All board members — regardless of their investment background and experience — need to understand the strategy and decisions made with regard to the foundation's investments. This can be accomplished in a number of ways (see above for specific ideas).

- **Excise tax on net investment income:** Private foundation endowments are subject to an excise tax of at least 1 percent, and up to 2 percent, of investment returns each year. These taxes are paid on realized net gains, and a portfolio with constant turnover will likely trigger the maximum tax payments. Although it may not be possible to avoid the maximum tax in any given year, families may wish to consider working with advisors who have sensitivity in managing the portfolio in a tax-efficient manner.

Just as the foundation's grantmaking goals and objectives may change over time, so may its spending and investment objectives and strategies. Keep in mind that program goals, rather than the performance of individual managers or asset classes, should drive these changes.

For more information about the self-dealing rules, consult with legal counsel or refer to resources listed in the Appendices. You may also wish to develop a conflict-of-interest statement to make clear the limitations on board member's interaction with the foundation. (See Facing Important Legal Issues, p. 59.)

Considering the Role of Future Generations

At some point, you and your board will need to determine what the role of the next generation will be with regard to the foundation's investments. Common questions that families face in this area include:

- Should the next generation have the option of changing spending policy?
- How can we best prepare the next generation to manage the investments of the foundation?
- What guidelines can we provide the next generation with regard to the investments of the foundation?

Developing these guidelines can be an important and potentially time-consuming task.

Reducing Investment Costs

By reducing costs, a foundation board may be able to adopt a more conservative portfolio, yet still achieve the returns needed to maintain or increase purchasing power. Many smaller foundations look to an indexed approach to attain the excellent returns historically associated with equity markets, while minimizing investment costs. Three common methods for developing a portfolio with limited investment costs are mutual funds, separate account managers, and self-implementation:

- **Mutual Funds.** Mutual funds are the vehicle of choice for many smaller foundations. Advantages include ease of implementation, moderate costs, low thresholds for investment, and a huge selection of alternatives. On the downside, mutual funds must maintain a cash reserve to meet redemptions, and returns are diminished accordingly. Also, because contributions tend to pour into mutual funds during market highs and flow out during market lows, mutual fund

investors are often forced into a "buy high/sell low" scenario by the managers. On the whole, however, mutual funds are an excellent choice for investing the endowments for smaller foundations.

- **Separate Account Managers.** Many foundations hire advisors to manage separate accounts on their behalf. Advantages include the potential for lower costs and negotiated fees; direct input to and feedback from the manager; and the potential for developing a customized portfolio, if the foundation is looking to minimize the excise tax on investments. This type of investing is appropriate for foundations interested in socially responsible investing or in developing other individualized approaches. Many of the better investment managers, however, have investment minimums ranging from several million to tens of millions of dollars. Thus, smaller foundations may be precluded from employing separate account managers. Moreover, even for those smaller foundations that are able to meet one manager's established minimum, diversification may be limited because the foundation endowment is not sufficient to meet the minimum for multiple managers with their various investment styles.

- **Self-Implementation.** The boards of many foundations are comfortable with making their own investment selections. Advantages to this approach include flexibility to customize the portfolio and minimal investment expenses (assuming the individual or individuals involved work without remuneration). Disadvantages include: a lack of expertise or experience, which may result in diminished returns; an inability or lack of time to deal with the sometimes overwhelming mechanics of the investment process (including custody considerations and recordkeeping); limitations on diversification (unless the foundation is of significant size); and a lack of time to monitor and review holdings, which may also result in reduced returns.

Several other low-cost management options exist, including the use of a bank or other financial institution, community foundations, and the use of pooled funds such as The Investment Fund for Foundations (see below). Options include:

- **Use of a custodian.** Smaller foundations or funds may choose to make use of existing relationships with the banks or other financial institutions that serve as their custodian. Because the foundation may already be paying the custodian for other services, it can often obtain competitive rates on investment management fees and other costs.

- **Community foundations.** In addition to their traditional grantmaking and administrative services for advised funds, some community foundations offer investment management services

to private foundations. Investment management fees are generally based on the type of fund that the family has, and are sometimes negotiable. Although the investment choices available through a community foundation may be limited because of existing relationships with managers, community foundations that group funds with managers may be better able to meet minimum asset requirements, and thus may be able to secure lower investment expenses for family foundations who use these services.

- **The Investment Fund for Foundations.** The TIFF Investment Program (TIP) — a family of commingled investment funds of grantmaking foundations — is an example of a pooled fund that is open to smaller foundations. TIP employs a performance-based fee system, and in the past has maintained relatively low investment minimums.

Revisiting Goals and Objectives

Just as the foundation's grantmaking goals and objectives may change over time, so may its spending and investment objectives and strategies. Keep in mind that program goals, rather than the performance of individual managers or asset classes, should drive these changes. Because well thought-out grantmaking and investment strategies often require that you stick with a philosophy over an extended

period, it is important that you allow these strategies time to develop without making radical or frequent shifts in approach.

Situations may develop, however, in which changing the spending policy and investment objectives may make sense. Specific reasons to consider revisiting the spending policy (and associated investment strategy) may include:

- **Underperformance:** Foundations should review their overall portfolio performance at least annually. In some cases, the board may find that the investment objectives are not being achieved over a period of time. This outcome could be because the investment objectives are not realistic, or the spending policy itself is too ambitious.

- **Sustained growth in the markets and economy:** In some situations, the opposite is true. The market occasionally experiences sustained periods of growth, which may lead to significantly higher endowments than expected. In such cases, the foundation might want to consider increasing its payout rate for an indefinite period of time.

- **Opportunities for significant social investment in a particular issue or cause:** In some cases, you and the board may identify a well-defined cause that you think the foundation might be able to correct with a substantial influx of funds. In such cases, revising the spending policy may be necessary.

fig. 9 Checklist of Fudiciary Responsibilities

1. Does the foundation file 990-PF and related state forms?　　Yes No

2. Does the foundation publish in a local newspaper the location and availability of the 990-PF?　　Yes No

3. Do staff and board periodically disclose to the governing body the nature of any personal or family affiliations or involvement with any organization that might be considered an act of self-dealing or a conflict of interest?　　Yes No

4. Do you believe that the board fully understands its legal responsibilities?　　Yes No

5. Does the board annually approve a budget and periodically review its implementation?　　Yes No

6. Do board members understand the data presented in regular financial reports?　　Yes No

7. Does the board have members with special expertise who give advice and leadership in:
   a. Long-range fiscal planning?　　Yes No
   b. Investment practices?　　Yes No
   c. Fiscal management?　　Yes No
   d. Budget review?　　Yes No
   e. Analysis of audit reports and recommendations?　　Yes No

8. Do you feel that the board fully accepts its responsibility for prudent fiscal management?　　Yes No

9. Does the board or a board committee hold regular meetings with its investment advisors or investment staff?　　Yes No

10. Does the board get adequate and comparative information on the investment portfolio's performance?　　Yes No

11. Does the board have a policy to guide those responsible for selecting/monitoring foundation investments?　　Yes No

12. Are you generally satisfied with the performance of the foundation's investment managers?　　Yes No

13. Does the board or an appropriate board committee take direct responsibility for voting on shareholder resolutions affecting companies whose stock the foundation owns?　　Yes No

14. Does the board have a conflict-of-inherent policy statement that all directors and officers are expected to execute?
   a. Should it be reviewed for substantive content? Yes No
   b. Was it, in fact, signed by all directors　　Yes No

15. Was there a meeting at which a director disclosed a conflict of interest regarding a decision?　　Yes No

16. If so, was there an adequate record in the minutes of that disclosure?　　Yes No

17. Was there a vote on the issue to which the director had a conflict?　　Yes No

18. If so, was there a quorum (as defined by the statute of incorporation) for such a vote?　　Yes No

19. If so, was there a vote of an adequate number of disinterested directors?　　Yes No

20. What material is distributed in advance of board meetings?
   a. Minutes of last meeting?　　Yes No
   b. Current financial statements?　　Yes No
   c. Current reports of committees?　　Yes No
   d. Summaries of decisions to be made?　　Yes No

SOURCE: Compiled from the Guidebook for Directors of Nonprofit Corporations of the American Bar Association. Republished from Appendix E. *Investment Issues for Family Funds: Managing and Maximizing Your Philanthropic Dollars.*

- **Decision to sunset the foundation:** Whether you make this decision on your own or with the family, or whether this is a choice that will be made at some point in the future, the decision to sunset or spend out the foundation will have radical implications for how the foundation spends and invests its resources.

A Final Word: Reviewing the Checklist

John Craig, executive vice president and treasurer of the Commonwealth Fund, offers the following checklist for managing a family foundation endowment:

- Does the foundation have a clear spending policy? Does that policy reflect a consensus among trustees regarding the life expectancy of the foundation?
- Do members of the investment committee have relevant experience for overseeing the management of the endowment?

- Are members of the investment committee fully engaged in the foundation's mission and equally attentive to its grantmaking?
- Does the foundation have written investment guidelines for the endowment as a whole and for individual managers? Do these guidelines include targeted allocations to named asset classes with permissible ranges for each?
- Is the allocation of the endowment among asset classes regularly monitored? Is corrective action taken when market trends cause allocations to veer beyond the targeted ranges?
- Does the investment committee report at meetings of the board of trustees on the endowment's recent and long-term performance?

SOURCE: John E. Craig, Jr. "Understanding Trustee Responsibilities and Duties," *Investment Issues for Family Funds: Managing and Maximizing Your Philanthropic Dollars.*

These questions provide a helpful context for the types of conversations and decisions you and your board will be making in the future regarding the investment of your foundation's endowment and the role of the family in that process. You probably will not be able to answer "yes" to each of these questions at this time. As you review the development of your strategy, policies, and practices, consider revisiting these questions at each board meeting until you feel comfortable with your answers. As John Kunstadter, president and long-time trustee of the Albert Kunstadter Family Foundation, once wrote,

In the end, your satisfaction and joy will come not so much from good investments, but from the grants you have made, the lives you have affected for the better, the Earth which is a little better place for your efforts. There are many roads to these goals, as many roads as there are foundations; so use your common sense, don't take up with the latest fad, keep things in perspective, and your foundation will gladden your heart as you see it accomplish your goals.

GRANTMAKING and COMMUNICATIONS

IV

FIGURES

ESTABLISHING GRANTMAKING INTERESTS and PRIORITIES

by Deanne Stone

Grantmaking is the central activity of your family foundation and the purpose for its existence. It is your family's opportunity to exercise influence in areas that matter most to you. As grantmakers, you move beyond just talking about issues to looking for answers. You can think of your foundation as a mini-Congress and your board as a committee charged with developing policy. Your task is to figure out how to turn your family's concerns into a foundation vision.

Thinking like a policymaker is a serious undertaking; your decisions affect the lives of many people who count on foundation funding. To meet that responsibility requires study, contemplation, and hard work. At the same time, it can be one of the most rewarding activities of your life. Imagine the joy of knowing that your efforts have enriched the lives of others. Imagine the satisfaction of seeing situations improve through the intervention of organizations your foundation funds. As an added bonus, you will meet exceptional people through this work: colleagues, community workers, activists, researchers, and the recipients of programs you fund. Their efforts will inspire you, challenge you, and expand your thinking. And, along the way, you will likely uncover strengths, talents, and a social wisdom that you never knew you had.

As a grantmaker, you open your foundation doors to a wide field of organizations that are unfamiliar to you. What system will you use to invite grant proposals? How often will your board meet to vote on grants? How will you determine what organizations to fund, how much to give, and for how long? Will you fund local organizations, statewide, nationwide or, possibly, internationally? To make those decisions, you will have to develop specific grantmaking guidelines and procedures.

Clear, well thought out guidelines are the keys to good grantmaking. How you structure them is as much an expression of your values and beliefs as your mission statement. Some decisions will be easy; others touch on individual beliefs about the purpose of

philanthropy that may stir debate in your family.

It would be misleading to suggest that the intricacies of grantmaking are easily grasped. Those of you accustomed to making decisions on the basis of profit and loss sheets may be frustrated by the ambiguities and uncertainties of grantmaking. In some cases, the impact of your grants will not be easy to measure and, in others, not evident for years to come. Expect to go through periods when you feel overwhelmed by the amount of information you have to absorb and when you doubt that you have made the right choices. Most people do. Grantmaking is not a native talent; it is learned by doing. Be assured, though, that with each grantmaking cycle you will feel a little better prepared, a little more comfortable, a little wiser.

The first year of grantmaking is a period of rapid learning and a time to avoid hard and fast rules. After you complete your first year, you may want to reassess your guidelines and grantmaking process and, perhaps, even change your mind about program interests. That is why the watchwords for this phase are: *proceed slowly.*

Translating Mission into Grantmaking

If you are like most founders, you were a donor long before you established your foundation. In charge of your personal charitable giving, you were free to respond to requests for donations from friends, from alma maters, and from direct-mail solicitations. You could write checks of whatever size you chose and, if you wanted, you could go overboard in one year and trim back on your giving in the next.

After you start your family foundation, you may still continue your other forms of giving. As you learn more about grantmaking, you may want to have more formal grantmaking guidelines, policies, and procedures. In fact, it is the discipline that grantmaking imposes on funders that attracts many wealthy individuals to foundations

Some founders come to the foundation with a clear sense of purpose. They have already decided on the mission

and program areas for their foundations. Others invite family members to participate in deciding the direction of the foundation. Even after they have chosen their mission, some families still have trouble finding a focus for their grantmaking. This is especially true when family members have diverse interests or when they see so many areas of need that they can't decide what to concentrate on.

TIP ➤ If your family is having trouble identifying program interests, consider hiring a consultant to help you. An experienced consultant knows the right questions to ask, keeps the discussions on track, and leads the board to a conclusion.

Shortly after setting up a charitable remainder trust at age 96, Nathanael Berry's grandfather died without leaving instructions for how he wished the money to be used. It was left to nine family members to choose a mission and program areas for the Sandy River Charitable Foundation in Maine. Nathanael, a family member and the executive director, drew up 20 questions to survey the family's interests. "We were all over the map," says Nathanael, "but we found common interests that balanced the board members' desires to be connected to their local community with the recognition of incredible need worldwide." The foundation's international focus reflects the Berry family's com-

position; two siblings are Korean, Nathanael's daughter is Paraguayan, and a sister-in-law is Thai. "The key point in choosing a mission," says Nathanael, "is to understand that you can reach your objectives in myriad ways. My family has tithed 10 percent of our income for as long as I can remember, so when we were ready to start funding, we knew where to look."

TIP ➤ Circulate a survey to board members listing 15 to 20 possible program interests. Ask each person to indicate his or her top three choices. The tally from the survey will indicate the overlap or lack of overlap of interests. It will also give you a starting point for discussion.

Family interest in the program areas is critical. If family members are not engaged in the work of the foundation, they will likely perform their board responsibilities perfunctorily or decline to serve at all. Equally critical are community needs. You want to be sure that the programs you fund respond to pressing concerns of the populations you target. Before your board meets to select program interests, encourage family members to spend the next few weeks researching possible funding areas. Your discussions will be more fruitful if board members come to the meeting prepared to defend their interests with facts, and not just with feelings and opinions.

fig.
1 Ways to Educate Yourself About Community Needs

- Call your Regional Association of Grantmakers. (To find the office closest to you, go to the Website, www.cof.org. Click "Links and Networking.")

- Call your local community foundation and ask to talk with a program officer.

- Consult foundation trustees funding in your areas of interest.

- Interview staff and clients in organizations that interest you to learn what services are needed.

- Assemble a focus group of local community workers and academics who have experience in and an understanding of the topics you are exploring.

- Search the Internet or go to a public or university library.

- Attend relevant workshops and conferences.

- Research the availability of services by acting as if you were a client in need of those services.

For 25 years, Maxine and Jonathan Marshall published a daily newspaper in Scottsdale, Arizona. In the late 1980s, they began talking about selling it. Having enjoyed such a long involvement in their local community, they couldn't imagine not being a vital part of its activities. They decided to use a portion of the profits from the sale of their business to set up a family foundation.

One problem that concerned them was the growing number of homeless people in the Phoenix area. But before they could know where to direct their grants, they had to learn what kind of help was most needed: How many homeless programs existed in the area? What services did they provide? And what needs were still unmet?

With their background in the news business, the Marshalls knew how to find the right people to answer those questions. "All you need is one knowledgeable person in the field to begin networking," says Maxine. "That person will suggest others who, in turn, will suggest still others."

The Marshalls gathered together a group of experts from varied disciplines to brief them on the problem. They included the head of the largest homeless shelter in the state, a minister who had gone underground to live among the Phoenix homeless, a professor of anthropology and recognized expert on the homeless, an architect concerned with designing low-cost housing, a volunteer worker at a homeless shelter, and a formerly homeless woman who had become an advocate for the homeless. Learning about the problem from different perspectives allowed the Marshalls to identify areas where their small foundation could be most effective. They decided to direct their funding to small, grassroots projects providing services to neglected populations.

Learning about a program area takes time. For that reason, it's best to begin by focusing your grantmaking on one or two program areas. As mentioned in Facing Important Legal Issues, p. 59, new foundations have 2 years to meet their first 5 percent payout. By limiting the number of program areas in the first 2 years, you will have more time to delve into the issues, to meet with the people already working in these areas, and to ease into your grantmaking responsibilities.

Although it is important to choose program interests carefully, you are not locked into your initial choices. Circumstances change, and your original reasons for funding a particular program area may no longer apply. Social and economic conditions fluctuate, new research findings may become available, and new trustees who have different funding interests may join your board. Many grantmakers suggest staying with the same program areas for at least 3 years. That is sufficient time for the board to determine whether the program areas are a good fit for the foundation and to notify grantseekers of changes.

Developing a Grantmaking Strategy

Your mission and program areas give purpose and focus to your grantmaking, but they do not tell you how to implement it. For that you need a grantmaking strategy, which can be succinctly expressed in your grantmaking guidelines. Guidelines are the specific policies and procedures that you develop to structure each phase of your grantmaking program: the application process, screening and evaluating proposals, and awarding grants. Whether your foundation accepts unsolicited proposals from grantseekers or whether it solicits proposals from specific organizations, your guidelines will define who you are and what you hope to accomplish.

The grantmaking strategy expressed in your guidelines could cover, in addition to your mission, foundation history, and program areas, such topics as:

- Geographic focus of your grantmaking;
- Whether you accept unsolicited or solicited proposals;
- Whether you support projects only or general operating expenses as well;
- Range of size of grants; and
- Range of length of grants.

Grant guidelines also typically describe how to apply for a grant and the dates of your funding cycle (application deadlines, allocation meetings of the board, notices to applicants, and dates of grant awards).

Mission and guidelines play crucial roles: They establish the foundation's identity in the public mind and show the community that the foundation sees itself as a public steward. Well-articulated mission and guidelines can position your foundation to be more effective in its grantmaking and to advocate more forcefully for the kind of change that you envision.

The trustees of the Lillian M. Berliawsky Charitable Trust discovered the values and mission of the trust by revisiting the life experiences of the founder. Lillian Berliawsky was the daughter of immigrants who settled in New York City around the turn of the 20th century. She and her sister set up a retail business, and they succeeded handsomely. Lillian Berliawsky left an estate in excess of a million dollars for philanthropy.

The trustees discovered grantmaking themes when they researched her life: supporting economic self-sufficiency for women and girls, bringing arts to communities that lack access to them, and creating a welcoming climate for philanthropists, no matter how modest. These themes provided the trustees with the material with which to

Guidelines are the specific policies and procedures that you develop to structure each phase of your grantmaking program: the application process, screening and evaluating proposals, and awarding grants.

fig. 2 — Written Guidelines Are Valuable

Written guidelines are helpful to your foundation and grantseekers because they:

- Keep you focused on your mission;

- Make a public statement about your grantmaking interests and goals;

- Serve as a checklist for screening and evaluating proposals that are the best matches for your foundation;

- Provide objective criteria for rejecting proposals that do not meet your requirements;

- Influence the quality and quantity of proposals you receive; and

- Save grantseekers from pursuing fruitless leads.

fig. 3 — Guidelines That Attract the Right Grantseekers

- Use plain, direct language and avoid jargon, trendy terms, and abbreviations known only to those inside the field.

- Underscore your grantmaking philosophy and goals with statements such as, "We give top priority to programs that …," or "We prefer to support organizations that …."

- Include list of most recent grants.

- List the types of organizations, programs, and program areas that you *will not* consider.

take? Mission and guidelines are a declaration — and an affirmation — of a positive course in an imperfect world. By putting them out there, we are taking a stand on behalf of a better future." (For more information and family examples, see Virginia Peckham, *Grantmaking with a Purpose: Mission and Guidelines,* available from the National Center for Family Philanthropy.)

Having clear, specific guidelines will reduce the number of misdirected proposals you receive, but they will not entirely eliminate them. There will always be inexperienced grantseekers who, out of eagerness or desperation, fail to read guidelines carefully. And there will always be others who will read them and still try to persuade you that their proposals fit your mission when they clearly do not.

TIP➤ Keep a running tally of the inquiries and proposals you reject and your reasons for rejecting them. Is there is a pattern to the types of misdirected proposals you receive? Is something in your guidelines misleading grantseekers about your mission? You may want to ask a colleague to review your guidelines.

You may not be ready to publicize your guidelines when you first begin making grants. Even so, it's a good exercise to jot down guidelines for your private use. After you have completed a year of grantmaking, you may want to revise

develop a mission for the trust, and the grant guidelines.

To some, the mission and guidelines may seem at first glance to be mere "boilerplate," says one trustee of the trust. "But they are much more. Without a well thought out and expressed set of directions, how would we know which direction we should

your guidelines before publicizing them. In fact, it's a good idea to make a practice of reviewing guidelines periodically. As you become more experienced, your thinking about how to achieve your grantmaking goals will likely change.

Whether you are a founder writing the guidelines alone or a family hammering out the details together, it is important to be aware of your options. There are many ways to shape your grantmaking program. This section will help you make the choices that are right for your family and foundation.

Finding a Geographic Focus

Traditionally, family foundations have supported programs in communities to which family members have a connection: the founders' birthplace, the city or state where the family created their wealth, and the hometowns of current board members. As family members become more scattered geographically — living in different cities, regions and, sometimes, in different countries — foundations must decide where to draw geographical lines.

Consider these questions: Is your foundation more likely to achieve its grantmaking goals by keeping a narrow geographic focus? However, if the focus is too narrow, will family members living in different communities feel disconnected from the foundation's grantmaking? On the other hand, if the

foundation funds in all the communities where family members live, will you risk diffusing the impact of your grants?

Two years ago, Leslie Dorman and her husband John founded the Sterling Foundation in Los Angeles. Leslie brought with her 16 years of experience working in nonprofit organizations as a grantseeker and, later, as an executive director of a family foundation. When she and her husband began planning their family foundation, they took to heart a lesson she had learned in her professional career: New and small foundations do best when they keep a narrow focus. They decided to fund programs for teenagers and to limit their geographical area within Los Angeles. "At first we considered funding in all of Los Angeles," says Leslie. "But it is so large and has so many problems that we decided to narrow our focus to just a few neighborhoods. That way we can get to know the people and the organizations in the area, and we can better judge what kind of support they need. Later on, we can consider whether to broaden our geographic focus to other neighborhoods in Los Angeles."

The Stocker Foundation made a different choice. When it started, all the trustees lived in Lorain, Ohio — the hometown of the founders and the place where they built their business. Then, two members of the second generation moved to another

state. The board spread out farther when the third generation signed on: five live in different cities and one in a foreign country. The family feels an enduring commitment to Lorain, and it has pledged to continue to support local programs even when family members no longer live there. At the same time, the surviving donor wanted the foundation to fund programs in the towns where family members lived. By doing so, she hoped the younger generation would be more involved in their own communities and develop a stronger connection to the family foundation. (For a more comprehensive discussion of this topic, see Deanne Stone, *Grantmaking with a Compass: The Challenges of Geography,* available from the National Center for Family Philanthropy.)

Choosing Between Solicited and Unsolicited Proposals

Over the past decade, a growing number of grantmakers have chosen to solicit proposals rather than invite unsolicited proposals from grantseekers. Soliciting proposals can work in two ways: You can contact organizations whose work you admire and invite them to submit a proposal to your foundation. Or, if you have identified a particular problem that you want to address, you can put out a Request for Proposals (RFP). Soliciting proposals helps you to stay focused on your mission and avoid having to read misdirected proposals.

This approach makes sense for new foundations, especially if you do not have staff. By controlling the volume of proposals you receive, you have more time to learn about your program areas. The drawback is that you can limit your access to new ideas and risk missing out on some excellent programs. The growing trend toward soliciting proposals has had some drawback for grantseekers, too. By reducing the pool of funds for which all grantseekers can apply, it can favor organizations known to grantmakers and make it harder for small or less sophisticated groups to gain notice.

TIP ➤ You can begin by soliciting proposals. Later, when you feel more comfortable with your grantmaking responsibilities and more knowledgeable about your program areas, you may want to reserve a percentage of your grants budget for unsolicited proposals.

Small vs. Large Grants: Which Is Better for You?

An ongoing debate among grantmakers is whether foundations can best accomplish their goals by making many small grants or fewer large ones. The truth is that either can be effective or ineffective. A small, carefully targeted grant can have a big impact, and a large, ill-conceived grant can make little or no difference to the community. What matters is not the size of the grant but how it is used. (To learn more about

this topic, read Paul Ylvisaker's *Small Can Be Effective* in Virginia M. Esposito, ed., *Conscience & Community: The Legacy of Paul Ylvisaker*, p.359.)

The approach you choose may come down to who is going to do the work. As grantmakers, you are bound to give due diligence to each proposal. Making many small grants requires considerably more time than making a few larger grants. It is important to consider how much time you have to review proposals and visit organizations. If you are committed to making small grants but lack the staff (family volunteers or paid program officers) to carry it out, check with your local community foundation. It may have already researched the organizations you are considering funding. It can advise you on their findings and save you some time.

The JoMiJo Foundation is a small foundation in Northern California founded by three brothers. (The name is an amalgam of the first syllable of each brother's first name.) The foundation is funded with income from a trust set up by their grandfather. Because the brothers do not yet have access to the principal, their grants budget is limited. Their challenge was figuring out a strategy to support a range of projects helping the destitute and disadvantaged in the three geographic regions where the brothers live. They decided to target small, grassroots organizations

where their small grants would have the biggest impact. Last year, JoMiJo awarded 21 grants ranging between $3,000 and $5,000." Three thousand dollars doesn't sound like much," says Jonathan Frieman, JoMiJo's executive director, "but for some grassroots organizations that's more than 10 percent of their budget."

JoMiJo can give out so many small grants because Jonathan, the foundation's full-time director/program officer, is willing and able to handle most of the responsibilities by himself. A single man with a private income, he has chosen to make philanthropy his full-time profession. Paying expenses out of pocket, Jonathan travels among the three cities where the foundation funds to scout promising organizations. He reports back to his brothers, who have full-time careers and families, and together they decide on the grants. The brothers did not grow up in a family with a tradition of philanthropy, so they are learning together. "Working as a team," says Jonathan, "has been a kick. This is what we want to do with our money, and this is what I want to do with my life."

Like Jonathan, Sandy Buck serves as the full-time executive director and program officer for his family foundation, Horizon Foundation. The all-family board is made up of his parents, his brother and sister-in-law, and Sandy and his wife. Sandy, a former teacher and coach, had chaired the development committees at his children's school for years and was active in his community. When his parents set up the Horizon Foundation, Sandy volunteered to run it. Like Jonathan, Sandy is not paid. "I do this work for the sheer love of it," says Sandy, an upbeat, outgoing personality. "Every day that I come into the office is a new learning day. I see my job as keeping my ear to the ground, looking for good ideas, and finding the best ones to fund. Getting out in the community is my favorite part of this job."

Although the other board members do occasional site visits, the responsibility for meeting with grantseekers is primarily Sandy's. After three years of making many small grants, the board felt burdened by having to review so many proposals. "We started out by making 25 grants per cycle," says Sandy. "Last year we decided to cut in half the number of grants and increase the size of the grants. Now everyone is more relaxed, and the process is running more smoothly."

The Sandy River Charitable Foundation has an annual grants budget of $2.5 million, and its grants range in size from $20,000 to $300,000. Some family members wanted to fund small grassroots projects, too, but to do so would require hiring more staff. "We weren't ready to hire staff, but we wanted to respect those family members' wishes,"

says Nathanael Berry. "Our foundation is based in Maine, a state with fewer philanthropic dollars and many small efforts. We decided to give money to the Maine Community Foundation to help establish regional funds with local boards that, in turn, would give out small grants to community efforts."

When you first begin grantmaking, it is generally best to stick to the size of grants you announce in your guidelines. Occasionally, however, you may come across a project that you want to fund on a larger scale. In those instances, many family foundations prefer to bend their rules rather than miss the chance of funding a promising program that can further their mission.

Short- vs. Long-Term Grants: Which Is Appropriate?
Another ongoing debate among grantmakers is the appropriate length of a

---

fig. 4

Why Some Grantmakers Prefer Multiyear/Short-Term Grants

WHY SOME GRANTMAKERS PREFER MULTIYEAR GRANTS

- Gives new projects adequate time to get up and running;

- Recognizes that complicated projects need more time to develop;

- Eases grantmakers' workload by reducing the number of proposals they have to review for each cycle;

- Allows the foundation to build a portfolio of grantees aimed at fulfilling its mission;

- Gives grantseekers a break from writing yet another proposal; and

- Allows grantees to make important organizational decisions for more than a year at a time.

WHY SOME GRANTMAKERS PREFER SHORT-TERM GRANTS

- They don't want to commit money to a project before they know how it is progressing.

- If they tie up too much money in multiyear grants, they may not have money to invest in new proposals that interest them or to meet changing or emergency community needs.

- They worry that multiyear grants breed dependency.

grant. One-year grants are still the most common, but an increasing number of funders are giving out multiyear grants. Again, one is not better than the other. What matters is that the length of the grant fits the goals of the project.

All grantmakers want their grants to succeed, but oftentimes they withdraw funding before the programs have had a chance to take hold. One year is enough time to start a program but usually it is not enough time to stabilize it. Today, multiyear grants are typically given for three years, but there is nothing magical about that number. Three years may be a reasonable time for many new programs, but a very ambitious program may need more sustained support before it is stabilized.

In the early years of the Marshall Fund, Maxine and Jonathan Marshall shied away from giving multiyear grants. Over the years, however, they gained confidence in their ability to monitor multiyear grants with the same vigilance that they gave to one-year grants. "We give out the money in 6-month installments," says Maxine. "That way we can keep tabs on how the organizations are doing and whether they've run into any problems. We also require grantees to submit written progress reports every 12 months to see whether the organizations have run into any problems. Some foundations also make interim

visits to the organization but our system has worked well for us."

TIP ➤ In your first year of grantmaking, it is probably best to limit your grants to 1 year. Once you have a better understanding of the field and feel more at home with the grantmaking routine, you may consider giving multiyear grants.

TIP ➤ Regional Associations of Grantmakers (RAGs) have begun to publish common grant application forms that grantmakers can use. The forms are easy for grantmakers to adapt to their uses, and make applying far easier for grantseekers. A list of RAGs can be found at www.rag.org.

---

fig. 5 — What Grantmakers Commonly Require Grantseekers to Include in Applications

- One-page cover letter, including a brief description of the project, its cost, specific amount requested in the proposal, names of other foundations applied to, and name of a contact person;

- Proposal narrative with an executive summary, need statement, project description (including evaluation, project budget, fact sheet for applicant, conclusion);

- Appendix;

- Copy of most recent tax-exemption letter indicating 501(c)(3) status;

- Current list of board members and their affiliations;

- Current list of staff and their qualifications to lead and manage project; and

- Supplementary materials (annual reports, videos, brochures, or published articles). If you do not want to receive these materials, say so.

TIP ➤ Make life easier for your board members by requiring grantseekers to submit proposals in a standardized format. State your requirements regarding paper size, spacing, use of bulleted items, and placement of page numbers. In reading through proposals, trustees often want to pull out some pages for reference later. For that reason, it's better to have applicants secure proposals with elastic bands or sturdy paper clips rather than putting them in binders or folders.

fig.
6

Example of a Grant Application Form

The Marshall Fund of Arizona offers these guidelines to grant applicants:

APPLYING FOR A GRANT
Preliminary requests should be made in a one- or two-page letter. The letter should describe the mission and vision of the organization, the intended project, why it is needed and how it will be implemented. The initial request should be kept short and to the point.

In addition, a budget for the specific grant should be submitted as well as a budget for the organization, a copy of the IRS 501(c)(3) letter, a list of the board of directors, and a letter from the board chair stating board approval of the request.

If the proposed meets the Marshall Fund's guidelines and interests, the applicant will be asked to provide further detailed information for review and consideration by the board of directors. Final approval rests with the board of directors.

GUIDELINES
Grants will be made only to tax-exempt organizations that qualify under Section 501(c)(3) of the Internal Revenue Code. Grants will be made primarily to support new and innovative programs.

Grant requests must include short- and long-term goals and defined measurable outcomes. Grants that indicate collaboration and coordination with other organizations will be looked upon favorably.

fig.
7

Selecting a Proposal Application Form

You want to make the application process as smooth and simple as possible for your board and for your grantseekers. To weed out proposals that are off the mark, many family foundations request a letter of inquiry (LOI) before inviting a full proposal. An LOI is a one-to-two page summary of the grantseekers' project. While they are useful in screening proposals, they can also work against applicants who are not skillful writers by denying them the chance to fully explain their programs.

Before spending hours developing your own application form, review the many common application forms already in use. The National Network of Grantmakers in San Diego publishes one, as do many Regional Associations of Grantmakers groups. Common application forms vary from one organization to another, so you will want to look at several before selecting the one you like best. In the end, you may still prefer to develop your own, either because you have

particular funding interests or because you believe you can improve on available designs.

In selecting an application form, consider these questions:
- How can we make this form simpler for us and for grantseekers?

- Will this application form bring us the best possible proposals? If not, how can we change it?

- What else can we do to make the application process easier for us and for prospective grantees?

TIP➣ **Be sure to tell grantseekers whether you prefer that they contact you by telephone or by letter. If you do not want telephone inquiries, say so.**

Supporting General Operating Expenses

The trend in grantmaking over the past decade is for foundations to give grants for projects rather than for general operating expenses. Currently, fewer than 14 percent of grants are given for general expenses. The question for grantmakers is not whether to fund an organization's project or its operations. The more important questions to ask are: What do we want to achieve by funding this organization? And can we be more helpful by funding programs or by strengthening the organization?

The French American Charitable Trust in San Francisco is one of a handful of family foundations that gives grants primarily for general operating expenses. Other foundations are taking different steps to ensure that the programs they support will flourish. A new foundation in California, for example, routinely tacks on an extra percentage to program grants for operating expenses. The founder explains: "After visiting organizations last year and seeing what a hard time they were having paying their bills, I asked myself, 'How can we expect programs to succeed when the organizations running them aren't financially stable?' My husband and I decided that if we liked a program well enough to fund it, we should support the organization, too. Now we look at each program grant with the organizational infrastructure in mind, and we routinely add 10 to 25

percent for general operating expenses. We get to know the organizations before we fund them, and we trust them to be the best judges of how to spend the money."

Other foundations recognize nonprofit organizations' needs for general operating funds, but they worry that unrestricted grants will create dependency. These foundations prefer to fund line items in the organization's budget.

Said one trustee, "We look for something specific we can fund that will strengthen the programs we invest in. Last year, we funded a staff position for one program and, in another case, we paid for computer training. This year, we're funding an accountant to spend 6 months helping an organization set up a more professional financial system. We want to help the organizations, but we also want to know where our money is going."

---

fig. 8

Why (Most) Grantmakers Favor Project/ General Support Grants

WHY (MOST) GRANTMAKERS FAVOR PROJECT GRANTS

- Projects capture their interest.

- The connection between projects and the foundation's mission is clear.

- Project grants are easier to evaluate than general support grants.

- Grantmakers can point with pride to successful projects.

WHY (SOME) GRANTMAKERS FAVOR GENERAL SUPPORT GRANTS

- Help organizations doing good work achieve financial stability.

- Ensure that the programs they fund can continue to operate.

- Allow grantseekers to be forthright in asking foundations for what they really need rather than for projects they think foundations will fund.

- Allow grantseekers to concentrate on the daily business of running their organizations instead of taking time to create new programs repeatedly in order to get funding.

- Respect grantees' judgment to use the money wisely.

To help grantmakers think strategically about grantmaking, Stephanie Clohesy, a consultant in Cedar Falls, Iowa, developed a chart, A Spectrum of Philanthropic Options: A Situational Approach for Choosing the Right Grantmaking Tool for the Issue or Need. "The biggest challenge for beginners," says Clohesy, "is to get in touch with who and where they are at this moment in time. The chart helps them identify which options best suit their board as well as the needs of the community or the potential grantee." Clohesy identifies five grantmaking strategies:

1. **CHARITY:** provides immediate, altruistic assistance to someone in need
   Examples: disaster relief, soup kitchens and food banks
   Relationship: usually given to an organization serving immediate human needs
   Timeframe: usually short term

2. **SYSTEMS OF SERVICE:** develops a system or network of services that comprehensively addresses continuous or repetitive needs shared by many people
   Examples: a regional network of food banks, a health-care delivery system, a program for linking together organizations
   Relationship: grantee links individual service providers that meet targeted need
   Timeframe: usually multiple years but for a finite project

3. **EMPOWERMENT:** delivers needed services while positively changing the capacity of a person or group of people
   Examples: youth recreation services aimed at leadership, civic, or personal development; economic development programs with a leadership development component
   Relationship: grantee provides service or links multiple organizations to provide it
   Timeframe: usually multiple years

4. **ADVOCACY/SOCIAL CHANGE:** enables groups of people to work together to change systems and/or public policies (sometimes in connection with providing services, education, information, and empowerment)
   Examples: National Network of Neighborhood Associations, National Council of La Raza, Environmental Defense Fund
   Relationship: usually the funder or group of funders and coalitions or associations of organizations or some other form of constituent affiliates
   Timeframe: usually 3 to 5 years for a finite project model

5. **MARKET MODELS:** (Venture Philanthropy and Social Entrepreneurship); strategic assistance comprised of grants and/or investments for entrepreneurial endeavors that often bridge nonprofit and for-profit structures. This approach combines innovative solutions with sustainability plans that go beyond a traditional charitable/philanthropic base of support (earned or enterprise income)
   Examples: www.ShopforChange.com, Entrepreneurs Foundation, Women's Technology Center
   Relationship: usually an intensive, hands-on relationship in which funders and social entrepreneurs function as partners. Funders provide other support beyond financial capital
   Timeframe: usually multiple years and through multiple stages: seed support, startup, operationalizing, mezzanine-level (second stage of development to stabilization), and long-term sustainability

Clohesy encourages new grantmakers to ask themselves: Which of these options reflect your beliefs and values? What is realistic given your personalities, backgrounds, and time schedules? How much time are you willing to invest in learning about the issues and working with the organizations? Is your preference to address immediate needs or to foster social change?

Because of the extensive media coverage of high-tech entrepreneurs, many new grantmakers are attracted to the venture philanthropy model. Clohesy cautions them to think carefully before jumping into it. "Venture philanthropy may be the right choice for a foundation that has a staff or volunteer services to form a partnership with grantees," says Clohesy, "but it is too intensive a starting place for most beginners."

The Spectrum of Options can also be used as an assessment tool at the end of your first year of grantmaking. "This is the time to step back and look at what you've done," says Clohesy. "Given what you've learned, where do you want to go next?" The most effective grantmakers employ a variety of grantmaking options. In any one funding cycle, they may make some grants to meet immediate needs, others to foster empowerment, and still others to promote social change. You will probably start off favoring one or two strategies, but your emphasis is likely to shift over time as new trustees join the board bringing new knowledge and know-how, and in response to changing social and economic conditions.

Publicizing Your Guidelines

In the interest of promoting accessibility and accountability to the public, foundations are encouraged to publicize their guidelines. Printed guidelines do not have to be fancy or cost much money. You can type them on a single sheet of paper or print a simple brochure on your computer.

More and more family foundations prefer to post their guidelines on their websites. That way they can easily update the information without having to spend time and money reprinting and mailing guidelines. The websites of The Foundation Center (www.fdncenter.org) and the Association of Small Foundations(www.smallfoundations.org) provide links to the websites of private foundations. If you do not want to have your own website or if you want to wait awhile before creating one, contact The Foundation Center or the Association of Small Foundations to find out how you can post your guidelines on their websites.

Not all family foundations choose to publicize their guidelines. For personal reasons, some prefer to do their grantmaking quietly. They may live in small towns and want to avoid calling attention to themselves. Or they may keep a low profile to prevent their grantmaking activities from affecting relationships with friends and neighbors. Others worry that publicizing guidelines will invite more applicants than they can respond to or ever hope to fund.

In the past, choosing not to publicize guidelines may have afforded foundations privacy. Today, trustees no longer have that luxury; grantseekers can easily obtain information about foundations on the Internet. Given that reality, foundations have even more incentive to publicize their guidelines. By defining who you fund, you actually have more control over who contacts you than foundations that don't. Grantmakers who develop clear and specific guidelines report an increase in high-quality proposals within their funding interests and a decrease of inquiries outside their funding interests.

> **GOOD ADVICE** Understand the legal limits of what you can do. Let your imagination fly. Put yourself in the other person's shoes.
>
> NATHANAEL BERRY OF
> THE SANDY RIVER CHARITABLE FOUNDATION

Getting Ready for Grantmaking

In addition to tasks related to your grant guidelines, a second set of tasks relates to the mechanism of processing grant applications, namely:

- Setting funding cycles;
- Screening proposals;
- Arranging site visits; and
- Preparing the board docket.

Determining the Grants Formula

The formula you devise to divide your grantmaking budget depends on family interests and relationships as much as on your grantmaking strategies. Typically, foundations divide the budget by program areas, by communities where board members live, or by geographic regions.

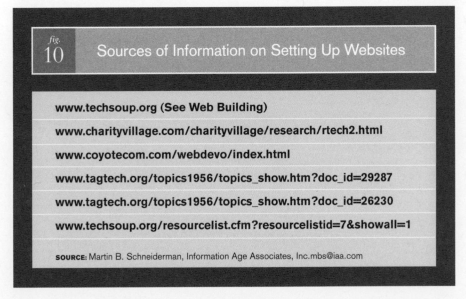

fig. 10 Sources of Information on Setting Up Websites

www.techsoup.org (See Web Building)

www.charityvillage.com/charityvillage/research/rtech2.html

www.coyotecom.com/webdevo/index.html

www.tagtech.org/topics1956/topics_show.htm?doc_id=29287

www.tagtech.org/topics1956/topics_show.htm?doc_id=26230

www.techsoup.org/resourcelist.cfm?resourcelistid=7&showall=1

SOURCE: Martin B. Schneiderman, Information Age Associates, Inc.mbs@iaa.com

fig. 11   Grantmakers Have Many Methods of Support

Grantmaking commonly — but not always — supports a specific project. A grantseeker submits a proposal to the foundation to fund a specific project and, if approved by the board, the foundation writes a check to the organization. While this is the most common kind of grant, it is only one of many types of support foundations can offer to grantees.

You may discover that circumstances and conditions dictate different responses. A standard project grant may be the best way to fund an innovative or proven program, but not the best way to help a fledgling organization or one under pressure to raise money quickly. The following types of support can be used effectively by family foundations of all sizes:

- **Project support:** to fund the specific project and outcome outlined in the applicant's proposal and approved by your board.

- **Seed money:** to launch a new organization or new program. The money can be used for planning or for staffing and operations.

- **Emergency fund:** to allow an organization to respond to immediate community needs or to see an organization through a crisis.

- **Restricted funds:** to limit use to purposes specified by grantor, such as a particular population or region.

- **General operating support:** to allow grantees to use grants according to their discretion, whether for administration, fundraising, overhead, or stabilizing the organization. (See sidebar)

- **Capital grants:** to help grantees finance the construction or renovation of a building and to purchase land, equipment, or a facility.

- **Endowments:** to help grantees gain financial stability by establishing or increasing the organization's endowment. Grantees cannot touch the principal but can use the income generated by the endowment for general operating expenses.

- **Research:** to further research projects conducted by universities, medical institutions, and think tanks.

- **Matching/challenge grants:** to help or encourage an organization to raise money by pledging to match a fixed amount raised from other sources. Grantors may match the money raised dollar for dollar or by a specified ratio

- **Collaborative grants:** to join with like-minded funders to support large or complex projects that no one funder can undertake single-handedly.

- **Impact grants:** a large, one-time gift, typically to launch a fundraising or endowment campaign.

- **Scholarships/awards:** to support or honor outstanding individuals who excel in areas supported by the foundation. (The IRS imposes strict regulations on grants given to individuals, including obtaining approval for the grants before they are distributed. Many foundations prefer to give the grants to the institutions or nonprofit organizations for the benefit of particular individuals.)

- **Program related investments (PRIs):** to give nonprofit organizations access to capital by providing low-interest loans, loan guarantees, or equity investments for projects such as community revitalization, low-income housing, and micro enterprise development. PRIs are not outright grants but loans the organizations are expected to repay by a specified period.

- **Technical assistance:** to allow grantees to hire consultants/trainers to strengthen the organization's management, fundraising, board development, or leadership. Grantors may also give grants directly to nonprofit management organizations to provide free trainings to current or past grantees.

fig.
12

Devising a Grants Formula

You enjoy the widest latitude in deciding how to allocate your grant funds. You need only ensure that the grants conform to legal requirements.

You can direct your entire grant fund to one nonprofit organization, to several nonprofit organizations within the same field of interest (such as education or the environment), or you can aim at targets of opportunity as they arise. You're the boss when it comes to deciding on a grants formula. This characteristic is one of the great strengths of the private (family) foundation, and one of the central appeals that the private foundation holds for founders.

Consider these two approaches. On founder is determined that grants will support education of youngsters from low-income backgrounds what are interested in science. This founder might adopt at the outset a formula that allocates grants as follows:

- **10 percent** to a public education campaign about opportunities in science;

- **60 percent** to build a scholarship endowment in a local public high school; and

- **30 percent** to build a scholarship endowment at the founder's alma mater.

Another founder also has strong ideas about the grantmaking strategy (to support new American music composition), but as startup day approaches, other members of the family begin to speak up. A couple of the founder's siblings and children advocate for environmental grants and the grandchildren want money to support Native American causes. Then, after much reflection, the founder's spouse weighs in with a proposal to support a local arts program.

This founder's problem is that family pressure is accompanied by very strong and well-presented reasoning. The family debates the familiar trade-off: a few large, focused grants accomplish more (it is argued) than do several smaller, more scattered grants. But, the point is made that foundations can trigger more support, generate activity, and effect change with small grants as well as large one. The founder finally settles on this formula:

- **50 percent** to support new American music composition, with grantees largely selected by the founder;

- **20 percent** to support environmental activities, with recommendations for grantees made by family members interested in that field;

- **20 percent** to support Native American causes, with recommendations for grantees made by family members interested in those causes; and

- **10 percent** for discretionary grants to be made by the founder with suggestions from family members.

GOOD ADVICE ≻ No one formula for dividing the grants budget is better than another. What's important is that the one you choose suits your family. Some families function best with strict rules for dividing the grants budget; others prefer a more flexible policy. You know your family best — and you will get to know them even better by working together. If you generally get along well and know how to negotiate compromises, you may do well with a looser approach to dividing the budget. If, however, your family members tend to be competitive or concerned that one person or branch is getting more than the other, you will have to take extra care to devise a formula that is acceptable to everyone. Often arguments over how to divide the budget are not so much disagreements over proposals as symptoms of spoken and unspoken rivalries between individual board members, generations, or family branches.

GOALS OF THE FOUNDERS

Sam and Celia Sanders established the Sanders Family Foundation to share and continue a philanthropic legacy with their children and future generations. Sam and Celia did not intend to spend out the foundation, and indeed had named the foundation as a primary beneficiary of their estate. They did want, however, to see the results of the foundation's grantmaking in their lifetimes, and to realize the joy that came through giving with other family members.

DECIDING ON A SPENDING POLICY

The first step for determining payout was to decide on a spending policy. Sam, Celia, and the rest of the Board decided on a spending policy with an annual payout objective of 8.5 percent — significantly above the required 5 percent minimum payout rate. The foundation's investment advisors explained to the Sanders that this payout rate, combined with the costs of inflation and the administrative costs required to run the foundation, would almost certainly erode the real value of the foundation's initial endowment over time. The Sanders, however, were eager to accomplish as much as possible with the funds they had allocated, and wanted to see the results of their philanthropy in their lifetimes. They also realized that the long-term value of the endowment would be significantly increased by the testamentary gifts they had planned.

DETERMINING PAYOUT

The Sanders Foundation's investment assets at the start of the most recent year were valued at $19.5 million. At the beginning of the year, the board estimated an average value for the foundation of $20 million throughout the year, factoring in their expectations of a gradual appreciation of the assets.* Thus, with an annual spending policy of 8.5 percent, they projected a total payout for the year of $1.7 million ($20 million x 8.5 percent).

The foundation board meets quarterly to decide on grants, and awards approximately one-fourth of the annual grant payout at each meeting. During each of the first three quarters of the year they awarded grants totaling $1.275 million ($425,000 per quarter for three quarters). This left them with approximately $425,000 to distribute at the final meeting of the year, give or take any unexpected gains or losses in the average value of the endowment throughout the year.

CARRYOVER CREATES FLEXIBILITY FOR FUTURE YEARS

Because their spending policy was well above the 5 percent minimum requirement, the Sanders did not have to be concerned with the exact amount of the fourth quarter payment. Indeed, because they were well over the required payment (see box), the Foundation was able to "carry over" approximately $735,000 (the amount that their

payout exceeded the required amount) toward payout over any or all of the next five years. Although they did not intend for their spending policy to change in the coming years, Sam and Celia were happy to know that due to the fact that they had exceeded the required payout for several years running, they could easily afford to scale back grantmaking for a year or two if they decided they needed to review the direction or some other aspect of the foundation's future.

DETERMINING THE MINIMUM REQUIRED PAYOUT
for the Sanders Foundation

ITEM	AMOUNT	EXPLANATION
Foundation Assets	$20,000,000	12-month average fair market value of foundation's assets*
Cash Reserve	– $ 300,000	Law allows up to 1.5 percent of endowment value to be "held for charitable purposes"
	$19,700,000	
		Law requires a minimum 5 percent payout
Payout rate	X .05	
	$ 985,000	This indicates that the foundation has qualified to reduce its tax on investment income from 2% to 1% for year (see Additional Resources)
Excise Tax Credit	– $ 20,000	
		Payout may be met through grants, administrativeexpenses, and other qualified distributions
Minimum Payout Requirement	$965,000	

---

*While there is no specified formula for how to calculate required payout, a monthly average is generally accepted as one of the most straightforward and reasonable approaches. To get the average fair market value, add up the value of the endowment on the last day of each month, and divide by 12.

ADDITIONAL RESOURCES

For technical issues related to payout, please consult your advisor or accountant. For additional resources on calculating payout, please see:

- "How to Calculate Your Payout," National Network of Grantmakers
  http://www.nng.org/html/ourprograms/campaign/calculate_table.htm

- "Calculating the Required Distribution," from *Family Foundation Handbook*, Aspen Publishers, Inc., Washington, DC: 2001, Section 7.04, pages 7-30 to 7-39.

- *Family Foundations and the Law*, Council on Foundations, Washington, DC: 2002, pages 25 - 26 and 40 - 41.

Jason Born

You may divide the funds equally among all areas, designate a larger share for an area that has special interest to the family, or let the quality of the proposals dictate the size of the grants.

Setting Funding Cycles

Funding cycles vary widely among family foundations. They may give out grants annually, biannually, quarterly, or all year round. The cycle you choose will depend on board members' schedules and how much effort is required to bring them together. If, for example, your family is spread across the country or if the younger generation has full-time careers and young children, you may arrange to meet only once a year and hold conference calls in between. Whatever funding schedule you choose, you will want to map out a timetable for the entire grantmaking process far in advance to alert board members to important dates. And to be on the safe side, assume that preparing for your first funding cycle will take longer than expected.

Ferdinand and Susanna Colloredo-Mansfield set up The Alces Foundation in Massachusetts in 1999. (Alces is Latin for "Moose," Ferdinand's nickname.) The foundation is small, and Moose and Susanna could have just as easily turned the money over to a community foundation. But they wanted their three adult children living in different states to learn about philanthropy. They also

fig. 14 Timetable for Grant Cycle

DATE	TASK
_____	Letter of inquiry deadline (optional)
_____	Application deadline
_____	Acknowledge receipt of proposal with card or form letter
_____	Initial screening meeting
_____	Notify applicants of status of proposal
_____	Complete site visits
_____	Complete all other fact-finding
_____	Prepare docket
_____	Mail packets to board members
_____	Allocations meeting
_____	Notify applicants of final decisions
_____	Mail checks to grantees
_____	Receive reports from grantees (6 months or 12 months)

wanted the family to have more contact and to learn about and respect each other's interests and concerns.

Because of its small size, The Alces Foundation gives grants only to nonprofit organizations it invites to submit proposals. In the first year, the family agreed that each trustee would bring in proposals from grassroots organizations doing exciting work in their communities. When it came time to deliver the proposals, the three younger trustees had none, Moose brought in two, and Susanna had found 12 projects she wanted to fund. The board realized that

they would have to be more specific in their instructions and to design a funding schedule that fit the trustees' busy lives.

Now the board talks by phone in January and as needed until grants are awarded in May. The trustees start their research early so that they will have plenty of time to visit organizations and to determine their needs before the spring board meeting. Susanna has been a volunteer with nonprofit groups for 30 years and an advisor to foundations. She is the one who provides technical assistance to organizations from which they solicit proposals. "We seek out cutting-edge groups that are under-funded," says Susanna. "Some of them have never written a proposal before we contacted them. We give them as much help as they need to produce a good proposal, and they can always call us if they have questions. We want them to succeed, and to do so they have to know how to write proposals."

Most foundations still require grantseekers to deliver their proposals by mail. With the widespread use of the Internet, today some foundations accept application forms via e-mail. In fact, The Sandy River Charitable Foundation encourages it. "We try to be flexible," says Nathanael Berry. "We also accept information about an organization's financials that they've posted on public websites — either on their own or on sites such as www.guidestar.org." The Sandy River Charitable Foundation is willing to go a step further to accommodate grantseekers. It accepts proposals applicants have written to other foundations as long as grantseekers rewrite sections to address Sandy River's interests.

Screening Proposals

However you initiate the grantmaking process — with a letter of inquiry, solicited proposals, or unsolicited proposals — you will receive more requests than you can fund. To ensure that proposals get a fair hearing, it is recommended that at least two people — trustees or staff — read and discuss the proposals. Different perspectives on a project or issue can mean the difference between a proposal being rejected or accepted for further consideration.

Your initial screening procedure might involve these elements:

- Develop a checklist of criteria for screening proposals. The checklist can be used in the initial screening process and again in the formal review process to help board members focus their thoughts.
- After reading each proposal, put it in one of three stacks: interesting, questionable, outside guidelines.
- To learn more about the "questionable" proposals, consider calling colleagues or your local community foundation. They may have information about the organizations and programs that would help you decide whether to consider or reject the proposals.
- Decide how many proposals your board can reasonably manage in your first funding cycle. Let's say that you can fund 10 proposals. Go through stack #1 again and select the 15 strongest candidates, anticipating that at least five will not make the final cut.
- Notify applicants of the status of their proposals promptly. Nonprofit organizations put their hard work and hopes into each proposal. The sooner they hear from you, the better they can plan their fundraising efforts.

More and more family trustees are recognizing the advantages of having a mentor to guide them through their first year of grantmaking. Some are most comfortable with an informal mentor relationship: meeting or talking periodically with someone whose ideas, values, and achievements they admire. Others prefer a formal relationship, such as hiring a consultant to act as an advisor or coach. And, then there are those like Maxine and Jonathan

---

fig. 15

Sample Postcard or Form Letter

To those organizations whose proposals you will consider: "Thank you for sending us your proposal for _____. We are interested in it and have placed it on our docket for review by the board on _____. We will contact you if we need additional information _____ or to arrange a site visit."

To organizations you have screened out: "Thank you for sending your proposal. Because it does not fall within our guidelines or current funding priorities, we regret that we cannot consider your proposal. We wish you luck in finding other funding."

fig.
16

Becoming a Knowledgeable Grantmaker

As a grantmaker, you want your grants to have the maximum impact on the communities you target. One way to make that happen is to become an expert on your program areas and the organizations that share your goals. A list of resources for doing research on program areas was presented at the beginning of this chapter. Here are additional suggestions:

1. Attend professional workshops and conferences.

2. Join your local Regional Association of Grantmakers. (For a listing of regional associations, go to www.rag.org.)

3. Join an affinity group of colleagues working in the same program area. (For a listing of affinity groups, go to *www.cof.org*. Click "Links and Networking.")

4. Volunteer to serve on professional committees and panels.

5. Start a library of professional books and publications in your foundation office. Request The National Center for Family Philanthropy's catalog of publications prepared for family foundations. Subscribe to professional journals such as *Foundation News & Commentary* (a publication of the Council on Foundations) and *The Chronicle of Philanthropy.*

6. Make use of the Internet. Subscribe to The Foundation Center's free *Philanthropy News Digest*, a weekly update of news about philanthropy, www.fdncenter.org. (The Foundation Center, 79 Fifth Avenue, New York, NY 10003 Tel: (212) 620-4230 Fax: (212) 691-1828.)

7. Invite academics, city leaders, and community activists to brief your board on topics bearing on your mission.

8. Arrange bus tours for your whole board to visit neighborhoods where you fund or consider funding organizations.

9. Talk with staff and clients of nonprofit organizations. They are among the best sources of information about what the community needs.

Jonathan Frieman had 17 years of volunteer experience behind him when he and his brothers started their foundation, JoMiJo. He had done legal work for homeless advocacy groups and sat on boards of nonprofit organizations. What he lacked was hands-on grantmaking experience. Jonathan set out to educate himself. He turned to local family foundations for guidance on the nuts and bolts of grantmaking. Then, for help in thinking about program areas, he consulted with More than Money, an organization located in Massachusetts that promotes philanthropy and shares his views on working for social change.

To broaden his grantmaking experience, Jonathan joined Threshold, a project of the Tides Foundation in San Francisco. An invitation-only group, Threshold brings together wealthy individuals to fund projects and sharpen their grantmaking skills. Jonathan also volunteered with Catalog for Giving, a group that published an annual guide to charitable giving. Serving on the committee researching organizations for teens — one of JoMiJo's funding areas — Jonathan learned about exciting projects around the country. Of his efforts to educate himself, Jonathan says, "I have three professional degrees. Now philanthropy is my fourth."

fig.
17

Possible Criteria for Judging Applicants

- The purpose of the proposal and its compatibility with the foundation's mission;

- The mission and history of the applicant;

- The community needs served;

- The amount of the grant request and what share other grantmakers are funding;

- Plans to sustain the effort in the future; and

- Desired outcomes and how they will be measured.

fig.
18

Why Grantmakers Make Site Visits

GRANTMAKERS MAKE SITE VISITS TO:

- Get to know the staff and the work of the organization firsthand;

- See the neighborhood in which the organization is located;

- Observe programs in action;

- Speak with clients served by the organization;

- Develop a better understanding of how they can help the organization;

- Broaden their understanding of issues in their program areas;

- Shape their thinking about future grants;

- Judge whether the proposal accurately represents the organization; (Proposals can be deceiving. Those written by professional grantwriters can make a so-so organization shine. Conversely, a less artfully written proposal can disguise the merits of an excellent program.)

- Build relationships with grantseekers; and

- Be reminded of the importance of the work they do.

Marshall who organized a group of their peers. "When we started out," says Maxine, "we rounded up a group of small funders in our area. For the next two years, we met informally every two months to talk over issues and share ideas. It was an invaluable experience for all of us."

TIP ➤ If your foundation prefers not to hire paid staff, consider bringing in interns to help you manage the grant process. Graduate students working toward degrees in your program areas may welcome the opportunity to work for a foundation. They can be excellent resources, alerting you to new research findings and to academics doing important work. You may also want to develop relationships with knowledgeable people in your area who can advise you on proposals and developments in the field.

Arranging Site Visits

Once you have completed the screening process, you may want to make appointments to visit as many applicants as you can. Although you can learn a lot about an organization from reading the proposal, having phone conversations with staff, and doing background research, most grantmakers agree that there is no substitute for a site visit. (See Sample Policies and Forms, p. 239, for a site visit report.)

As fact-finding missions, however, site visits have limitations. Grantseekers regard site visits as they do written proposals: opportunities to sell their program. Their job is to present their organization in the best light and to withhold information that would damage their prospects of getting the grant. That approach, says Jonathan Frieman, can be self-defeating. He encourages applicants to be honest with him. He tries to win the trust of grantseekers with his directness. "I tell them not to tell me what they think I want to hear. I can't help them unless I know what their situation really is and what they really need."

The eagerness of grantseekers to make a good impression may tempt you to make encouraging comments about their prospects. Please restrain those impulses. Few things are worse than raising grantseekers' hopes and then disappointing them. To avoid any confusion about the purpose of your visit, remind grantseekers that you represent your board and that you are there to learn more about their organization.

It is usually best for two board members to do the site visit together. That way you can compare impressions of the organization. You may also want to invite your mentor or a consultant to go along with

you on your first few visits. There is nothing wrong with admitting to the applicant that you are new at grantmaking and just learning to ask the right questions. If anything, grantseekers will probably be more forthcoming with you.

Because family members today live in different parts of the country, most foundations ask family members to conduct site visits in their home communities. Some, however, set aside a small percentage of their grant budget for travel expenses so that a few family members can visit organizations together. These foundations regard expenses associated with site visits as the cost of doing business and as part of their board's education.

After more than a decade of doing site visits, Leslie Dorman is more convinced than ever that they are indispensable to good grantmaking. "You can't make grants from your desk," she says. "Grantmaking becomes an art when you get the feeling for the people running the organizations and receiving the services." To relax the staff and to learn more about them, she starts the interview by getting them to talk about themselves. "I ask them how long they've been with the organization and what they enjoy about their work. I want them to know that I'm interested in them, too, not just in the organization. If the staff feel comfortable with you, they will talk more openly." For Leslie, site visits are a reminder of why she has worked in this field for more than 25 years. "Problems today are so huge that I sometimes feel as if nothing can change. Then I go on a site visit and meet wonderful people doing important work, and I leave feeling hopeful again."

Ensuring a Fair Hearing

There are likely to be times when the interests of individual family members fall outside the stated guidelines of the foundation. While your foundation may make some accommodation for that (see Discretionary Grants Programs, p. 185), other families find that focusing on their shared mission is the best way to accomplish that mission and fulfill their public trust.

Preparing the Board Docket

If your foundation does not have a designated staff person — program officer or grants administrator — consider appointing a committee of board members to share the work of preparing the docket. If board members are geographically dispersed, it may be best for one person to assume responsibility for the docket.

To give members sufficient time to study the proposals, packets should be mailed 2 to 4 weeks before the board meeting. The packet includes the full proposal, requested supplementary materials, and a report to the board. The report is a summary of the proposals' strengths and weaknesses plus any additional relevant information board members have gathered from visiting grantees and conferring with other knowledgeable sources.

Sandy Buck recalled the first time he prepared the docket for the Horizon Foundation. "It was so thick that board members were practically crying about the amount of reading required. We looked around for short cuts." Because Sandy makes most of the site visits for the foundation, a colleague suggested that he write a two- or three-paragraph summary of each proposal for the board, including recommendations for the size of grants. "The summaries represent my best judgments," says Sandy, "but that doesn't mean that everyone accepts them. Rather, they give the others something to bounce off of and keep the discussion moving. This approach works well for us, and my family appreciates that it requires less of their time and focuses their attention on the most pertinent information."

Your board must decide whether to award grants on the basis of majority vote or consensus. A common misconception is that consensus requires 100 percent agreement. If that were the case, boards would rarely, if ever, reach consensus. Consensus is reached when all the board members can accept the decision, even if it isn't perfect. Another misconception is that voting by consensus works only when board members are like-minded. In fact, many boards that have diverse political and religious views use it successfully. What is required is a reasonable degree of flexibility: board members who judge proposals on their merit and who have the willingness to let go of an established position when it is out of step with the others.

Working together as grantmakers allows family members to get to know one another in a different realm. You may discover new sides to family members' personalities and a depth of feeling about issues or particular proposals that you never imagined. Sometimes, you may also be surprised by the vehemence with which a family member can fight for a proposal about which others feel lukewarm. When these situations arise, you will be relieved to have clear grantmaking guidelines to fall back on. Sometimes, in these instances, discretionary funds can defuse disagreements by allowing family members to use their funds to support organizations they like but which haven't won over the whole board.

Saying "Yes" and Saying "No"

Foundations can reduce the gamble of investing in riskier organizations by developing grant agreements with grantees. In the agreement, you spell out the expectations for both the grantor and the grantee. You also include a schedule of payments that you may or may not wish to link to evaluations of the grantee's progress. Then, if at any time the grantee is not living up to the agreement, you can discontinue payments.

One of the more difficult tasks for the grantmaker is having to say "no" to hopeful grantseekers. In fact, some new grantmakers find it so hard to say no that they procrastinate in notifying applicants. And, when they finally do contact them, they try to soften the blow with ambiguous language. More often than not, attempts to be kind will only mislead and frustrate the people you tried to protect.

The way to be most helpful to grantseekers is to talk straight to them. Grantseekers want answers to three questions: Do they still have a chance to get funding? Should they resubmit their proposal for the next funding cycle? How can they improve their proposal?

If grantseekers have no chance of getting a grant from your foundation, give them a clear "no." With volunteer management, it can be difficult to get back to everyone in detail. For those who can, the effort can be educational and satisfying for both funder and grantseeker.

"I worked as a fundraiser," says Sandy Buck of the Horizon Foundation, "and I remember how angry I felt when foundations sent me a two-line boilerplate rejection letter. That's why I make a point of giving applicants an explanation of why we rejected them and tying it to something specific in their proposal." Jonathan Frieman of the JoMiJo Foundation prefers to contact applicants by phone to explain why the foundation did not fund their proposals. If the proposal shows promise, he will work with the applicants to strengthen their request.

The Sandy River Charitable Foundation considers each grantee on a case-by-case basis. "Our board has spent a lot of time discussing exit strategies," says Nathanael Berry. "We want to fund organizations long enough to get them on their feet, but we don't want the grants to turn into subsistence grants." In one case, the foundation funded a full-time position for a development director for 1 year and provided an additional challenge grant amounting to half again the funded salary. In the second year, it made a smaller grant to pay half of the development director's salary. And, in the third year, it renewed the challenge grant only.

Evaluating Outcomes

After all the hard work that you have put into the funding process, you want to know what the organizations you funded accomplished. Evaluations do not have to be costly or time consuming. What you want to know is how the programs fared and whether your grantmaking process contributed to their success or failure.

Typically, grantmakers evaluate grantees after one year. Oftentimes, however, that is not sufficient time to judge a program's performance. Programs that collapse and close their doors are obvious failures. Others fall prey to the usual organizational demons: poor leadership or management, undercapitalization, and the unexpected — illnesses, natural disasters, and changing economic and political conditions. But, in many other cases, it simply isn't possible to assess accurately after one year whether a program succeeded or failed. This is especially true of programs designed to affect behavioral changes. Occasionally, participants may show dramatic changes after one year, but more often the changes are subtle or don't show up for years.

This does not mean that you should stop requesting 1-year reports. Organizations can always benefit from periodically assessing their policies and goals. But foundations have to have reasonable expectations for programs that address difficult problems and what they can

Grants Agreements

fig.
19

Typically, grantmakers think of evaluation as something done after the grant has been made. In fact, it is more useful to ask yourself questions before you award the grant. What do we hope to achieve with this grant? How will we recognize the organization's progress? What will success look like? Clarifying expectations allows you and your grantees to stay focused on the goals. It also can avoid misunderstandings and disappointments down the road.

Large foundations have routinely used grants agreements to spell out their expectations of grantees. Now, more and more small and mid-size foundations are also discovering their value. In addition to outlining the program expectations, grants agreements can spell out legal requirements, preferences regarding publicity, and other issues that protect the foundation and ensure common understanding. They take time to write, but the time is well spent.

Write a letter to each grantee outlining the requirements of the grant. The requirements repeat the objectives the grantee enumerated in the proposal. Tell grantees that you would like them to address each of the objectives in their final report to you. (If the grant is large, you may request a brief interim report.) Encourage the grantees to contact you quickly if they have questions or want to clarify the objectives you have listed.

The original objectives often have to be modified once a project gets underway. However, if grantees make any significant changes, tell them that you expect them to notify you. Finally, remind grantees that the purpose of the report is to allow you to learn from them. The insights they share help you to sharpen your thinking about grantmaking. (See Sample Policies and Forms, p.235, for an example of a grants agreement forms.)

Ways to evaluate grantees' performance:
- Send questionnaire to grantees at the end of six months and/or one year;
- Ask the grantees to provide written self-evaluations;
- Have staff or trustees check in with grantees periodically by phone or in person;
- Hire a consultant to talk with grantees;
- Meet with other funders in your area who have funded the same groups; and
- Host a meeting with grantees to evaluate the application process.

TIP ➤ **Be sure that your reporting requirements are commensurate with the size of your grants. Do you have the same reporting requirements for all grantees, regardless of how much money they received? Are you asking grantees who receive small grants to spend more time writing reports than the value of the grant they received?**

Some people question the value of asking grantees to evaluate their performance. They argue that grantees tell grantors only what they want to hear. It is true that grantees tend to be self-protective. After all, why should they be expected to say anything that would

achieve. Grantmaking is rife with uncertainties and ambiguities, and often the best that you can expect after one year is that the programs are moving in the right direction.

Some foundations hire professional evaluators to assess their grants but most foundations, especially smaller ones, don't have the money or the need to make such formal or elabo-

jeopardize their chances of getting future funding? Yet the experience of the Marshall Fund demonstrates that grantees can be disarmingly honest when they believe that the grantors are after helpful information and not looking for reasons to discontinue funding the grantees. "We send questionnaires for the 6-month and 12-month grant reports to our grantees," says Maxine Marshall, "and ask them to report the mistakes they made and what they would do differently. We've been amazed at how truthfully grantees respond to those questions. We appreciate their honesty because it helps us to rethink how we do things, too."

TIP➤ The purpose of conducting evaluations is to make use of what you learn. Be sure to set aside time to discuss your findings at a board meeting or retreat. Consider, too, convening a meeting with grantees to talk about what they learned from the experience and how they think the process could be improved. And you may want to call your local RAG to check on upcoming workshops on evaluation where you can exchange ideas with colleagues.

GOOD ADVICE➤ "The best advice I ever got about grantmaking came from Gene Wilson, formerly of the Arco Foundation and now with the Kauffman Foundation in Kansas City. He told me that we must always remember that our money is essentially worthless without the nonprofit organizations that serve the clients we want to reach. It is only through these agencies that we are able to fulfill our own goals. We must always be respectful of grantees and conduct our business in the spirit of true partnership."

LESLIE DORMAN, THE STERLING FOUNDATION

---

fig. 20 Breaking Down Barriers Between Grantmakers and Grantseekers

More family foundations are reaching out to nonprofit organizations than in the past, but grantseekers and grantmakers are still often isolated from one another. Neither knows enough about the other and when they do talk, they tend to talk only about matters related to proposals. In doing so, they miss the opportunity to exchange information about their larger body of work and experience. As a grantmaker, you can learn about the bigger issues by:

■ Visiting grantees midway through the grant. On the second visit, grant proposals are not on the line and grantees can be more relaxed and more forthcoming about their work and the challenges they face.

■ Hosting meetings or going to meetings sponsored by community groups or state associations of nonprofits where you can meet grantseekers.

■ Serving on panels on which trustees and grantseekers are seen as equals.

■ Hosting meetings with grantees to talk about program areas and to hear their ideas of how to address community needs.

Special Grantmaking Opportunities

Using Discretionary Funds

Discretionary grants are grants made at the discretion of individual trustees or other authorized individuals, without the standard review process by the whole board.

Over the past decade, a growing number of family foundations have designated a portion of their grantmaking budget for discretionary funds.

The popularity of discretionary funds stems from their versatility. They can be used to:

■ Reward family and non-family trustees for their hard work;

■ Reward staff (usually executive directors) for outstanding service, or allow them to respond to immediate needs within the foundation grant guidelines;

fig. 21

Discretionary Grants Programs

REASONS FAMILIES ESTABLISH DISCRETIONARY GRANTS PROGRAMS

Many families find that discretionary grants can be an effective way of encouraging and rewarding trustee participation. Common reasons for developing a discretionary grants policy include:

1. To encourage the ongoing participation of geographically dispersed boards.

2. To help trustees with basic ideological differences get along together, and keep their focus on the core grantmaking of the foundation.

3. To encourage trustees' interest in philanthropy and specific issue areas.

4. To recognize and encourage outside board and volunteer service.

5. To allow for quick turnaround and response to national disasters and local emergencies.

6 To train new or future trustees in the work of the foundation and the grantmaking process.

7. To bring clarity to the overall grantmaking of the foundation, by requiring that all other (non-discretionary) grants must fit strictly within the program areas of the foundation.

REASONS FAMILIES DO NOT ALLOW DISCRETIONARY GRANTS

The majority of family foundations do not use discretionary grants. Some of the most common reasons they give for not allowing discretionary grants include:

1. Family foundations are supposed to be about family — by allowing individuals to make their own grants, you take the family out of the decision.

2. Family foundation grantmaking is not intended to be about one's personal prerogative.

3. The full board is legally required to approve all grants, and allowing discretionary grants — without developing a formal review and approval system — may increase the likelihood of self-dealing or conflict of interest in grants (or at the very least, it may increase the perception of this).

4. Ensuring that discretionary grants are made to eligible grantees and filling out the necessary paper work for a large number of small grants takes significant time and effort.

5. Discretionary grants that are outside of standard guidelines can send mixed messages to grantees and potential grantees, particularly where grants lists are included in the annual report and/or other printed materials.

6. Discretionary grants that do not support the goals and purpose of the foundation make it more difficult for the foundation to be effective in reaching its stated long-term goals.

7. Some family members may feel that discretionary grants are a substitute for a personal responsibility to give and families may not want to encourage this attitude.

8. Once the practice of discretionary grants is started, it can be difficult to keep it from escalating, with a growing percentage being allocated to discretionary grants each year. This is especially true if the number of trustees is increasing as the generations participating in the foundation increase.

SOURCE: Jason Born, "Discretionary Grants: Encouraging Participation … or Dividing Families?" *Passages*. Washington, DC: National Center for Family Philanthropy, 2001.

- Stimulate interest in giving among family members who lack enthusiasm for the foundation's program areas;
- Encourage family members' participation in their own communities;
- Motivate and train young family members to participate in philanthropy;
- Diffuse tension stemming from disagreements over grants;
- Allow board members who do not have much personal wealth to give more generously than they could manage on their own;
- Discourage pressure to use the grant budget for pet projects;
- Include family members in the family's philanthropy who are not serving on the board (e.g., by dividing discretionary funds among family branches to donate as a family unit); and
- Recognize the volunteer services of board members by making small grants to nonprofit organizations where they serve.

Foundations vary widely in how they use discretionary funds. Some allow family members to donate funds to any bona fide nonprofit organization of their liking. Others stipulate that the funds be given only to organizations that fall within their guidelines.

Some family foundations steer clear of discretionary funds, which they regard as potentially troublesome. They believe that:
- Discretionary grants undermine the purpose of the foundation as a family endeavor based on shared values and aims;

fig. 22 A Foundation Cannot Pay a Personal Gift Pledge

Your foundation cannot pay a personal charitable pledge of a family member, trustee, or other "disqualified person," which includes certain relatives and staff members. For a private foundation to use foundation assets to satisfy the personal obligation of a disqualified person is an act of self-dealing. Once any disqualified person makes a personal pledge, it becomes a personal debt or liability. (For details on disqualified persons, please see Facing Important Legal Issues, p. 59.)

fig. 23 Board Responsibilities for Discretionary Grants

Like all grants from a private foundation, the board of directors as a whole is legally responsible for approving any and all discretionary grants by trustees. In practice, the approval of these grants is often delegated to one trustee (such as the chair) or to a trusted staff person who is given responsibility for ensuring that the grantee is an eligible 501(c)(3) organization, and that there is no self-dealing or conflict of interest associated with the grant. It is particularly important to pay attention to the self-dealing rules. Due to the nature of these gifts, discretionary grants may be more prone to run afoul of self-dealing rules (regardless of the intentions of the individual trustee)." (Excerpted from *Discretionary Grants: Encouraging Participation…Or Dividing Family?* Available from the National Center for Family Philanthropy.) (For a discussion of the rules on self-dealing and conflict of interest, please see Facing Important Legal Issues, p. 59.)

- Foundation money should not be used for individual giving or be seen as a substitute for individual giving;
- Discretionary grants are not subject to the same standards of review;
- Discretionary grants confuse grantseekers about the foundation's purpose; and

- The discretionary budget can grow unwieldy as the number of family members multiplies.

The term "discretionary fund" should not be interpreted too loosely. These grants are subject to the same legal requirements as any other grants the foundation makes. To avoid legal problems, appoint either the board chair or a staff person to review all discretionary grants before checks are sent, or include a list of proposed discretionary grants in the board docket for consent review by all board members.

Remember, your Form 990-PF is readily accessible to the public on the Internet. The 990-PF lists your foundation's grants — including discretionary ones. Discretionary grants are written on foundation checks, and the name of your foundation will probably appear on the organization's list of donors. You may view these as grants from individual board members; the public is not likely to see that distinction.

To avoid confusing or misleading grantseekers about your giving, list your discretionary grants separately from your board-approved grants. Explain the purpose of the discretionary grants and why some may fall outside your stated guidelines.

Taking Risks

With well over one million tax-exempt organizations in the United States, foundations have virtually unlimited funding options. Yet, most foundations fund a relatively small universe of nonprofit organizations. Everyone wants to back winners: programs that have met or exceeded expectations, led to positive changes, or become models for others to replicate. But if all foundations funded them exclusively, think of how many innovative and promising programs would never have a chance to flower.

Foundations are relatively unfettered by government interference or public scrutiny — and for a purpose. They are in a position to find creative solutions to stubborn social problems, and that entails the willingness to experiment and risk failure. No foundation would be foolhardy enough to bet all its money on long shots, but you can take risks on promising — if untried people and projects — and take steps to limit your risk.

Maxine and Jonathan Marshall of the Marshall Fund have not shied away from funding controversial grassroots projects, what they call "leap of faith grants." One of their first grants — and one of which they are still most proud — was providing seed money for a shelter for prostitutes and their children in South Phoenix. "We got a request from a former prostitute who wanted to offer temporary shelter and AIDS education to prostitutes," says Maxine, "but she couldn't get any funding. Our seed grant got her started and enabled her to get a large grant from the Robert Woods Johnson Foundation. Ten years later, the organization is still running."

The term "discretionary fund" should not be interpreted too loosely. These grants are subject to the same legal requirements as any other grants the foundation makes.

As you prepare to launch your grantmaking program, you may want to post these watchwords above your computer: Take One Step at a Time, Make Use of All the Resources Available to You, and Don't Be Afraid to Move Forward.

The Sandy River Charitable Foundation takes an innovative approach to supporting riskier projects. It sets aside 5 percent of its assets for making high-risk investments. "This arrangement gives us a lot of flexibility to make different kinds of investments," says Nathanael Berry. "For example, recently we gave a loan at 5 percent to a local organization to use for a capital building fund." Nathanael emphasized that this type of loan is not to be confused with a typical Program-Related Investment because it is *not* money taken from the grants budget.

How to be Helpful Beyond Giving Grants

Giving grants is but one way foundations can help grantseekers and grantees. As you extend your contacts in the field, you can consider offering other forms of support:

- Write letters or make phone calls of support to other foundations;
- Make referrals to other funders that may be interested in the organization's work;
- Host grantwriting workshops to ensure that all applicants are better prepared to seek funding;
- Host meetings to bring together grantmakers with similar funding interests to discuss ways to support grantees;
- Participate in meetings to introduce grantmakers to grantseekers;
- Host meetings to bring together grantees working on the same issues to exchange information and ideas;
- Provide technical assistance to strengthen management and fundraising; and
- Allow grantees to hold occasional meetings in foundation boardroom.

(For more information on this subject, see Paul Ylvisaker's *Small Can Be Effective* in Virginia M. Esposito, ed., *Conscience & Community: The Legacy of Paul Ylvisaker*, p.359.)

Summing Up

This chapter began with the caution, "proceed slowly," and it closes with the same reminder. After reading so much about grantmaking, you should have a good idea of both the complexity and flexibility of the grants process. Not long from now, much of the process will become second nature for you and your management, and you can focus more on the important decisions you and your family members will be making. Grantmakng may never be entirely easy, however; because it expresses power, it must be taken seriously.

As you prepare to launch your grantmaking program, you may want to post these watchwords above your computer: Take One Step at a Time, Make Use of All the Resources Available to You, and Don't Be Afraid to Move Forward. In learning grantmaking, as in learning any other discipline, expertise is acquired through action. Be assured, however, that with each grantmaking cycle you will feel a little better prepared, a little more confident, and a little wiser. Grantmaking has the potential of being one of the most satisfying and involving efforts you and your family will ever undertake. Enjoy the adventure.

Some family foundations and their grantees have begun to venture into the realm of public advocacy, both directly and through their grantmaking. But they should do so carefully, with a firm understanding of the Internal Revenue Service groundrules.

A foundation may conduct "advocacy" in support of a particular viewpoint, so long as the advocacy does not "cross the line" and become political activity or fall into a prohibited category of "lobbying." Advocacy can take the form of advertisements, brochures, pamphlets, books, seminars, or lectures.

Advocacy becomes "political activity" — and taxable — only when it involves statements that support or oppose the election to office of a particular candidate or the conduct of a voter registration drive. Advocacy becomes "lobbying" — and *may* be taxable — if it seeks to affect a legislative body's vote on particular legislation, either through direct appeals to legislators and their staffs or appeals urging members of the general public to contact legislators and their staffs about particular legislation or urging them to vote a particular way on a referendum or bond issue.

Advocacy expenses should not be taxable when a foundation can demonstrate that it is merely making available to legislators or the general public the results of its nonpartisan analysis, study, or research on an issue, or providing technical advice or assistance in response to a written request from a government body, committee, or subcommittee, or acting in "self-defense." "Self-defense" lobbying would be advocacy for or against legislation that would affect a foundation's existence, its powers or duties, its tax-exempt status, or the deductibility of contributions to it.

A foundation may make a grant in support of advocacy by another organization, but not if the activity is something that the foundation itself may not do under the "lobbying" and "political activity" rules.

Recognizing the growing role of advocacy by foundations, the Council on Foundations has created The Paul Ylvisaker Award for Public Policy Engagement — so named to honor one of the leading thinkers and writers in 20th century American philanthropy and a family foundation trustee for many years. This award celebrates grantmakers that help "set the agenda for public consideration and debate." In 2002, The McKnight Foundation, a family foundation in Minneapolis, was selected as the first recipient of this award because of its stance in persuading public and private agencies to resume responsibility as a community for successful transitions from welfare to work. Since 1997, McKnight has committed $27 million to help welfare reform succeed in Minnesota.

Another leading example is the work by the Pew Charitable Trusts to strengthen democratic life in America. Pew's objectives are to restore public trust in elections, increase the civic engagement of young Americans, and improve public understanding of and confidence in government.

INFORMATION IS READILY AVAILABLE

The biggest barrier to more family foundation support of advocacy and lobbying, many observers believe, is the widespread assumption in philanthropy that such activity is illegal. Information on IRS regulations regarding advocacy and lobbying is available but not widely understood. As a result, many lawyers, trustees, and executives in the field have adopted an ultra-cautious approach to advocacy.

The IRS has clarified the groundrules for private foundations and nonprofit organizations to engage to public advocacy and lobbying. Information on IRS rules is available from various sources, including Charity Lobbying in the Public Interest (CLPI), initiated in 1998 by Independent Sector. The three major activities of CLPI include:

- Coordinating a network of persons in several states that provide education and training about lobbying, voter education, and other forms of government relations;

- Working with colleges and universities that provide studies in nonprofit management to encourage and support course offerings that relate to lobbying and nonprofit-government relations; and

- Supporting efforts to provide a web-based location (charity.lobbying@Independent Sector.org) where leaders of charities can learn about lobbying, voter education, and effective government-relations.

A FINAL NOTE

Grants may not be made for the purpose of supporting political activity by a grantee, and a foundation may wish to develop procedures to ascertain whether grantees are engaging in activities, political or otherwise, that make them unsuitable recipients of foundation funds.

Family foundation trustees would do well to ask legal counsel to develop a memorandum of law to guide the board in this whole area. The board might then adopt a resolution setting out its policy on advocacy and lobbying, which could also become part of its grantmaking guidelines.

JOHN SARE AND JOSEPH FOOTE

FIGURES

COMMUNICATING
Enhancing Process, Participation, and the Public Face of Your Foundation

By Vincent Stehle

After considering finances, legal issues, family dynamics, and grant-making, the last thing you might wish to consider is developing a communications strategy. For many new foundations, the preferred communications strategy can be summed up in a phrase: "The less said the better."

But there are lots of good reasons for you to publicize the work of your foundation — and its grantees. Family foundations use communications to:

- Expand the base of potential charitable partners (especially grantees), thus helping to find nonprofit organizations that are best suited to carrying out the foundation's mission;
- Inform the community and generate community support for initiatives;
- Create a supportive environment for grantees; and
- Spread the results of grantees' work to a larger audience.

The Information Age has brought awesome communications capabilities to any desk with a PC sitting on it. Family foundations now routinely use email, websites, PC-published reports, listerv distributions, and other techniques to communicate with one another, keep trustees and family up to date, and disseminate information.

Fortunately, a growing number of foundations are becoming sophisticated in media relations, publishing, and online communications. As a result, there are many well-established practices and resources to help you choose the proper communications strategy.

For some larger foundations, communications is a full-time job. The Henry J. Kaiser Family Foundation is an operating foundation that devotes most of its resources to creating and disseminating information about health care. According to Drew Altman, president of the Kaiser Foundation, "We are in the information, not the grantmaking, business." You will most likely not want to take such an aggressive approach. But there are myriad ways to provide information and to support communications efforts of grantees that fall within the reach of even the smallest foundations.

At a minimum, you have an obligation to provide basic financial details when your foundation receives inquiries from the public, as part of the bargain of not paying taxes. Likewise, most grantmakers recognize a basic responsibility to provide information about eligibility to prospective grant applicants. But at a more strategic level, foundations are learning that they can only achieve their larger objectives if they engage in some form of communications.

Rapid improvements in information technology have greatly increased the flow of information about all types of institutions. Internet search engines, online discussion lists, and email have made it much easier for grantseekers, journalists, and others to find out about a foundation's activities. As such, it is now much harder for a foundation to operate in obscurity.

All communication begins with listening.

— ANON

Information resources available to grantseekers and others researching foundation activity have expanded exponentially in the past decade. The Foundation Center and its associated research libraries, operating throughout the country and online, provide information on nearly 60,000 foundations. And Guidestar, an online search service run by Philanthropic Research, Inc., is attempting to publish financial and program information about all charities and foundations.

The two key concepts that drive much of the scrutiny of foundations today are accountability and transparency. And both of these concepts are amplified with greater access to information. As part of the more skeptical ethos ushered in by the national tragedies of Watergate and the war in Vietnam, public institutions of all types are held to a higher standard of accountability than they were before. Public officials and institutions now have to continually earn the trust of a questioning public, and foundations are no exception.

Transparency is a related concern, more commonly discussed in the conduct of business affairs. Transparency means that an enterprise conducts its affairs in a way that makes decision processes and financial transactions open to scrutiny, as a way to prevent corruption and to ensure the most effective use of resources. Foundations have greater flexibility and latitude than government agencies in determining how they spend their money. But there is no way to escape the sense that an increasingly curious public wants to know

how and why foundations spend their resources the way they do.

This chapter explores communications from two perspectives, first looking inward at family matters and then looking outward to the community and the world.

The chapter addresses five subjects:
- Thinking about privacy and the family;
- Developing a communications strategy;
- Learning about communications basics;
- Finding communications resources; and
- Communications can support the mission.

---

fig. 1 — **Ideas on Communications for the New or Small Family Foundation**

- Consider how communications can facilitate your own internal operations, such as communication among trustees via email, a "family" page on a website (probably by password), and communications with contractors and advisors.

- Look at ways to get out the important messages to be found in your Mission Statement and grant guidelines: issue an announcement, a press release, or a brochure; go on community television; create a listserv for grantees.

- Develop an annual reporting mechanism that complements your Form 990-PF and is right for your family foundation style. For example, you can send a photocopy of the annual report to those you hope to involve or to those who request information. A photocopy saves time and money.

- Talk with other founders and trustees in your community who share funding interests, and ask for ideas on how to get the word out.

- If you do not accept unsolicited proposals, say so. Many family foundations begin by funding organizations they know, while researching new ones.

- Think about how communications can help your grantees and add "bang to your grant dollars." Draft procedures for and standard language on how nonprofit organizations can and cannot use your foundation name in their communications.

- Develop a strategy for responding to press inquiries before it's an issue.

- Consider the advantage of a communications advisor as an ad hoc or retained consultant or firm. Such a professional can help you during the startup phase and be available later, as needed.

Thinking About Privacy and the Family

At the outset, it's important to acknowledge the common urge to operate anonymously. There are several good reasons why donors might seek to operate foundations in anonymity. But whatever the impulse, giving anonymously is not really an option when a donor decides to establish a foundation under United States tax law. By virtue of the tax benefits extended by the government, foundations have an obligation to operate for public purposes and to make regular reports to the public. Private foundations have long been required to provide information about their operations, especially since 1969, when a major overhaul of tax laws greatly increased formal scrutiny of foundation affairs.

Limiting Public Knowledge and Access

Many founders and their families are concerned about the effect of publicity on the family. They may have heard about grantseekers buttonholing them in public places. They may have read stories suggesting that persons of wealth may face threats to their personal security.

In fact, with one exception, the founder and the foundation can achieve a high degree of anonymity. Aside from the Form 990-PF, you can keep your family and foundation activities very private. You do not have to list the foundation in the telephone book, maintain an office available to the public, print foundation letterhead or business cards, issue printed or electronic grant guidelines, publicize your grants, or accept offers from well-meaning nonprofit organizations that want to honor you and the foundation with a bronze plaque. Your lawyer can write the grant checks.

One foundation that follows a limited public knowledge approach is the Jerry Taylor & Nancy Bryant Foundation in

---

fig. 2 — No Cloak of Secrecy: Anonymous Giving

Look at any list of donors and you are sure to find a familiar name: anonymous. Throughout the ages, anonymous giving has been greatly admired and deeply rooted in the practice of philanthropy. Maimonides, the 12th Century Jewish philosopher, is the most commonly cited among many influential thinkers who have argued that giving is most virtuous when it is done privately and selflessly. Even today, many donors want to keep their good works quiet out of modesty and humility,

There are also selfish — but no less compelling — reasons to conduct philanthropy anonymously. Some donors feel that public displays of philanthropy can bring unwanted attention to their wealth, thereby leaving family members vulnerable to threats to their personal security.

Some donors may even entertain the romantic notion of being a latter-day John Beresford Tipton, the unseen force in the old television program, "The Millionaire." Each week, Tipton's assistant, would deliver a tax-free check for $1 million to an unsuspecting beneficiary. (Perhaps less well-remembered are the distressing consequences of Tipton's essentially manipulative style of giving.)

On a more mundane level, some people believe that providing too much information about a foundation's operations can lead to a flood of unsolicited proposals. By operating in secrecy, some donors feel that they can maintain better control of their giving, devoting themselves more fully to thinking about who to support and less to the task of turning everybody else down.

Whatever your reason, if you want to carry out your philanthropy in total anonymity, using a foundation is not the way to do it. In the first place, it's not legally possible, given the public reporting requirements of the federal government. But even more importantly, foundations function more effectively when they operate with some degree of public accountability.

Washington, DC, which maintains a low profile, mostly out of a sense of family style. Because the foundation does not accept unsolicited grant proposals, it does not issue grant guidelines; it has no website, publishes no annual report, and does not alert the media to grants. "We have kept our foundation as simple as we possibly can," Nancy Bryant says. "Basically, I'm the staff person. I don't want to be inundated with the workload, if we accepted unsolicited grants. I keep a statement of guidelines that I send to charities that interest us."

She adds: "We state in our form 990-PF that we do not accept unsolicited grant proposals. The nonprofit community pretty much honors that position. We receive maybe one or two such proposals a year. If we do receive an unsolicited letter of inquiry, I send a form letter stating that we are limited to a defined geographical area, focus only on specific issues, or are limited in resources and cannot make a grant at this time."

GOOD ADVICE ➢ **Access to information in some families is unequal. Young people and especially women don't always have equal access to financial and other types of information. Therefore, they are often unempowered. It's important for information related to the foundation to flow freely to all family members.**

ALISON GOLDBERG, BOARD MEMBER AND DAUGHTER OF THE FOUNDER, ROBERT P. & JUDITH N. GOLDBERG FOUNDATION

fig. 3 **Foundations Can Define and Redefine**

In a rapidly changing society, one of the most valuable processes is taking a new or another look at issues that have long been, shortly will [be], or should be on the public agenda. There is too often a lag in public perception and recognition; foundations can play an effective part in defining and redefining those issues through research, analyses, conferences, seminars, publicity, or simply reporting their own considerations and grant results.

PAUL YLVISAKER

"Small Can Be Effective," in *Conscience & Community: The Legacy of Paul Ylvisaker.* Virginia M. Esposito, Ed. New York: Peter Lang, 1999, p. 364. (First published as an occasional paper for the Council on Foundations, April 1989.)

Developing a Communications Strategy

Communications occupies such a large part of American life that you may find it advantageous to develop a communications strategy for the foundation.

There are many reasons for you to view communications in a positive light. It's not just an obligation or an unavoidable annoyance. Communications is an opportunity, and in some ways, it is essential for a foundation to communicate to achieve its full potential.

For all of these reasons, and more, if you are thinking of setting up a foundation today, consider how you intend to communicate its activities.

There is a growing consensus among foundations that communications efforts are central to the work of philanthropy. It is a realization that foundations are much more than merely financial conduits that dispense money to worthy causes. In many ways, foundations are information institutions, gathering and dispensing knowledge along with financial support. And if they don't convey that knowledge to a wider audience, it is a largely wasted effort.

In an influential *Harvard Business Review* article, Michael Porter and Mark Kramer argue that foundations can only justify their existence if they do more than merely transfer money. Foundations create value in four ways, according to Kramer and Porter, founders of the Center for Effective Philanthropy. In order of increasing impact, foundations add value beyond their financial contributions by:

- Selecting the best grantees. Like investment advisers, foundations channel resources to their most productive use by studying a range of organizations and selecting the groups that are most effective.

- Signaling other funders. Foundations can attract additional resources from other funders who follow their lead, when they can show that their grantees are especially effective.

- Improving the performance of grant recipients. Grantmakers greatly increase their impact when they offer more than financial support, providing management assistance, advice, and access to networks of funders and other peers.

- Advancing the state of knowledge and practice. Foundations produce the greatest value to society when they promote research and support projects that seek to produce increasingly effective responses to social problems.

The common thread in each of these approaches is that each of them requires foundations to communicate what they are doing to a broader audience, whether that means potential grantees, others working in a particular field, policymakers, or members of the general public.

Foundations communicate in many ways and for many reasons, but they can be boiled down to three basic categories of activity:

- Efforts to publicize their own work and the work of their grantees. Foundations routinely publish annual reports and press releases, commission research papers, and communicate with reporters and editors about grants and other foundation activities.

- Support for communications projects of grant recipients. Foundations frequently pay for the publishing, media relations, and advocacy activities of nonprofits, in many cases as part of grant support.

- Efforts to sustain and create nonprofit media programs. Backing groups like public television, public radio, and a range of other nonprofit media projects, a small group of foundations supports the infrastructure over which most public interest programs are carried.

For most donors thinking about setting up a new foundation, developing an effective advocacy campaign may be a low priority. It is one thing for the Robert Wood Johnson Foundation or the Pew Charitable Trusts, each of which employs dozens of communications workers, to be concerned with such a campaign. It is quite another for a small, startup family foundation to do so. Traditionally, new foundations have focused on supporting direct services at the local level. But now, even a small foundation with few or no staff members, can engage in a sophisticated communications strategy intended to shape popular opinion and public policy.

As you bring your foundation into being, choosing a communications strategy can be one of the most important decisions you will make. How or whether you will publicize the activities of the foundation and its grantees will

fig. **4**   **Sending the Message via Television Programs**

The Mayday Fund, which focuses on how pain is understood and treated, works with W.E. Duke & Co. to advance the message that pain should be addressed in Hollywood. In this project, screenwriters are educated about pain and its care in the hopes that the message will become part of programs, including dramas and soap operas.

fig.
5

Possible Elements of a Communications Strategy

Assume that a family foundation's mission can be advanced by connecting with key audiences throughout the community. The foundation's strategy might contain these steps and elements:

YEAR 1

- Establish goals for a communications strategy, and ensure that goals further the foundation mission;
- Select critical portions of the Mission Statement as the focus for messages to be offered to the community and key audiences;
- Identify key audiences, such as community leaders, local government officials, our sector of local nonprofits, and the public;
- Explore, with professional media advisors, optional approaches, such as sending messages via grantees, donor groups, etc.;
- Determine methods (neighborhood meetings, focus groups, etc.) of finding out about community feelings, values, opinions, historical problems, etc., and select methods that generate a constant stream of information from the community;
- Establish a procedure for making the Form 990-PF public and available;
- Talk with current and potential grantees about publicity: who will handle it, how the foundation's name and interests can be protected, what the goals are, etc.;
- Examine and cost out optional methods of reaching key audiences, such as convening meetings, direct mail, newspaper and radio/TV ads; and
- Create pilot communications products and develop capability to deal with the news media.

YEAR 2

- Arrive at longer term agreement with a communications firm;
- Narrow focus of the messages and select modest elements of the communications strategy for implementation;
- With grantees leading the effort, launch the strategy with a low-key briefing of local media;
- Follow up with meetings with key community leaders, government officials, key editors and reporters, potential collaborators in funding, etc.
- Open website for posting of the Form 990-PF, Mission Statement, Grant Guidelines, and other important information; and
- Publish the First Annual Report and distribute to key audiences.

YEAR 3

- Publish the Second Annual Report and distribute to key audiences;
- Form advisory group of grantees to advise the foundation on its communications strategy; and
- Appoint a qualified family member or hire an outside professional part-time to handle communications.

help to shape the way it is regarded — by the general public, news media, and governmental officials.

A Strategy Can Grow Over Time
The Helen Bader Foundation in Milwaukee is a family foundation started by the family of Helen Bader a few years after her death in 1989. The foundation started with no communications staff member. In the first year, the foundation trustees retained a small Milwaukee public relations firm to help advise them on how to inform the nonprofit world of the existence of the foundation. "We knew we wanted to do great things, but we also knew we could not do great things without great grant applicants," says Daniel Bader, now president of the foundation.

Early on, the foundation cultivated contacts in the media, setting up one-on-one meetings with local reporters who covered education, for example, to

fig. 6   Marco Polo Inquiry Group: A New Approach to Communications

In October 2000, a group of 14 funders got together to discuss how their foundations might be transformed by the digital age and other external forces. Group members represented foundations of all sizes, mostly from the California area. Identifying themselves as the Marco Polo Inquiry Group, each committed to working within their foundations — and among other foundations — to communicate and share new ways to optimize assets, networks, knowledge, and expertise and to participate fully in their communities' most critical problems in more powerful ways. Although the work of this group is far from complete, it has begun developing an indepth communications framework that emulates lessons of the famous explorer, Marco Polo. The following seven-issue framework developed by the group — essentially a creed — lays out a full range of strategies that foundations can choose to apply as they work to achieve their missions:

- **A larger ecosystem.** In our foundations, whatever the size or focus, we need to make our walls more permeable: to become more connected to the world and the other players around us, more attuned to what others expect of us, and to where we add value to a larger purpose. We need to become better consumers of ideas and experience from other players and sectors and more skilled at designing joint responses to shared needs.

- **Cultural adaptability.** The wired world is changing the fundamental nature of our political, organizational, and social life. It sets up high expectations for open access, transparency, rich and "storied" data, knowledge sharing, and rapid response time; it flattens hierarchies, calls boundaries into question in both positive and negative ways, and makes "linking to learn" and "learning by doing" the order of the day. Most of our foundations are ill equipped culturally to operate in this world.

- **Customer satisfaction.** We find the idea that foundations "don't have customers" (or don't operate in a marketplace, or don't have anything analogous to bottom-line accountability) to be misleading and shortsighted. For us to be the organizations we want to be, performance matters. The measure of performance is not just the evaluated outcomes of our grants. It's also the value our customers—be they donors, grantees, elected officials, or program partners—experience from our work.

- **Knowledge.** We need to get better at learning from and with others, at recognizing grantees as the source of much of "our" knowledge, at enabling others as knowledge creators, at turning grant output into usable knowledge for others, and at determining what skills, systems, and cultures inside foundations best support this knowledge work.

- **Communications as leadership.** The drive for change in foundations comes most directly to the leaders at the top. It demands of us a different set of skills and priorities than we have traditionally been asked for. It compels us to value and practice communications as a leadership skill — for its full power to help build cultures of teamwork, learning, innovation, and responsiveness inside the foundation, and to put the full weight of our foundations behind the work of building constituencies for equity and change outside our foundations.

- **Cross-foundation work.** Creating a culture of shared work and shared learning across foundations is profoundly important. Echoing the "silos" that exist within many of our foundations, we have developed as institutions our lone capabilities and identities. There is much we can learn for each other. There is much redundancy — deriving from our instinct to "invent it here" — to eliminate. And there is much potential in thinking of our different organizations as composing a system of problem solving.

- **Expanded accountability.** In distilling the themes above, we hold ourselves to a new definition of accountability. This new "high standard" of accountability is based on the conviction that unknown, isolated, and perceived-to-be-inflexible organizations will become less and less able to create value in our networked society — thus generating lower return on exempt assets and ultimately becoming less accountable in the context of public benefit.

SOURCE: Marcia Sharp, "Grantmakers in a New Landscape," *Foundation News & Commentary*, 43:2, March/April 2002. Members of this group include: Blueprint Research & Design, Inc., Irvine Foundation, Charles and Helen Schwab Foundation, Sobrato Family Foundation, Los Angeles Urban Funders, David and Lucile Packard Foundation, Omidyar Foundation, Wallace Alexander Gerbode Foundation, Dean and Margaret Lesher Foundation, California Community Foundation, Durfee Foundation, Humboldt Area Foundation, California Community Foundation, University of Southern California, Millennium Communications Group, Inc., Peninsula Community Foundation, Northern California Grantmakers, and Ewing Marion Kauffman Foundation.

explain what the foundation intended to do and how the nonprofit community might be involved in those plans. Within about a year and a half after startup, the foundation added a printed annual report to its communications repertoire. "The purpose was to keep the community posted on what had been accomplished, any changes in direction, and other matters of interest to grantseekers," Bader says. "The annual reports became increasingly reader-friendly, attractive, and informative."

As the foundation grew, the trustees decided to hire a communications staff member to oversee these activities. Press conferences and other events attended the launching of initiatives: photo ops with a grantee, for example, or a sit-down between a foundation program person and a particular reporter to explain the grant.

The core of the communications direc-tor's job is to prepare the annual report, oversee internal communications (keep-ing the board informed, for example), scheduling onsite visits, and so on. The foundation launched its website in 1997; Daniel Bader is highly proficient in com-munications technology and wanted capability to serve users in the founda-tion's statewide Alzheimer's program, in its rural outreach programs, and in its over-seas work in Israel. A website is a natural tool for these uses. "At the beginning, the website was essentially a mirror image of our annual report," says Bader. "We updated it maybe twice a year. Lately, we've gotten a lot more newsworthy, looking for profiles of interesting people and activities in the programs throughout the year. Also, we want to get information out there as events occur — great projects that the foundation has been involved with, recent grants, and other matters that offer a good way to keep the community informed more frequently."

The foundation maintains a clear set of guidelines on its website. Although the website is basically a public informa-tion tool, it also enables grantseekers to apply on line (fully 25 percent of proposals come in online).

Learning About Communications Basics

Knowledge of the basic tools of foun-dation communications will be useful to you. You may wish to employ some all, or none of them, but this primer will provide a basic menu from which to choose.

Understanding the IRS Form 990-PF

For starters, every private foundation must fill out and file a federal informa-tional tax return, Form 990-PF. Not only must you file the form with the federal government, but you must also make it available to members of the public upon request. Foundations have long had to file 990 forms, but recently the federal government has tightened its rules requiring foundations to make their reports more readily available to the public.

Moreover, Guidestar, a free online infor-mation service, posts copies of all foun-dation 990 forms to its site. (Guidestar also carries news from the Internal Revenue Service and other sources about developments on Form 990-PF,

fig. 7 Making Your Form 990-PF Public and Available

- Must file with the IRS by the 15th of the 5th month after the close of the foundation's fiscal year;

- Must make copies of the form available for public inspection; and

- Must provide copies of forms for the past three years to anyone who asks for them (if the foundation makes the form widely available, as on its web-site, it need not respond to individual inquiries for copies).

such as electronic filing of the form.) Altogether, the increasing awareness of the availability of your Form 990 means that your financial information will be made widely available to the public. Unfortunately, many charities and foundations have been careless in preparing their tax returns. According to the National Center on Charitable Statistics at the Urban Institute, more than half of all 990 forms are filled out incorrectly. But now, with wider access being made possible through technology, such mistakes are more consequential. At a minimum, you should carefully and accurately fill out your 990 form.

Given that your financial information is going to be made public to a wide audience, you may want to inform the public about your foundation by using one or more of the following simple methods. (After all, the Form 990-PF in an imperfect communications vehicle; Curtis W. Meadows, Jr., president emeritus of The Meadows Foundation and a lawyer, notes that the Form 990-PF was designed by the IRS for tax purposes, not as a communications vehicle.)

Publishing an Annual Report

Although not required by law, annual reports are considered by many foundations to be the most complete and straightforward way to handle a range of communications needs. Annual reports can include introductory essays by governing board members, usually the chairman, or by staff members, if

---

fig. 8 — An Innovative Approach

The Boone Foundation of San Marino, California, is a small family foundation that shares information about its work in a particularly innovative way. Trustee George Boone enjoys photography as a hobby and has made several videos about the foundation and its work. One, entitled "Grantmaking with a Passion," shows the work of several foundation grantees. Boone says that he videotapes whenever he sees the need to get out more information about a particular program. He believes that the videos are effective communications tools. "When someone asks, 'What does your foundation do?'" Boone says, "I hand them a brochure about the foundation and offer them a video."

SOURCE: Newell Flather, Mary Phillips, and Jean Whitney, *Governance*. Family Foundation Library, Virginia M. Esposito, ed. Washington, DC: Council on Foundations, 1997, p. 97.

---

there are any. They can also include detailed descriptions of each of the grants made during the year under review. They generally include a basic financial statement, accounting for assets and liabilities, grant payments and administrative expenses and other financial activity. And they generally include grant guidelines.

According to the Foundation Center, more than 75 percent of foundations with assets of more than $100 million published annual reports or other publications that described their giving. On the other hand, fewer than 5 percent of foundations with assets less than $5 million published such reports. Overall, fewer than one in five foundations of all sizes publish annual reports or other materials.

Family foundation annual reports reflect the full range of options. Some family foundations publish no annual report at all. Others issue a photocopy of a statement from the founder or the trustees. Many publish a simple pocket-sized brochure, while still others publish a full-color illustrated report that rivals the best of the Fortune 500 corporate annual reports. Quite a few offer a videotape. The content, design, and printing quality of the annual report reflect the tastes and values of the family foundation that issues it.

An example of a family foundation annual report is that of The Carpenter Foundation in Medford, Oregon. The foundation issues a 2-color, 10-panel brochure. One panel carries a four-paragraph President's Report, a one-paragraph Purpose Statement, and a

Contents of an Annual Report

The contents of your annual report are entirely up to you: no law or regulation requires you to file one. Annual reports typically contain:

- Name and location of the foundation, names of officers and trustees, and name of contact person and ways to reach him or her (telephone, mailing address, and email address);

- History of the foundation and biographical material about the founder;

- Mission Statement and a report of the past year on grantmaking activities undertaken to carry out the mission (grantees and grant amounts are often given);

- Vignettes or longer stories about grantee activities;

- Grant application guidelines, application submission procedures, and grantmaking decision cycles by the trustees;

- Financial statements for the past year; and

- An outlook section looking toward the year to come.

two-paragraph History. Financial Statements and a list of Trustees occupy another panel. Five panels list recent grants, one panel presents grant guidelines, and two panels are given to the front and back covers.

A similar but unique approach is that of the Dr. G. Clifford and Florence B. Decker Foundation, a family foundation located in Binghamton, New York. The 2001 annual report is a 10-panel, 1-color brochure that devotes fully 5 panels to a list of grants, carries financial information (assets, grant payments, and grants approved), presents grant application procedures, and contains a thoughtful mini-essay by Board Chair Ferris G. Akel on the year 2001 in review.

Large, national family foundations publish annual reports that are 50 to 100 pages long, are printed in color with photography, and carry in-depth stories about grantees and grantmaking activities. Some become noteworthy for excellence in editorial content. The annual essays by Margaret E. Mahoney, for many years president of The Commonwealth Fund, are still referred to in thoughtful discussions of important issues in family philanthropy. (Excerpts from her essay on trusteeships are included in the Governance chapter, p. 85.)

Publishing Grant Guidelines

Although many foundations publish their grant guidelines in their annual report, many foundations also publish, on paper and online, grant guidelines for wide distribution to potential grant applicants. You might worry that your foundation will be overwhelmed by proposals, but it's a rare complaint that a foundation has received too many good proposals. In any event, broadly publicizing what a foundation will support or its geographic restrictions also helps to limit the number of applications, by showing clearly what will fall outside a foundation's purposes. Of course, it is always possible not to issue guidelines and to state that a foundation does not accept unsolicited proposals.

Grantmaking guidelines assist both your foundation and those who are engaged in the grantseeking process by spreading the word on foundation mission, streamlining the application for foundation administrators, and helping grantseekers present themselves and their needs clearly and completely, without wasting their or their prospective funder's time. At a minimum, published guidelines provide a brief history of the foundation and its mission; detail the nature and size of grants and any restrictions; specify requirements for submitting proposals; describe the selection process; and set out policies regarding first-time grants, renewals, site visits, or contact with trustees. Formats for guidelines vary from simple foldout brochures to lengthier booklets, to electronic formats provided on the foundation website. (See Sample Policies and Forms, p. 228.)

GOOD ADVICE ➤ For the Gordon–Lovejoy Foundation, established in 1998 by Nicholas Gordon and Barbara Lovejoy, a simple website announces the small handful of grants to nonprofit organizations involved in promoting environmentally sustainable practices. With some justification, many small foundations are leery of the Internet, in fear that it will provoke a flood of unwanted solicitations. But the Gordon-Lovejoy Foundation offered a straightforward solution: "We kindly request that you do not send proposals and limit your correspondence to three pages."

---

fig. 10 — A Classic Set of Communications Tools

The Mayday Fund employs a set of communication tools to help it fulfill its charitable mission, which is "the alleviation of the incidence, degree, and consequence of human physical pain." Its tools include:

- Extensive use of electronic mail between trustees and staff members as well as with grant applicants and grantees;

- Posting of the foundation's mission statement, grant guidelines, and lists of grants made on the website of a grantee, for example, The Mayday Pain Project, which is located at www.painandhealth.org;

- Retention of a small communications firm, Burness Communications, to advise on communications generally, conduct appropriate research, and help develop effective tools for working with the public; and

- Use of the communications firm to plan public events, such as press conferences, which draw attention to Mayday's activities

Considering Named Gift Opportunities

You may wish to make a substantial gift to a cultural or educational organization or a hospital or clinic, or virtually any other large capital project, and permit the organization to acknowledge your generosity by naming a part of the project for you or someone you would like to honor. Most donors may think that they are the principal beneficiaries of such a memorial. But fundraisers will quickly point out that the institution also benefits, because a donor's public involvement often spurs others to join the effort.

In 1998, for example, Columbia University christened the Joseph L. Mailman School of Public Health in honor of the late industrialist on the occasion of a gift of $33 million from the Mailman Foundation, a family foundation. Phyllis Mailman said the gift was intended to reflect her late-husband's approach to philanthropy during his lifetime, in which he often urged other people to give. "The family's hope is that the gift may encourage other small family foundations to consider making such transforming gifts to really make a difference, to think about the possibilities of how they can make a statement. And to stop being shy about it. The time is now," she said.

Issuing Press Releases

A press release is a simple statement that informs members of the press and others about an upcoming or recent event or activity. You may wish to issue press releases concerning grants by your foundation. But it is more common for the recipient organization to draft a press release describing the project and acknowledging supporters as part of the statement. It can be useful for you to establish a policy about press releases, determine whether you want to participate or not, and decide who will handle calls and provide information for the beneficiaries when they want to create a release.

Basic Contents of a Press Release

- Date of release, when the media can publish the information;
- Name and telephone number of person for further contact and information;
- Headline that presents the key message;
- Lead paragraph that states the top news element: the What:
  - Where and When, if an event is being announced;
  - Who, if the news is about a person;
- Second paragraph that presents the Why and the How;
- Third paragraph with further details;
- Fourth paragraph with a quotation from the founder, a trustee, or other person in authority;
- Additional details;
- No longer than 400 words.

Press Release Announces Named Gift (Excerpt)

FOR RELEASE ON
October 29, 2001

Contact: Robert Tobon
414/224-6470, ext. 115

HELEN BADER FOUNDATION, IN LARGEST GRANT TO DATE,
Awards $5 Million for UW-Milwaukee's Focus on Aging

(Milwaukee) – The Helen Bader Foundation has awarded a five-year, $5 million grant to the University of Wisconsin-Milwaukee's School of Social Welfare, the largest grant in the Foundation's 10-year history and the largest grant ever received by a UWM school. In recognition of this gift, and of the Foundation's support of UWM over the past 10 years, UWM has renamed the School of Social Welfare in honor of the late Helen Bader, a 1981 graduate of the School.

The $5 million grant establishes an endowed chair in gerontology within the School of Social Welfare and the Helen Bader Scholarship Fund to assist UWM students throughout the university in preparing for careers in gerontology and age-related studies.

"In the next few years, there will be an urgent need to address the many day-to-day aspects of growing older," said Daniel Bader, son of Helen Bader and president of the Foundation. "UWM has a long track record of working with the community in developing fresh, creative approaches to aging. I know that my mother would be pleased that UWM will continue her passion for helping older adults live better lives."

Helen Bader earned her Masters in Social Work at age 53, after she and her former husband, Alfred, built the Aldrich Chemical Company. After graduation from UWM, she began working with residents at the Milwaukee Jewish Home and Care Center, where many older adults were living with Alzheimer's disease. She used music and dance to reach residents, and she worked at the Center until her death in 1989….

fig. 12

Sample Press Release (Excerpt)

FOR RELEASE ON
March 5, 2002

Contact: Robert Tobon
414/224-6470, ext. 115

PRISON VISITS HELP CHILDREN RECONNECT WITH JAILED MOMS
Helen Bader Foundation Awards $10,000 Grant to St. Rose Residence

(Milwaukee) – Women comprise just 12 percent of Wisconsin's prison population, yet their incarceration is more likely to create upheaval in their children's lives than for male inmates. In most cases, their children are sent to live with relatives or a foster family, an adjustment complicated by feelings of fear, anger, and self-doubt.

Since 2000, St. Rose Youth & Family Center Inc.'s Family Reunification Program has helped Milwaukee County children better understand the various issues that arise after their mothers are jailed. The Helen Bader Foundation, Inc. recently awarded a $10,000 grant to help the agency continue the program, the only one of its type in the county.

"In-person visits are the primary way of maintaining relationships," said Kenneth Czaplewski, St. Rose president. "Phone calls from prison have to be made collect, so the cost is prohibitively expensive for most families."

Through the program, the child and counselor travel together one Saturday each month to one of the state's far-flung prisons. The counselors prepare the children for what to expect during the visit, which is not held behind glass, but face-to-face. According to counselors in the program, visits tend to revolve around a shared activity or talking about everyday concerns....

Retaining a Communications Professional

However ambitious your communications plans, it is likely that you will not immediately hire a staff member specifically to carry out communications activities. You may assign a board member or a staff member to be the principal official handling these matters, but you may also wish to hire a communications consultant to help out. There are many public relations and communications consultants who can help you on an ad hoc basis, either to prepare an annual report or to generate press releases or any other communications task.

Examples of Press Releases on Websites

Glazier Family Foundation – Florida
www.glazerfamilyfoundation.com/latestnews.asp

Sobrato Family Foundation – California
sobrato.com/foundation/press.htm

The Spencer Foundation – Chicago, IL
www.spencer.org/index.htm

Waitt Family Foundation – California
www.waittfoundation.org/News/press_powerup.asp

Blandin Foundation – Minnesota
www.blandinfoundation.org/releases/New%20Senior%20Program%20Director%20Hired.Joselyn.February.2001.htm

George Gund Foundation – Ohio
www.gundfdn.org/news_f.html

Precisely what value does a communications firm bring to a family foundation, however, in addition to skills and experience that no family member may possess? The Mayday Fund responds that it works through teams that advise its trustees. The small communications firm ensures that the teams will be well informed about the mission of the foundation and alert to concerns of the trustees. "By having professional teams, the Fund is trying to send a message that the issues are serious and that they deserve expert attention," Executive Director Christina M.

fig. 13 — How a Press Release Can Further Your Foundation's Mission

A well-prepared press release can be of value in promoting the work of your foundation whether the release is prepared by you, a foundation trustee or staff member, a grantee, or another known, respected organization. For instance, a recent announcement that the Minneapolis-based McKnight Foundation, a family foundation, received the Council on Foundation's new Paul Ylvisaker Award was prepared by the Council, and provides substantial information about McKnight's efforts in support of welfare-to-work requirements. The release was posted to McKnight's website (www.mcknight.org) and has been widely distributed within the philanthropic community.

fig. 14 — Three Key Questions About Using a Communications Firm

The Mayday Fund has retained communications firms with considerable success. Through Executive Director Christina M. Spellman, the trustees gave these responses to three critical questions:

Why did Mayday hire a communications firm?
One of Mayday's goals is public education. The trustees agreed that a most effective way to educate the public was to have a well-coordinated communications strategy. The executive director at that time had followed the work of Burness Communications over the years and had been impressed by how persistent, innovative, and skillful the firm was. Also, as Mayday only has one staff person, working with a communications firm was equivalent to having a communications branch. The same strategy holds for our Hollywood Project.

How does it use the firm?
Mayday uses the communications firms it works with to help develop an issue, to design a creative and effective strategy, and to help to evaluate the success of communications proj-

ects as well as other types of grantmaking. When the executive director has a question about a grant request, she often asks for an opinion from Burness Communications if the project involves media or the public. In some ways, they function as a form of peer review.

What advice can Mayday give to new foundation founders on using a firm during the startup era?
A communications firm helps you to define who you are as part of the process of framing the messages that you wish to create. A firm also shares the best methods (and common practices) to achieve the goals. Part of this function is that communications advisors help the foundation founders to articulate what they hope to achieve while sharing realism about how to do it.

Spellman comments. "Finally, for a small staff, having communications advisors increases and enhances the ability to reach larger audiences."

Mayday uses the communications firm for specific purposes, not as a bin for routine mail. Day-to-day requests for information are handled in several ways: The foundation's director reviews all requests, responds to some directly, refers some to the communications firm, and sends some to a specific grantee or a known authority on the topic. Responses to mail are seen as an important information activity.

Communicating Online

In the past few years, the Internet has become a powerful and ubiquitous force in American society. In philanthropy, it has changed many things, including the way charities raise funds. The Internet can be an efficient and effective tool for even the smallest foundation, to publish whatever information it wants to make public. You may want to provide information online, in addition to that contained in your 990-PF, just to make sure you are shaping how people view the work of your foundation.

Many family foundations today use email extensively to communicate among family members; quite a few family foundations maintain limited-access websites or listservs that only family members or designated others can access for information about board

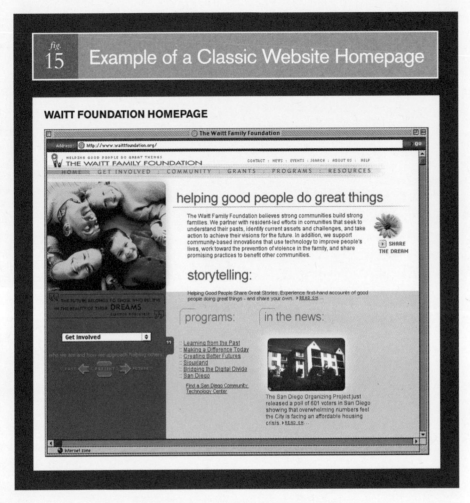

fig. **15** Example of a Classic Website Homepage

WAITT FOUNDATION HOMEPAGE

Many family foundations today use email extensively to communicate among family members; quite a few family foundations maintain limited-access websites or listservs that only family members or designated others can access for information about board meetings, discussions of grant applicants, and other inside-foundation and family business.

meetings, discussions of grant applicants, and other inside-foundation and family business. (Some family foundations still distribute a printed newsletter about family and foundation history, current grants, board activities, and the like — preferring print over electronics.)

Finding Communications Resources

The main reason most foundations don't publish information about their activities is they just don't have the time or extra hands to handle the work. But this reason may be less valid today than it was in times past. There are now many resources available that should make it much easier for small foundations, including those run completely on a voluntary basis, to provide basic information to the public.

Desktop and online publishing gives anyone with a personal computer the capability to publish information, without becoming involved in the long and laborious process of creating drafts and contracting with printers and distributors to publish information. In fact, if you decide to establish a website, you can easily post information about your foundation's activities without ever putting pen to paper. Beyond advances in information technology, many resources are available for every foundation that seeks to launch communications activities. The first stop for guid-

ance is the Communications Network, a Washington, DC-based affinity group (an organization of foundations with similar interests), whose express purpose is to:

- Raise awareness of the importance of communications in philanthropy;
- Expand and enhance the fields' communications capacities; and
- Provide resources to foundations and their grantees to help them make the most of that capacity.

The Communications Network carries out its goals by publishing guides, conducting workshops, and offering technical assistance and a wide range of other services, mainly for foundation trustees and staff. You can learn more about this affinity group by calling their offices at 202.887.4818, or visiting their website at www.comnetwork.org.

A comprehensive general guide to foundation communications, the *Grantmakers Communications Manual,* is published by the Council on Foundations and the Forum of Regional Associations of Grantmakers. The manual offers guidance in devising communications plans, by helping to determine who the audience is and how to develop messages

tailored to that audience. The manual details means for engaging board members and other volunteers, along with full-time staff and consultants, and gives detailed guidance on setting hourly pay rates for communications consultants. Although the full range of communications issues is discussed, the manual focuses mainly on media relations.

Much basic information exists on how to use communications tools. The Benton Foundation's website subject category, "Strategic Communications in the Digital Age: A best practices toolkit for achieving your organization's mission," is an excellent overview resource. This website features a broad range of resources, produced by Benton in cooperation with other nonprofit communications experts. It serves as a forum for foundations and nonprofit organizations that want to ask questions and share success stories, offers tips on designing and implementing media strategies and other communications plans, and carries outside reports concerning communications and information technology for nonprofit organizations. The Benton website address is www.benton.org.

The main reason most foundations don't publish information about their activities is they just don't have the time or extra hands to handle the work. But this reason may be less valid today than it was in times past.

of the projects and other activities your new foundation supports. Over time, your communications may even shape popular opinion and public policy.

Communications Can Support the Mission

Family foundations have different missions and different practices in their effort to serve the community and the public. Some families may prefer to operate quietly and without fanfare, while others may prefer to promote the excellent work of their grantees or advocate for change. In any case, founders are well advised to give communications some serious thought early in the founding stage.

Communications can, after all, support the mission. Communications can help to build a community of support for foundation activities, acknowledge hardworking nonprofit workers and volunteers, and — who knows? — maybe even encourage other families to start their own foundation.

---

fig. 16 Communications and Public Advocacy

If you want to help nonprofits shape public policy, providing support for advocacy communications can be a crucial element of success. According to "Now Hear This," a brochure published by Fenton Communications, there are three essential characteristics for an effective advocacy campaign. It must have:

- Clear, measurable goals;

- Extensive knowledge of whom you are trying to reach and what moves them; and

- Compelling messages that connect with your target audience.

For more information on laws and regulations on public advocacy by family foundations, and on examples of what family foundations are doing in this area, see Establishing Grantmaking Interests and Priorities, p. 159.

Other resources designed to help foundations and nonprofits interested in particular aspects and issues of communications include:
- The Strategic Press Information Network (SPIN) — a program designed to provide media training to progressive nonprofit public interest groups.
- The Annie E. Casey Foundation's *Using Strategic Communication to Support Families* — a technical assistance guidebook for organizations involved in the foundation's *Making Connections* program to strengthen families with vulnerable children. (This guide outlines the broad range of activities involved in strategic communications, beyond simply obtaining positive media exposure.)

- *Now Hear This: The Nine Laws of Successful Advocacy Communications* — a publication that offers strategic guidance to groups seeking to develop effective advocacy campaigns. Published by Fenton Communications, with support from the David and Lucile Packard Foundation, *Now Hear This* provides basic ideas on how to shape public opinion and policy debates through the effective use of strategic marketing and communications.

Use of these and other communication resources will help you develop a communications strategy that is right for you. That strategy can range from an information program aimed at a small and specialized audience, to a larger program that can inform increasingly wider circles

COMMENCEMENT

Celebrating the Creation of Your Family Foundation

The creation of your family foundation deserves recognition and celebration. You may have been involved in philanthropy for many years, you may come from a family with a long philanthropic tradition, or you may never have launched a philanthropic journey before. No matter, this moment is one of the most significant in your life. Founders always remember when and where they signed the papers establishing their family foundation.

The creation of a family foundation offers an opportunity for reflection, learning, and growth, both for you and for your family. This is a special time for completing your preparation for the great privilege and responsibility of grantmaking. It is quite likely that, by this point, the charter is in place, bylaws are written, tax exemption has been received, and countless other startup tasks have been accomplished. With this final chapter, you're also completing your first introduction to the ideas, information, suggestions, tips, and — most important — encouragement that fill the pages of *Splendid Legacy*. Now, the moment to begin is at hand, like a grand commencement.

Perhaps you'll find that this is a wonderful time to consider the profound responsibility that attends stewardship of a philanthropic enterprise. We hope you have found that *Splendid Legacy* captures and passes on the true spirit of philanthropy — giving without expectation of reward, dedication to the betterment of society, and preservation of humane values.

The spirit of philanthropy was embodied in the life of Paul Ylvisaker, a great inspirational leader of modern philanthropy. One of his most compelling essays on philanthropy graces these last pages of *Splendid Legacy*. Paul very much understood that your education as a grantmaker will be a lifelong process. So, too, will your family continue to learn, refine, and renew. Many more commencements will likely occur in your own philanthropic lifetime and that of your family foundation.

For now, however, enjoy this moment, and accept our sincere best wishes, as you and your philanthropic family embark on the journey of a lifetime. The ride will likely have many ups and downs; there will be great moments of celebration and even consternation, but it will never be dull. May you always travel in the spirit of inquiry, respect, responsibility, joy, and even awe.

THE SPIRIT OF PHILANTHROPY
And the Soul of Those Who Manage It

PRESENTED TO THE THIRTY-EIGHTH ANNUAL CONFERENCE OF THE COUNCIL ON FOUNDATIONS, ATLANTA, GEORGIA, MARCH 1987

by Paul Ylvisaker

"Philanthropy is not just another institution. It stands for something distinctive and special, with a tradition and necessarily a spirit which represent to society the nobler motives of altruism and the more humane consideration so characteristically missing in the worlds of business and politics."

Stewardship is a term that is healthily disciplining, but it is also too passive: it does remind us of the specific trusts we have accepted, but it does not suggest the creative roles we inescapably play. We are stewards not merely of money, but of a tradition — a tradition [that] is still evolving. And that makes us accountable not only for what we preserve but for what we create.

I'd like to brood with you over both the custodial and the creative responsibilities of philanthropic managers.

I'll be making some generalizations that suffer all the liabilities of half-truths. Fair warning à la Robert Wood, who once introduced me with the mischievous alert: "I want you to listen carefully to Paul Ylvisaker. He's always persuasive but not always right." Still, how else than by generalizing do we human beings communicate insights — or keep an audience awake?

Who are the managers of philanthropy? To start with, the seven or eight thousand who don't own the money but make their living giving it away (the "philanthropoids"), plus another nearly equal number of trustees who manage organized philanthropy without benefit — some would say, without burden — of paid staff, but essentially all responsible for discharging the fiduciary responsibilities involved in running foundations.

Even at that, we're talking about a meager fraction of Americans: only six out of 100,000 who are trustees of foundations, and only three out of 100,000 who are paid staff.

Philanthropy is not easy to generalize about, despite those meager numbers. There can't be a more esoteric human activity, nor one more extraordinarily diverse — especially given the vast assortment of trusts that exist and therefore of the responsibilities involved.

But it is not enough to take refuge in diversity. We have a name, and therefore an identity; we have a function, and therefore a set of personal and public responsibilities. In searching for the spirit of philanthropy, that quintessential that instructs us in how we should behave and what values we ought to symbolize, there are two traditions to explore.

First, that of charity, the older and better understood; it has become almost instinctive in ours and other cultures in its presuppositions if not always its practice. Its "pure theory" builds upon six elements:
1. Altruism, the subordination of self-interest.

2. Compassion and empathy as the best avenues to understanding.
3. Taking the perspective of "the least among us." John Rawls built this into his theory of justice: the just society is one which tests its actions by their impact on the condition of its least powerful members.
4. A readiness to affirm and to act alone.
5. A quest for better human condition, sometimes in its sense of perfection reminiscent of the search for the Holy Grail.
6. Giving as a one-to-one human encounter in a micro-world of personal relationships.

In juxtaposition to this tradition of charity, another has evolved, [which] we now call modern (organized) philanthropy. It has developed its own set of presumptions, adapted from and adapting to, another environment:

1. The environment in which it works the one in which institutions, rather than individuals, are the key actors. We have moved from the world of the one-on-one to that of institutionalized interaction.

Guard your own humanity. The first ethical commandment is to take care of yourself. This is not acting for number one; it means taking care of what you are or should be, so that you can radiate that out to others.

2. There is a separation of donor and beneficiary into a world of intermediaries. The original donor, if still involved, acts through trustees, who act through staff, who act through one or more layers of nonprofit agencies, who act through staff, who act through a filter of representatives of the class, or problems, ultimately being dealt with. And further distancing occurs with the growth of specialization.

3. A look past the immediate condition of persons to what we call root causes and systemic reform.
4. A tilt toward reason and dispassion as the best route to systemic understanding and change.
5. A consciousness of institutional image and self-concern, ranging from tax considerations and the explicit rationalization by corporations of self-interest in their charity, to the incessant search all of us are engaged in for a distinctive mission and focus.
6. A recognition of a public responsibility, with accompanying public disciplines and restraints — and the redirection of that search for the Holy Grail toward an even more elusive concept called the public interest.
7. A conscious engineering of power, not only through grants and leveraging but through processes such as convening in which the gift plays only a part. Also, an explicit recognition of playing a social role, not simply a personal one.
8. A shift from gift to negotiated contract. We do this to both provide discipline and an assurance of effectiveness by watching carefully the terms of the grant. We also, by that method, allow reciprocity and participation. It is not the Lady Bountiful, unilateral act, and therefore it is consistent with the nature of our time. But have the very words "gift" and "grant" become archaic? Think about the way you deal with applicants. It is a negotiated contract that we have come to, rather than a gift or grant.
9. A search for consensus in approach and resolution. Consensus is an institutional imperative in our times, simply to minimize the friction generated by institutions moving through a crowding social and political environment.
10. A bias in favor of excellence and a meritocratic elite, both as justifications in themselves for philanthropy, but also as the preferred vehicle for helping the less advantaged.

Let's be clear: each of these elements has its own rationalizing logic. I am not putting these things down, but describing them. Each has made its own contribution to the evolving tradition of philanthropy. Without what they represent, charity could never have developed into the equilibrating and distinctive social force it has become. Charity could not have adapted to the social, economic, and political transformations that have taken place in modern society.

But the change has produced an institution and a profession with internal tensions, if not outright contradictions. Philanthropy has evolved, as Joseph Schumpeter once analyzed capitalism to have evolved, to produce a routinization of progress. Good works in our time have become routine, which partly explains the paradox of organized philanthropy routinely turning out worthy grants with gray-flannel-suit regularity and rhetoric — just read all those foundation annual reports.

Have we moved from flesh-and-blood giving to dispassionate and depersonalized philanthropy?

Which of these two traditions — the charitable or the more recent — are we the custodians of? The answer is both. We are tested by how creatively we balance and resolve those contending logics and meld them into a concept and code of behavior that honor the imperatives of both traditions. This may seem, and partly is, just another version of the contemporary dilemma: how do we remain human in an institutional environment?

But it's not that; philanthropy is not just another institution. It stands for something distinctive and special, with a tradition and necessarily a spirit which represent to society the nobler motives of altruism and the more humane considerations so characteristically missing in the worlds of business and politics.

Each of us will find his or her own way of living with these tensions — each one's own resolution, each one's own way of contributing creatively to the evolving practice of philanthropy. But there are some guiding maxims and imperatives I would urge on you, though clearly they reflect my own biases and pieties. (You'll note there are eleven commandments. Anything to outdo Moses.)

1. Guard your own humanity. The first ethical command-

Guard the soul of your own organization, even from your own pretensions. Those of you lucky enough to be part of an institution that has a soul know what a precious environment it is.

ment, taught to me by a distinguished professor of ethics, is to take care of yourself. This is not acting for number one; it means taking care of what you are or should be, so that you can radiate that out to others. If you lose your own soul — whether to arrogance, insensitivity, insecurity or shield of impersonality — you diminish the spirit of philanthropy. The goal to aspire to is that you will be a distinguished human being who gives to the foundation as much an identity as you derive from it, and far more than the money you give or negotiate away. In a very real sense, you *are* philanthropy.

2. Guard the soul of your own organization, even from your own pretensions. Those of you lucky enough to be part of an institution that has a soul know what a precious environment it is. It's a secure environment within which distinctive personalities complement rather than compete with each other; it's an open environment in which hierarchy is respected but not imposed, and where posturing and game-playing are unnecessary; it's an institution in which values are explicitly and easily discussed, and there is a consistency between values stated and values played out; it's an organization [that] demonstrates its humanity equally in its responsiveness to the needs and sensibilities of its external constituencies and in the care with which it nourishes and grows in its own personnel.

3. Be ready to speak out and act on your own on those hopefully rare occasions when principle is at stake or the unspoken needs to be aired.

4. Constantly assess your own motivation, whether what you're arguing for reflects your own power-drive and personal predilections or a measured evaluation of public need and foundation goals. This goes for trustees as well as staff, and ranges well beyond the more apparent realm of conflicts and interest.

5. Scan the whole gamut of your foundation's activities to make certain they are consistent with the goals and spirit of the philanthropic tradition. Are the values that peek through the backpage listing of your investments the same as those featured in the pious opening pages of your annual report? In your convening function, are you more intent on demonstrating influence than on catalyzing and releasing community energies? Do your personnel policies and board compositions jibe with the affirmative action expectations directed at your applicants? Does the care with which you consider public needs and foundation policy match the exhaustive scrutiny you give to applicant proposals and budgetary attachments? Compile your own checklist of such questions; you'll find it an instructive and sometimes chastening exercise.

6. Constantly traverse the lengthening distance between the words used in foundation docket items and press releases and the ultimate impact and beneficiaries of the grants once made. Have the intended beneficiaries really benefited? Who are they, and how many of them are from among the least advantaged? Has the quest for a better human condition dissipated in the chase after some abstraction? Have verbalizations and the mere recital of good grants made substituted for demonstrable attainment of tangible goals?

Follow both routes to understanding, the compassionate as well as the analytical. No one can comprehend the universe who does not understand and care for the sparrow.

7. Be willing to open the black box of philanthropy to share with others the mysteries of values and decision-making. They may seem disadvantageous to you as a protective mechanism, but in reality they're a breeding place for personal and institutional botulism. An anaerobic environment is not a healthy one for the spirit of philanthropy, nor for the soul of a manager.

Be ready and willing to mix with the community, and with those closer to real life than you are. Engage in dialogue with others who have legitimate interest in what you're doing and who may provoke you into insights that seclusion may have kept you from. Consider another ethical commandment: always be ready to explain publicly your decision and your reasons for your actions. Don't wind up your organization so tight that competing ideas can't filter through.

8. Never stop affirming. When you find your battery of hope, excitement, and even idealistic naiveté so drained that you don't let an applicant finish a presentation without pointing out why it can't be done, it's time you departed for another profession. Philanthropy builds on the hope of rising generations; it lights fires rather than snuffs them out.

9. Follow both routes to understanding, the compassionate as well as the analytical. No one can comprehend the universe who does not understand and care for the sparrow.

10. Don't ever lose your sense of outrage. Bill Bondurant [*Executive Director, Mary Reynolds Babcock Foundation, 1974-92*] can't forget, nor can I after he related it, the wondering comment of an applicant who looked about Bill's comfortable office and lifestyle: "How, Bill, do you keep your sense of outrage?" There has to be in all of us a moral thermostat that flips when we're confronted by suffering, injustice, inequality, or callous behavior.

11. Don't ever lose your sense of humor. Organized philanthropy so easily dulls into pretentious drabness, and we all need the revitalizing spark of a good laugh, mostly at ourselves.

My own chastening reminder is the memory of a cocktail party at which I, Mr. Big Bucks from the Ford Foundation, was pontificating to all within earshot. To make a point even more impressive, I paused to pick up an olive. But what my bad eyes had missed was that it was actually a cigar butt. Any of you who have ever tasted one knows the abrupt and ignominious end of that pious performance.

Philanthropy — in the degree to which it fulfills the aspiration of its spirit and tradition — is a rare element in our social firmament, a salt that cannot be allowed to lose its savor. It is a distinctive function that, like religion, relies eventually and essentially on its moral power.

We diminish that force when we get absorbed in a mistaken quest for power of another sort, be it money or social and political influence. Philanthropic influence derives more from spirit than from social positioning or monetary domination. The love of that money is undoubtedly the most corrupting element in the grantmaking enterprise.

There is enough of an alien spirit already attaching itself to philanthropy — self-interest being an ancient example and partisanship and political manipulation a more recent one — without our failing to recognize and honor the spirit and tradition of which we are stewards.

The power of organized philanthropy can indeed corrupt. But conducted in a humane spirit, and with soul, it can also ennoble.

I was once asked to work for Joe Clark, then mayor of Philadelphia. When I inquired of him what the job was, *really*, he thought a minute and replied, "To help fight the battle for my mind." It was an irresistible challenge.

But what I'd ask of someone about to join us as a foundation manager would be quite another dimension: "Help fight the battle for our soul."

APPENDICES

VI

—A—

Adjunct (Associate) Board. An adjunct board is often used for involving next generation and/or community members in the work of the foundation.

Affinity Group. A coalition of grantmaking institutions that shares information or provides professional development and networking opportunities to individual grantmakers with a shared interest in a particular subject or funding area.

Annual Report. A voluntary report published by a foundation describing its grant activities and application procedures. It may be a simple typed document listing the year's grants or an elaborately detailed publication. A growing number of foundations use an annual report as an effective means of informing the community about their contributions activities, policies, and guidelines.

Articles of Incorporation. A document filed with the Secretary of State or other appropriate state office by persons establishing a corporation. This is the first legal step in forming a nonprofit corporation.

Assets. Money, stocks, bonds, real estate or other holdings of a foundation. Generally, assets are invested and the income is used to make grants. (See Payout Requirement.)

—B—

Beneficiary. The donee or grantee receiving funds from a foundation or corporate giving program is the beneficiary, although society benefits as well.

Bequest. A sum of personal or real property made available upon the donor's death.

"Bricks and Mortar." An informal term for grants for buildings or construction projects.

Building Campaign. A drive to raise funds for construction or renovation of buildings.

Bylaws. Guidelines for the operation of a nonprofit corporation, developed according to state law requirements. Bylaws often provide the methods for the selection of directors, the creation of committees and the conduct of meetings.

—C—

Capacity Building. A process funders use to assist nonprofit organizations in strengthening their internal operations to become more efficient and effective for those they serve.

Capital Campaign (or Capital Development Campaign). An organized drive to collect and accumulate substantial funds to finance major needs of an organization such as a building, major repair project, or endowment purpose.

Challenge Grant. A grant that is made on the condition that other funds must be secured, either on a matching basis or via some other formula, usually within a specified period of time, with the objective of stimulating giving from additional sources.

Charitable Deduction. The portion of a gift to a qualified charity that is deductible from an individual's federal income tax, individual's gift tax, or individual's estate tax.

Charitable Organization. An organization that is eligible to receive charitable donations and is tax-exempt under federal tax law.

Checkbook Philanthropy. Spontaneous, responsive giving by a donor sometimes without personal involvement. Often involves giving small amounts in an unplanned manner.

Committed Funds. A portion of a donor's budget that has already been pledged for future allocation.

Community Foundation. A type of foundation formed by broad-based community support from multiple sources: trusts, endowments, individual contributions or private foundation grants. A community foundation often serves both its community and the donors who live in that community. All community foundations are classified as public charities.

Conflict of Interest Policy. Written policy developed within a foundation to address conflict of interest issues between trustees and potential grantees in a manner that is fair both to potential grantees and to the foundation trustee with whom they have a relationship. The policy details what is — and what is not — acceptable behavior on the part of the trustee.

Corporate Foundation (Company-Sponsored Foundation). A type of private foundation that receives its income from the profitmaking company whose name it bears but which is legally an independent entity. Corporations may fund these foundations with a donation of permanent assets or give periodic contributions that are generally based on a percentage of the company's profits.

Corporate Giving Program. Funding that is distributed, other than through a foundation, to meet corporate contributions goals. Often such a program is handled by the public affairs or public relations office. A corporate giving program is not subject to the same reporting requirements as a private foundation.

—D—

Decline (or Denial). The refusal or rejection of a grant request. Some declination letters explain why the grant was not made, but many do not.

Declining Grant. A multi-year grant that becomes smaller each year, in the expectation that the recipient organization will increase its fundraising from other sources.

Deferred Gift. A gift that is committed to a charitable organization but is not available for use until some future time, usually the death of the donor.

Demonstration Grant. A grant made to establish an innovative project or program that, if successful, will serve as a model and may be replicated by others.

Designated Funds. A type of restricted fund in which the fund beneficiaries are specified by the grantors.

Directors & Officers Insurance (D & O Insurance). D & O Liability Insurance is designed to help protect the Directors and Officers of a foundation against claims other than those for personal injury, property damage, or loss of property.

Discretionary Funds. Grant funds distributed at the discretion of one or more trustees, which usually do not require prior approval by the full board of directors. The governing board can delegate discretionary authority to staff.

Disqualified Person. Substantial contributors to a private foundation, foundation managers, certain public officials, family members of disqualified persons and corporations and partnerships in which disqualified persons hold significant interests. Financial transactions between disqualified persons and foundations are in violation of self-dealing rules, except as specified by law.

Donee. The individual or organization that receives a grant.

Donor. The individual or organization that makes a grant.

Donor Advised Fund. A fund in which the donor exercises the privilege of making nonbinding recommendations to the governing body as to which public charity or charities should receive a grant from this fund.

Donor Collaborative (Cooperative Venture). A joint effort between or among two or more grantmakers. Partners may share in funding responsibilities or contribute information and technical resources.

Donor Designated Fund. A fund held by a community foundation where the donor has specified that the fund's income or assets be used for the benefit of one or more specific public charities. These funds are sometimes established by a transfer of assets by a public charity to a fund designated for its own benefit, in which case they may be known as grantee endowments. The community foundation's governing body must have the power to redirect resources in the fund if it determines that the donor's restriction is unnecessary, incapable of fulfillment or inconsistent with the charitable needs of the community or area served.

—E—

E-philanthropy. Term used to describe the variety of methods of giving using the Internet. Many sites have been developed that accept donations in addition to providing information regarding nonprofit groups.

Endowment. A bequest or gift that is intended to be kept permanently and invested to create income for an organization or foundation.

Excise Tax. The annual tax of 1 or 2 percent of net investment income that must be paid to the IRS by private foundations.

Expenditure Responsibility. When a private foundation makes a grant to an organization that is not classified by the IRS as tax exempt under Section 501(c)(3) and as a public charity according to Sections 509(a), it is required by law to ensure that the funds are spent for charitable purposes and not for private gain or political activities. Such grants require a pre-grant inquiry and a detailed written agreement. Special reports on the status of the grant must be filed with the IRS, and the organizations must be listed on the foundation's 990-PF.

—F—

Family Foundation. A private foundation whose funds are derived from members of a single family. One or more family members continue to serve as officers or board members of the foundation and play an influential role in governance and grantmaking.

Financial Report. An accounting statement detailing financial data, including income from all sources, expenses, assets and liabilities. A financial report may also be an itemized accounting that shows how grant funds were used by a donee organization. Most foundations require a financial report from grantees.

501(c)(3). Section of the Internal Revenue Code that designates an organization as charitable and tax-exempt. Organizations qualifying under this section include religious, educational, charitable, amateur athletic, scientific or literary groups, organizations testing for public safety or organizations involved in prevention of cruelty to children or animals. Most organizations seeking foundation or corporate contributions secure a section 501(c)(3) classification from the Internal Revenue Service (IRS). Note: the tax code sets forth a list of sections—501(c)(4-26)—to identify other nonprofit organizations whose function is not solely charitable (e.g., professional or veterans organizations, chambers of commerce, fraternal societies, etc.)

509(a). Section of the tax code that defines public charities (as opposed to private foundations). A 501(c)(3) organization must also have a 509(a) designation to further define the agency as a public charity. (See Public Support Test.)

Form 990. The tax information form filed annually with the IRS and the state's Attorney General's office by tax-exempt organizations and institutions with gross revenue of more than $25,000 except religious. This tax return includes information about the organization's assets, income, operating expenses, contributions, paid staff and salaries, names and addresses of persons to contact, and program areas.

Form 990-PF. The IRS form filed annually by all private foundations. The letters "PF" stand for "Private Foundation." The IRS uses this form to determine if a private foundation is complying with the Internal Revenue Code. The 990-PF form lists foundation assets, receipts, expenditures, compensation of officers and a list of grants made during the year.

Funding Cycle. A chronological pattern of proposal review, decisionmaking and applicant notification. Some donor organizations make grants at set intervals (quarterly, semi-annually, etc.), while others operate under an annual cycle.

—G—

Gift Fund. Commercially sponsored donor-advised fund typically formed by a mutual fund group or similar financial institution offering some grantmaking assistance to donors. Gift funds function like private foundations, but at a lower cost, and provide all the tax benefits available for contributions to a public charity. They do not provide the unlimited control that is inherent in a private foundation.

Giving Circle. An organization of people who meet regularly to share information and to make joint giving decisions.

Giving Pattern. The overall picture of the types of projects and programs that a donor has historically supported. The past record may include areas of interest, geographic locations, dollar amount of funding or kinds of organizations supported.

Grant. The award of funds to an organization or individual to undertake charitable activities.

Grant Monitoring. The ongoing assessment of the progress of the activities funded by a donor, with the objective of determining if the terms and conditions of the grant are being met and if the goal of the grant is likely to be achieved.

Grantee. See Donee.

Grantee Financial Report. A report detailing how grant funds were used by an organization. Many grantmakers require this kind of report from grantees. A financial report generally includes a listing of all expenditures from grant funds as well as an overall organizational financial report covering revenue and expenses, assets and liabilities.

Grantor. See Donor.

Grassroots Fundraising. Efforts to raise money from individuals or groups from the local community on a broad basis. Usually an organization does grassroots fundraising within its own constituency—people who live in the neighborhood served or clients of the agency's services.

Guidelines. A statement of a donor's goals, priorities, criteria and procedures.

In-Kind Contribution. A donation of goods or services rather than cash or appreciated property.

Independent Foundation. A private foundation in which members of the board of directors are not related to the original donor(s).

Internal Revenue Service (IRS). The federal agency with responsibility for regulating foundations and their activities.

—J—

Jeopardy Investment. An investment that is found to have jeopardized a foundation's purposes. The result of a jeopardy investment may be penalty taxes imposed upon a foundation and its managers. While certain types of investments are subject to careful examination, no one type is automatically a jeopardy investment. Generally, a jeopardy investment is found to be made when a foundation's managers have "failed to exercise ordinary business care and prudence."

—L—

Letter of Inquiry (Query Letter). A brief letter outlining an organization's activities and a request for funding sent to a prospective donor to determine if there is sufficient interest to warrant submitting a full proposal. This saves the time of the prospective donor and the time and resources of the prospective applicant. (See Preliminary Proposal.)

Letter of Intent. A grantor's letter or brief statement indicating intention to make a specific gift.

Leverage. A method of grantmaking practiced by some foundations. Leverage occurs when a small amount of money is given with the express purpose of attracting larger funding from other sources or of providing the organization with the tools it needs to raise other kinds of funds. Sometimes known as the "multiplier effect."

Limited Life. Length of life of a foundation that is limited by the donor(s). The charter may require that the assets be distributed after a certain number of years.

Limited-Purpose Foundation. A type of foundation that restricts its giving to one or very few areas of interest, such as higher education or medical care.

Loaned Executives. Corporate executives who work for nonprofit organizations for a limited period of time while continuing to be paid by their permanent employers.

Lobbying. Efforts by any group or organization to influence legislation by influencing the opinion of legislators, legislative staff and government administrators directly involved in drafting legislative proposals. Lobbying activities by public charities are limited by Section 501(c)(3) of the tax code. Public charities may lobby as long as lobbying does not become a substantial part of their activities. Private foundations generally may not lobby except in limited circumstances such as on issues affecting their tax-exempt status or the deductibility of gifts to them. Conducting nonpartisan analysis and research and disseminating the results to the public generally is not lobbying for purposes of these restrictions.

—M—

Matching Gifts Program. A grant or contributions program that will match employees' or directors' gifts made to qualifying charitable organizations. Specific guidelines are established by each employer/foundation. (Some foundations also use this program for trustees and other foundation-related individuals.)

Matching Grant. A grant or gift made with the specification that the amount donated must be matched on a one-for-one basis or according to some other prescribed formula.

Mission Statement. A mission statement reflects the foundation's core values and reason(s) for existing. It should capture what the foundation does, why it does it, how it does it, and for whom it does it. A mission statement broadly addresses the current and future purpose(s) of the foundation.

Mission-Related Investing. A specific type of socially responsive investing that attempts to align an institution's mission with its investment strategies.

—N—

Nonprofit. A nonprofit is an organization whose purpose is to serve a public good rather than make a profit; net earnings are not distributed to the owners or shareholders (as in a private corporation) or to the members, but are retained for the purpose for which the organization was established. The organizational form and use of volunteers varies enormously across the sector. The sector would include hospitals, universities, religious organizations, cooperatives, charities, voluntary organizations, economic and trade associations (the association is nonprofit even though the industry which it represents is not), among many others.

Not-for-Profit. Not-for-profit organization is a synonym for nonprofit organization.

—O—

Operating Foundation. A type of private foundation that carries out its own charitable programs rather than making grants to other organizations to accomplish charitable purposes. To qualify as an operating foundation, specific rules, in addition to the applicable rules for private foundations, must be followed.

Operating Support. A contribution given to cover an organization's day-to-day, ongoing expenses, such as salaries, utilities, offices supplies, etc.

Organizational Effectiveness. Organizational effectiveness generally refers to the structures and systems that allow an agency to grow, adapt, innovate, and take advantage of new opportunities resulting in improved internal processes and external outcomes for their clients.

—P—

Pass-Through Foundation. Foundations that receive funds and make distributions to donees, with little or no principal remaining with the foundation.

Payout Requirement. The minimum amount that a private foundation is required to expend for charitable purposes (includes grants and necessary and reasonable administrative expenses). In general, a private foundation must annually pay out approximately 5 percent of the average market value of its assets.

Perpetuity. Length of life of a foundation that is deemed perpetual by the donor(s). The donor may wish to establish the foundation in perpetuity to enable the family tradition to continue after his or her death.

Personal Gift Pledge. Pledge made by a disqualified person of a foundation. Self-dealing rules preclude payment by a foundation of any obligation of a disqualified person, even a charitable pledge.

Philanthropy. Philanthropy is defined in different ways. The origin of the word philanthropy is Greek and means love for mankind. Today, philanthropy includes the concept of voluntary giving by an individual or group to promote the common good. Philanthropy also commonly refers to grants of money given by foundations to nonprofit organizations.

Pledge. A promise to make future contributions to an organization. For example, some donors make multi-year pledges promising to grant a specific amount of money each year.

Post-Grant Evaluation. A review of the results of a grant with the emphasis upon whether or not the grant achieved its desired objective.

Preliminary Proposal. A brief draft of a grant proposal used to learn if there is sufficient interest to warrant submitting a proposal.

Private Foundation. A nongovernmental, nonprofit organization with funds (usually from a single source, such as an individual, family or corporation) and program managed by its own trustees or directors, that was established to maintain or aid social, educational, religious or other charitable activities serving the common welfare, primarily through grantmaking. "Private foundation" also means an organization that is tax-exempt under Section 501(c)(3) of the tax code and is classified by the IRS as a private foundation as defined in the code.

Program Officer (Program Associate, Public Affairs Officer or Community Affairs Officer). A staff member of a foundation or corporate giving program who may do some or all of the following: recommend policy, review grant requests, manage the budget and process applications for the board of directors or contributions committee.

Program-Related Investment. A loan or other investment (as distinguished from a grant) made by a grantmaking organization to a profitmaking or nonprofit organization for a project related to the foundation's stated purpose and interests. Program-related investments are often made from a revolving fund; the foundation generally expects to receive its money back with limited, or below-market, interest, which will then provide additional funds for loans to other organizations. A program-related investment may involve loan guarantees, purchases of stock or other kinds of financial support.

Proposal. A written application, often accompanied by supporting documents, submitted to a foundation or corporate giving program in requesting a grant. Most foundations and corporations do not use printed application forms but instead require written proposals; others prefer preliminary letters of inquiry prior to a formal proposal.

Prudent Investor Rule. This rule defines the duty owed by a trustee to the beneficiary in making "prudent" investment decisions for the beneficiary's benefit. Initially, this only required that the actions taken by a trustee be those of a man of prudence, discretion, and intelligence. Over the years, however, the 1830 statute has been revised: It is now commonly referred to as The Third Restatement of the Prudent Man Rule.

Public Charity (Public Foundation). A nonprofit organization that receives at least one-third of its annual income from the general public (including government agencies and foundations)—the so-called public support test, which can also be satisfied if the foundation meets an absolute minimum public support test equal to at least 10 percent of all support, and also has a variety of other characteristics which make it sufficiently "public." Some make grants, while others engage in direct service or other tax-exempt, charitable activities serving the common welfare.

Public Support Test. Tests designed to ensure that a section 170(b)(1)(A)(vi) or 509(a)(2) public charity is responsive to the general public rather than to the private interests of a limited number of persons. The organization must normally receive more than one-third of its financial support from the general public.

—Q—

Qualifying Distributions. Expenditures of a private foundation made to satisfy its annual payout requirement. These can include grants, reasonable administrative expenses, set-asides, loans and program-related investments, and amounts paid to acquire assets used directly in carrying out tax-exempt purposes.

—R—

Regional Association of Grantmakers (RAG). Nonprofit membership associations of private and community foundations, corporations, individuals and others committed to strengthening philanthropy in the geographic areas in which they operate, within the United States.

Requests For Proposals (RFP). Request sent by foundations to organizations that might qualify for funding within a specific program of the foundation. The RFP lists project specifications and application procedures.

Restricted Funds. Assets or income that is restricted in its use, in the types of organizations that may receive grants from it or in the procedures used to make grants from such funds.

—S—

Seed Money. A grant or contribution used to start a new project or organization.

Self-Dealing. An illegal financial transaction between a private foundation and a disqualified person(s). There are a few exceptions to the self-dealing rule, including the compensation of disqualified persons by a foundation for services that are necessary and reasonable. Violations of this rule result in an initial penalty tax equal to 5 percent of the amount involved, payable by the self-dealer.

Set-Asides. Funds set aside for future payments. If a foundation demonstrates successfully to the IRS in advance that the funds will in fact be paid within 60 months and that the project can better be accomplished by such a set-aside than by an immediate grant, the full appropriation may count in the first year.

Site Visit. Visiting a donee organization at its office location or area of operation; meeting with its staff or directors or with recipients of its services.

Social Investing (Ethical Investing and Socially Responsible Investing). The practice of aligning a foundation's investment policies with its mission. This may include making program-related investments and refraining from investing in corporations with products or policies inconsistent with the foundation's values.

Social Venture Fund. Charitable fund whose donor invests their expertise as well as their money, providing support and requiring accountability of nonprofit organizations just as venture capitalists do in business enterprises. (See Venture Philanthropy.)

Spend Out (Spend Down). Process used by foundations to deplete assets resulting in the closing of the foundation.

Strategic Planning. Strategic planning is a disciplined effort to produce fundamental decisions and actions that shape and guide what a foundation is, what it does and why it does it. Strategic planning involves the entire process of defining the future direction and character of the foundation, and of attempting over an adopted timetable to attain the desired state to accomplish related goals and outcomes.

Supporting Organization. An organization created primarily to fund the activities of one or more existing public charities. There must be a close relationship between the supporting organization and one or more such public charities.

—T—

Tax-Exempt Organizations. Organizations that do not have to pay state and/or federal income taxes. Tax-exempt status can be obtained by applying to the IRS and, in most states, the Attorney General's Office.

Technical Assistance. Operational or management assistance given to a nonprofit organization. It can include fundraising assistance, budgeting and financial planning, program planning, legal advice, marketing and other aids to management. Assistance may be offered directly by a foundation or corporate staff member or in the form of a grant to pay for the services of an outside consultant. (See In-Kind Contribution.)

Tipping. The situation that occurs when a grant is made that is large enough to significantly alter the grantee's funding base and cause it to fail the public support test. This failure can result in the grantee's conversion to a private foundation and would also require expenditure responsibility on the part of the grantor.

Trust. A legal device used to set aside raised money or property of one person for the benefit of one or more persons or organizations.

Trustee. The person(s) or institutions responsible for the administration of a trust.

—U—

Unrestricted Funds. A grant that does not specifically stipulate how the money is to be spent by the grantee. (Note: In community foundations, Unrestricted Funds refer to funds the foundation holds that are not designated by donors and may be granted at the discretion of the board of the community foundation.)

—V—

Venture Philanthropy. Charitable funding where donors invest their expertise as well as their money, providing support and requiring accountability of nonprofit organizations similar to what venture capitalists do in business enterprises. Donors may assist nonprofit organizations in the planning, launch, and management of new programs or social purpose enterprises. In addition to grants, venture philanthropists provide networking, management advice and an array of other supports to organizations within a given portfolio of charitable investments. (See Social Venture Fund.)

Virtual Foundation. Refers to the transition from grantmaking through mail and face-to-face meetings to grantmaking by email and Internet transfers. Such a foundation may exist only on the Internet and be capable of transferring money from philanthropists to organizations globally.

This glossary is adapted with permission from a version that appeared in the Family Foundation Library series [Council on Foundations, 1997, Virginia M. Esposito (editor)]. As significant edits were made to the text and more than 40 new entries were added, the National Center for Family Philanthropy is solely responsible for its content. ⁕ The Family Foundation Library series is available from the Council on Foundations at www.cof.org.

The National Center for Family Philanthropy is indebted to Elizabeth Watkins, graduate student at the Center on Philanthropy at Indiana University and an intern at the National Center, for her work on this glossary.

SAMPLE POLICIES AND FORMS

CONTENTS

VII. APPENDICES

In addition to the documents listed in this section, other policies and forms are available from the National Center. These include:

- Articles of Incorporation;
- Bylaws;
- Common Evaluation Form; and
- Personnel Policies.

Membership Selection Procedures

- The Board of Trustees elects all board members.

- Individuals elected to board membership should possess characteristics described in "Trustee Qualifications and Values," which has been endorsed by the board.

- There are _____ seats on the board. There is/is no requirement that all of the seats on the board be filled.

- To promote stability and continuity on the board, no more than three board members should be elected in any given year. No more than two new board members should be elected in any given year.

- The intent of the board is to have a minimum of one and a maximum of two lineal descendants from the family of each of [the donor's] three children on the board each year. If lineal descendants are not available and qualified, then a maximum of two family members may be considered to serve on the board. The majority of the trustees should be members of [the donor's] family.

- It is helpful for the board to have at least one member from outside [the donor's] family.

- The term of office is three years. However, a trustee may be elected for a term of less than three years if the board determines a shorter term is appropriate in order to reduce the number of trustees elected in subsequent years or for any other appropriate reason.

- Trustees may be elected for more than one term.

- Board membership is a serious obligation. If a trustee misses two regularly scheduled meetings in any year, his or her term as a trustee may be terminated upon board review.

- If at all possible, board members should give the board formal notice at least two meetings before they plan to retire from the board.

- The board will select a nominating committee to nominate new board members for consideration by the full board. The nominating committee should consist preferably of one person each from each of the family's branches.

EXCERPTED FROM *The Trustee Notebook: An Orientation for Family Foundation Board Members*, by Robert Hull, National Center for Family Philanthropy: 1999.

Conflict of Interest Policy

OUR POLICY:

The Self Family Foundation encourages board members to play an active role in the community by serving as board members or otherwise being involved with a wide spectrum of nonprofit organizations. This means that, from time to time, potential conflicts of interest or appearance of such conflicts will inevitably arise. It is the Foundation's policy to deal with such conflicts as openly as possible.

Conflicting involvements include but are not limited to the following:

- Foundation board members serving as board members of applicant organizations.

- Immediate family members of Foundation board members serving on applicant organizations.

- Foundation members or their immediate families being employed or doing business with applicant organizations.

In the case of such conflicts or the appearance thereof, Foundation board members and/or staff are expected to disclose the conflict prior to making any grant-related decisions. Once such a disclosure is made, the remaining board members will determine if there is a potential conflict of interest. Should it be determined, the board member involved shall abstain from voting and shall not participate in the discussions of the applicant organization other than to provide information of a technical nature or answer specific questions that may be raised by other board members.

In cases where the Foundation's board of trustees decides to award a grant to an organization and one or more of the Foundation's board members abstains from voting as a result of conflict of interest or the appearance thereof, such grants and board member will be identified in the official minutes of the meeting.

A roster listing each board/staff member and organizations on whose boards they or immediate family member serve, are employed by or have a business relationship with, will be maintained by the Foundation president.

Grant Guidelines

GRANT GUIDELINES

The _____ is a private family foundation established in _____ by _____ to continue the family tradition of commitment to enhancing the quality of life of the community through grants to qualified charitable organizations.

In carrying out its mission, the Foundation considers a wide ranged of proposals within the following areas: arts, education, health, human services, environment, and public interest. Currently, the Foundation has a special interest in _____. The Foundation encourages collaborative efforts and integrated, comprehensive proposals.

FUNDING POLICIES

Grants are made only to non-profit charitable organizations which are tax exempt under Section 501 (c) (3) of the Internal Revenue Code, or to public governmental units. Generally, grants are limited to projects that benefit the citizens of _____. Occasionally, projects that benefit the state of _____ as a whole may be considered.

The Foundation prefers to support proposals for new initiatives, special projects, expansion of current programs, capital improvement or building renovation.

The Foundation does not consider support for annual campaigns, endowments, sectarian religious activities or requests under _____. Grants are not made to individuals.

Grants from the Foundation are usually awarded for one year only. For projects in those areas in which the Foundation has a special interest, requests for multi-year funding and general operating support may be considered.

Only one grant application may be submitted in any twelve-month period. Organizations receiving grants are required to complete an evaluation report within twelve months after receipt of the funds.

REVIEW PROCESS

The Board of Directors meets in the spring and fall to consider grant requests. Application must be received by March 1 or September 1 to be acted upon at the following meeting.

Applications are welcome and encouraged to discuss their proposal with the Foundation's staff either by telephone or in person. Upon receipt of the completed proposal, staff may request additional information or schedule a site visit. Members of the Board of Directors prefer not to be contacted directly.

APPLICATION PROCEDURES

To apply, submit one (1) set of the following items. Please do not staple materials or place them in a bound notebook.

1. Grant Application form completed, dated and signed by the Chief Executive Officer o Chairman of the board of the organization.
2. Proposal of not more than two pages which includes (in this order):
   a) A short introductory paragraph with a concise statement of the purpose of the request and the amount requested;
   b) A detailed project description covering the issue being addressed, what will be different and why it is important; the outcomes to be achieved; the plans for accomplishing the outcomes and project timetable; capacity of your organization to carryout the plans; if this is a collaborative effort, the role of each partner; how you will evaluate the success and effectiveness of the program;
   c) A brief description of the history, mission and activities of your organization.
3. Project Budget including both anticipated sources of income and projected expenditures.
4. Organization Operating Budget for the current fiscal year including income (sources and amounts) and expenditures.
5. Board of Directors list with affiliations or occupations.
6. Financial Statement audited if available, for the most recent complete fiscal year.
7. Copy of IRS 501 (c) (3) Determination Letter.
8. Optional Materials may be submitted but are not required.

Grant Application

HOW TO APPLY FOR A GRANT ELIGIBILITY

Grants are awarded for projects consistent with one or more of the Helen Bader Foundation's program areas. Grants are given only to U.S. organizations that are tax exempt under Section 501(c)(3) of the Internal Revenue Code or to government entities. Grants will only be approved for foreign entities that meet specific charitable status requirements. The Foundation does not provide direct support for individuals, such as individual scholarships.

The Foundation often funds multiple-year projects, but rarely for a period of more than three years. All grants approved for more than one year are conditional and are subject to annual review and approval before funds for subsequent years are released.

The Foundation is an affirmative action employer and grantmaker. Eligible applicants are expected to adhere to all non-discrimination laws.

APPLYING FOR A GRANT

Organizations interested in applying for a grant should follow these steps:

PHASE ONE

Complete the attached one-page preliminary application form to formally make a request for funding. This form introduces both the applicant organization and the proposed project or program to the Foundation. Mail, fax or e-mail the one-page preliminary application form prior to the scheduled Board meetings (see deadlines for 2001-2002). The preliminary application is also available online at www.hbf.org.

The Helen Bader Foundation will also accept the Common Application Form, which is endorsed by the Donors Forum of Wisconsin.

Shortly after its receipt, the Foundation will respond in writing regarding the status of the letter of application.

PHASE TWO

The Foundation will notify applicants when there is an interest in exploring the grant request further, and a full proposal will be requested and site visits and/or meetings scheduled. Full proposals must be mailed or hand-delivered, as faxed or e-mailed copies will not be accepted. All of the above information is essential for each proposal to be considered. Supplemental videos or other materials cannot be returned to the applicant.

The appearance of the proposal will not be used as criteria; a simple, readable format is encouraged. The following materials are required:

Description of Organization
(Limit to five single-spaced, printed pages)
- Background of organization
- Mission and objectives
- Description of target group(s)
- Type(s) of program(s) offered
- Major accomplishments
- Number of staff
- Current annual operating budget (income and expenses)
- Attach strategic plan and/or marketing materials (if available)

Complete Project Description
(Limit to five single-spaced, printed pages)
- Need for the project and how the need was determined
- Expected results of the project
- Means for measuring the project's results
- Plans and timetables for implementation
- Staff responsible for implementation
- Project's actual or projected expenditures and revenues for the project period

Financial Information

- Organization's actual or projected expenditures and revenues for the past, current, and upcoming fiscal years, and your budget vs. actual year-to-date statement
- Plans for sustaining the project's funding upon the expiration of Helen Bader Foundation funding
- A list of other funding sources applied to for support of the project
- A complete copy of the most recent financial statement of the applicant organization and, if available, a copy of the report or opinion as prepared by an independent accountant

Legal Information

- A copy of the IRS determination letter concerning Section 501 (c)(3) status and private or non-private foundation status
- A copy of the most recently submitted IRS Form 990 with Schedule A
- The names of the organization's directors or trustees; please indicate the titles of the officers of the board of directors, including which board officer will sign the required legal documents

Deadlines

Preliminary applications should be submitted as early as possible. Due to the volume of requests to the Foundation, the submission of an application by the published deadlines does not guarantee that the grant request will be considered at the Board meeting immediately following that deadline. The Foundation will make every effort to meet the needs of the applicant.

The Board of Directors meets twice each year to make grant decisions. Preliminary applications and full proposals must be received by 5 p.m. on the deadline date.

Preliminary Application Form	Full Proposal	Board Meeting
January x, 2002	January x, 2002	May 2002
July x, 2002	August x, 2002	November 2002
January x, 2003	February x, 2003	May 2003

The grant policies, guidelines, programs, application requirements, and funding decisions are the responsibility of the Board of Directors. These items may be modified by the Board of Directors at any time in its sole discretion.

Geographic Restrictions

Geographic Restrictions for the following grants programs include:

- Alzheimer's Disease and Dementia: National (with priority to Wisconsin organizations)
- Economic Development: Greater Milwaukee
- Education: Greater Milwaukee
- Jewish Life and Learning: Greater Milwaukee
- Sankofa – Neighborhood Renewal: Milwaukee

Foundation Name

The Helen Bader Foundation reserves the right to maintain the exclusive use of its name. Helen Bader made donations to charitable organizations for many years in a quiet and dignified manner, and the Foundation wishes to continue with her style and does not ordinarily accept requests to name facilities or programs.

Requests that are Denied

The Foundation receives a multitude of grant requests for worthwhile projects. Unfortunately, more than 70 percent of the requests are not funded simply because the demand exceeds the Foundation's resources. A denial is not necessarily a reflection of the quality of the grant request or applicant organization.

Applicants are welcome to resubmit a grant request. However, before reapplying, it is advantageous to discuss with the reason for the initial denial with the appropriate member of the program staff.

Grant Application (continued)

This preliminary application form must be completed when submitting an initial grant request prior to a detailed full proposal. If requested, a full proposal is due within 30 days after submission of this preliminary proposal.

1. Name of Applicant Organization: (Please Use Full Legal Name) _____

   Employer Identification Number (EIN): _____

2. Street Address/P.O. Box: _____

   City: _____ State: _____ Zip: _____

   County: _____ Country: _____

3. Phone: ( ) _____ Fax: ( ) _____

4. Website: _____

5. Contact Person: Mr./Ms. First Name _____ Last Name _____

   Title: _____ Phone: ( ) _____

   E-mail: _____

6. Name of Applicant Organization's Chief Executive Officer/Executive Director:

   Mr./Ms. First Name _____ Last Name _____

7. Names of Applicant Organization's Officers of the Board of Directors:

   Chairperson: Mr./Ms. First Name _____ Last Name _____

   President: Mr./Ms. First Name _____ Last Name _____

   Secretary: Mr./Ms. First Name _____ Last Name _____

   Vice President: Mr./Ms. First Name _____ Last Name _____

   Treasurer: Mr./Ms. First Name _____ Last Name _____

8. Date applicant organization's fiscal year begins: _____

9. Indicate the program area or fund within the Foundation for which this application should be considered:

   ❐ Alzheimer's Disease and Dementia   ❐ Education   ❐ Sankofa – Youth Development

   ❐ Economic Development   ❐ Jewish Life and Learning   ❐ Directed Grants

9. Title of Project: _____

10. Dollar Amount Requested: $ _____

    Year 1: $ _____ Year 2: $ _____ Year 3: $ _____

11. Date Project Started or Will Start: _____

12. Brief Project Summary (100 Words or Less; Use Back of Page if Necessary) _____

This form may be reproduced and/or e-mailed as a Word or Text attachment to info@hbf.org. Application form is also available online at www.hbf.org.

Grant Agreement

The grant to your organization ("Grantee") from the _____ foundation ("Grantor") is for the purpose (s) described below and is subject to your organization's acceptance of the terms and conditions herein. To acknowledge this agreement, to accept its conditions, and to be eligible to receive payment of the grant funds, **PLEASE RETURN TWO SIGNED COPIES TO THE FOUNDATION**. A countersigned copy will be returned to you for your organization's records.

GRANTEE:

Amount of Grant: _____ Date Authorized by Board: _____

Grant Purpose: _____

Special conditions of grant: _____

PAYMENT SCHEDULE: This grant will be paid upon receipt of two-signed grant agreements.

GRANTEE FURTHER AGREES:

1. The grant monies must be spent within one year of ward, for the grant purposes stated in this grant agreement.
2. The Foundation requires documentation of three (3) bids for every construction/renovation project and copies of permits where required by local jurisdictions.
3. To repay to Grantor any portion of the grant funds not used within one year or which were not used for the purpose (s) stated above; To submit to Grantor a post-grant report, with supporting documentation, one year following the receipt of grant funds awarded under this agreement, concerning the manner in which said funds were spent and the progress made in accomplishing the purposes herein;
5. To keep adequate records of expenditures to enable such records to be readily reviewed;
6. To keep records of such expenditures, as well as copies of any and all reports submitted to Grantor, for at least four years following the completion of the expenditure of grant funds;
7. To notify Grantor if any changes occur which could lead to a change in the Grantee's tax-exempt status or public charity classification and to repay to Grantor any unspent grant funds if the Grantee's tax-exempt status is revoked or it ceases to be a public charity;
8. To notify Grantor if any changes occur in the program or project for which funding is given, as specifically set out in the purposes and conditions of this grant agreement;
9. To fully cooperate with a representative of Grantor in evaluation the effective use of the funds awarded;
10. To use no portion of the grant funds to: 1) influence the outcome of any specific public election, or to carry on directly or indirectly any voter registration drive (either the meaning of Internal Revenue Code (IRC) Section 4945 (d) (2); 2) to carry on propaganda otherwise to attempt to influence legislation (within the meaning of the IRC Section 4945 (d) (1); or 3) to undertake any activity for any purpose other than a charitable, educational, etc. purpose described in IRC Section 170 (c) (2) (B); and
11. To repay to Grantor upon demand the full amount of the grant funds if there is a failure to comply with any provision of this grant agreement.

GRANTOR:

Name of Foundation: _____

By: (Board Chair or Executive Director) _____ Date: _____

The terms and conditions of this grant agreement have been read, are understood and are accepted, and it is confirmed that there has been no change in the tax-exempt status and public charity classification of Grantee.

GRANTEE:

Name of organization: _____

By (signature of authorized signatory): _____

Printed name: _____ Date: _____

Letters of Inquiry to The Stocker Foundation

- Any organization that has not previously submitted a proposal to The Stocker Foundation, received a declination the last time a proposal was submitted, or has not yet received IRS tax-exemption status **must first submit a Letter of Inquiry to the Foundation a minimum of six weeks before the submission deadline.**

- All Letters of Inquiry should be **no more than 2-3 pages** and should include:

  1. A brief summary of the project or need.
  2. A project budget that details how funding from The Stocker Foundation would be used (including the amount to be requested from the Foundation).
  3. All other funding pending or committed.
  4. A timeline of implementation.

- If your organization will be using a **fiscal agent**, please include a letter of support from the agent as well as the agent's 501(c)(3) exemption letter.

- If your organization received a **declination** the last time a proposal was submitted to The Stocker Foundation, please indicate what the name of the project was and when the declination was issued.

- Letters of inquiry must be received **6 weeks** before a grant deadline:

LETTER OF INQUIRY DUE	PROPOSAL DEADLINE*
April 1, 2002	May 15, 2002
July 1, 2002	August 15, 2002
December 9, 2002	January 15, 2003

  *If Trustees are interested in receiving a full proposal, staff will notify the organization within two weeks of the proposal submission deadline, and will give direction as to which cycle the proposal should be submitted.

- Funding is not guaranteed — Trustees will evaluate each proposal on its individual merits and in accordance with available dollars for that particular grant cycle.

Executive Director
Duties and Responsibilities

PROGRAM (60% OF TIME)

The Executive Director is responsible for overseeing all aspects of programming
for the Foundation, including:

- Works with the Board to establish the Foundation's general grantmaking focus and priorities.
- Reviews grant applications and response to letters of inquiry. Trustees will be expected to refer requests for support and oral inquiries to the Executive Director.
- Oversees the preparation of written agendas of grant proposal reviews and other matters requiring Board action.
- Oversees the preparation and presentation of special initiatives and reports to be considered for Board action.
- Oversees the conduct of public policy research related to community issues and future grant action.
- Meets with prospective applicants and discusses Foundation policies.
- Conducts grant reviews in the fields of art and the environment and making recommendation for Board action.

STAFF (20% OF TIME)

- Manages the Foundation's staff on a day-to-day basis, delegating responsibilities.
- Hires, performance evaluation, discipline and termination of employees.
- Recommends staff salary increases for review and approval by the Board.
- Recommends modification to and implementing Board-approved personnel policies and practices.

RELATIONS WITH COUNSEL (5% OF TIME)

- Confers with the Foundation Counsel on programs, projects, and other matters requiring legal assistance.

RELATIONS WITH INVESTMENT ADVISORS (5% OF TIME)

- Monitors the work of the Foundation's Investment Advisors and making certain that their reports are presented to the trustees in a timely manner.

PUBLIC RELATIONS (10% OF TIME)

- Represents the Foundation at important public events and overseeing all formal communications with the media.
- Supervises the preparation of the annual report and the other documents to be released to the public.

Knott Foundation Board Officer Descriptions

PRESIDENT: The President shall have the power: (1) to call special meetings of the trustees for any purpose(s); (2) to appoint and discharge employees and agents of the foundation; (3) to generally manage and control the business of the foundation and its assets; (4) to preside at meetings of the Board of Trustees; and (5) to generally perform all acts incidental to the office of President which are authorized by the Board of Trustees or required by law.

VICE PRESIDENT: The Vice-President shall, in the absence or incapacity of the President, preside over the meetings of the trustees and shall perform such other duties as may be authorized from time to time by the Board of Trustees.

TREASURER: The Treasurer shall: (1) perform all the duties customary to that office; (2) oversee the management of the funds and securities of the foundation by the money managers; and (3) have the general supervision of the books of account.

SECRETARY: The Secretary, or his/her designee, shall: (1) keep the minutes of meetings of the board; (2) have custody of the seal of the foundation and shall affix the same to documents when authorized to do so; and (3) perform all of the duties pertaining to that office.

Proposal Declination Letter

Dear _____:

Thank you for applying to the _____. Unfortunately, the Fund will be unable to make a grant in support of your project, "_____."
While your proposal advanced to the final stages of consideration by the Fund, it was not selected for funding. We appreciate the time and effort you have taken to provide us with information about your _____ and hope that there will be opportunities for us to collaborate in the future.

We wish you success in your efforts to contribute to the _____. If you wish to discuss your project further, please contact _____ at _____.

Sincerely,

_____

Site Visit Report

Visitors: _____

Date of visit: _____

Organization: _____

Amount requested: _____

Purposed of request: _____

1. Is there adequate talent in the leadership (board and staff) to make the program/organization a success?

2. Is there a probability of sustained change from our involvement — either within the organization or in the social problem being addressed?

3. Will our involvement (financial or other) help the organization succeed in gathering additional commitments from others?

4. Is there a better way to help, apart from the request as it stands?

5. Does this further our goal of increasing community-wide and neighborhood participation in meeting social needs?

Strengths: _____

_____

_____

Weaknesses: _____

_____

_____

Recommendation (full funding, partial, none, more?): _____

_____

_____

Perceptions of interview (were they knowledgeable about program, etc.): __

_____

_____

Other comments (e.g. ambience, etc.): _____

_____

_____

SOURCE: *The Trustee Notebook*, p.83.

Policy Statement of Trustees on Attendance at Foundation Events by Children of Members and Trustees

NORD FAMILY FOUNDATION

It is the policy of the The Nord Family Foundation to encourage full family participation in meetings, retreats, and conferences sponsored or supported by the Foundation. On a case-by-case basis, as determined by the Trustees, Trustees and Members may be reimbursed for a travel and related expense of their children accompanying them on Foundation business or alternatively, at home special expense [for] the care of children while the parent Trustee or Member is away from home on Foundation business. Such reimbursement shall be made only when the Trustees determine the reimbursement is necessary for the full participation in Foundation activities by the Trustee or Member parent. It is intended that in the execution of this policy parents retain the full responsibility for the appropriate care, conduct and participation of their children without expecting that the Foundation's committees or staff will assume this responsibility. Reimbursement paid by the Foundation may have income tax consequences to the Trustee and/or Member. The Foundation shall undertake any required reporting to the IRS for such reimbursements.

Trustee Qualifications and Values Statement

1. Interest in and concern for the _____ Foundation and its field (s) of operation.

2. A broad perspective on the problems of society and on issues relating to not-for-profit organizations.

3. Objectivity, impartiality and the ability to exercise good judgment.

4. Competence among one or more trustees in management, investment experience, familiarity with budgets, and knowledge of the law.

5. Capacity for harmonious teamwork, for arriving at and accepting intelligent group decisions. The ability to disagree while maintaining respect for fellow trustees.

6. Willingness to work: to give time and thought to the affairs of the foundation, to arrange one's personal schedule so as to be available to attend meetings, to serve on committees, to undertake special assignments, and to wrestle with issues of the foundation.

7. Practical wisdom: the capacity to see the whole picture, to recognize the validity of opposing arguments, to distinguish principle from expediency and to temper the ideal with what is realistically possible.

8. Commitment to the foundation as a whole and not to special interests or constituencies.

9. Commitment to the idea of philanthropic foundations and to acting in such a way that the foundation world is strengthened and not weakened.

10. Moral sensitivity to the act of giving, coupled with an empathy and passion for the need to give.

Adapted from: John Nason, *Foundation Trusteeship*, "Qualities of a Good Trustee."

BIOGRAPHIES

Editors

VIRGINIA M. ESPOSITO, Editor, is the founding president of the National Center for Family Philanthropy. A former vice president of the Council on Foundations, she served as founder and managing director of the Council's Program on Family Philanthropy. She has written and spoken on a broad variety of topics within the field of family philanthropy and served as editor for *The Family Foundation Library Series*, a four-volume set of comprehensive books on family foundation governance, management, grantmaking, and family issues. In addition to her work on resources for family donors, Ginny edited *Conscience & Community*, a volume of writings and speeches of the late Paul Ylvisaker, foundation trustee, educator, and former dean of the Graduate School of Education at Harvard University. A former teacher, Ginny is a graduate of Mary Washington College, and is a former policy fellow with the Institute for Educational Leadership. She serves on several boards and advisory committees dedicated to encouraging private philanthropy.

JOSEPH FOOTE, Associate Editor, is a professional writer and editor who specializes in philanthropy and social policy. He is a contributing editor of the National Center for Family Philanthropy. Joe's clients include Carnegie Corporation of New York, The Ford Foundation, the Joseph P. Kennedy, Jr. Foundation, the Council on Foundations, and Independent Sector. A former journalist, he has written and edited many reports for the White House, Cabinet Officers, and Congress, and was editor of both the Congressional and Independent Counsel investigations of the Iran-Contra Affair. He earned a B.A. *cum laude* at Williams College and a J.D. at the Harvard Law School.

ANDY CARROLL, Project Manager, is program director at the National Center for Family Philanthropy, where he manages several publications and research projects. Prior to joining the National Center, Andy served for five years as program coordinator for the Council on Foundations' annual conference. He helped the Council's membership develop the conference's program content, and he encouraged new and diverse voices in the grantmaking field to participate in program planning. Andy has 20 years of experience in management, administration, and program development for nonprofit organizations, including the Nature Conservancy, National Audubon Society, Wolf Trap Institute for Early Learning in the Arts, and Public Citizen. Andy has an M.B.A. degree from the University of Michigan and a bachelor's degree from Cornell University.

Authors and Contributors

DORNA L. ALLEN is a writer and editor living in Sandwich, Massachusetts. Following the satisfactions of raising a three-son family, she turned to a career of elementary school teaching on Cape Cod. As a Fulbright Exchange student, she taught in England for a year. Following retirement from teaching, Dorna spent several years in the family tree seed business. She is a *summa cum laude* graduate of Bridgewater State College in Massachusetts, and holds an M.Ed. from Cambridge College, Cambridge, Massachusetts.

JASON C. BORN is program director for the National Center for Family Philanthropy. Jason previously served as program coordinator for the Council on Foundations' Program on Family Philanthropy. He served as editor of the *Family Matters* newsletter for family foundations from 1995 to 1997, and managed the development of the Family Advisor series of information packets. He has authored and edited numerous articles and publications on family philanthropy, including Volume 2 of the National Center's Journal, *Investment Issues for Family Funds*. Other recent articles include, "Discretionary Grants: Encouraging Participation... or Dividing Family?" and "Supporting Organizations: Options, Opportunities, and Challenges." Jason earned a B.A. at Washington University in St. Louis, and holds an M.A. in economics from Tulane University in New Orleans.

PAUL BRAINERD has had three careers in his life: as a journalist, as a businessman, and currently as a community volunteer. In 1994, he founded The Brainerd Foundation, which is dedicated to protecting the environmental quality of the Pacific Northwest. The foundation is based in Seattle and supports grassroots-oriented projects that motivate citizens to get involved in efforts to protect the environment. He is a founding partner of Social Venture Partners, an effort to encourage business professionals to give back time, money, and expertise to their communities. In addition, he and his wife Debbi are co-founders of the Puget Sound Environmental Learning Center, currently under construction on 255 acres on Bainbridge Island. Focused on school-aged children, the Center will provide hands-on learning experiences that link science, technology, and the arts in a natural setting. Brainerd founded Aldus Corporation in 1984 to develop a new generation of page composition software that would allow business and creative professionals to perform page layout and design functions on the microcomputer. He coined the term "desktop publishing" for this new category, and in 1985 the company launched Aldus PageMaker desktop publishing software for use with the Apple Macintosh computer and LaserWriter printer. He served as president until 1994, when the company merged with Adobe Systems Inc. Brainerd's background includes extensive experience in journalism and dedicated publishing systems. Brainerd holds a B.S. in business administration from the University of Oregon and an M.S. in journalism from the University of Minnesota. He has received numerous awards for his business activities including Entrepreneur of the Year awards for Washington State and the Northwest region of the United States. In 1994,

Brainerd won Europe's prestigious Gutenberg Prize for his contribution to the advancement of the art and craft of the printing industry.

DEBORAH A. BRODY is senior program director at the National Center for Family Philanthropy. Before joining the National Center, she worked in marketing and business development for two Internet companies. Previously, as founding director of Grantmakers in Health's Support Center, she pioneered a new initiative to provide assistance to foundations formed from the sale of nonprofit hospitals. She spent 11 years at the Council on Foundations, first as director of Research and then as director of Private Foundation Services. Deborah is a frequent contributor to *Foundation News & Commentary* magazine and managed the National Center's *Faith and Family Philanthropy* Journal. She is a mediator for the District of Columbia Superior Court. She graduated with honors from Wellesley College, where she received the Ralph H. Ballard Award for distinguished work in American history, and she holds a master's degree in public policy from Georgetown University.

WILLIAM H. GATES, SR., is Co-chair & CEO of the Bill & Melinda Gates Foundation. Bill Gates, Sr., first answered his son's request to help use his resources to improve reproductive and child health in the developing world by directing the William H. Gates Foundation, which was established in 1994 and later merged with the Gates Learning Foundation to create the Bill & Melinda Gates Foundation in 2000. Gates guides the vision and strategic direction of the foundation. He earned his bachelor's and law degrees from the University of Washington, following 3 years of U.S. Army service in World War II. Gates, a founding partner at Preston Gates & Ellis, has served as president of both the Seattle/King County Bar Association and the Washington State Bar Association. Gates has served as trustee, officer, and volunteer for more than two dozen Northwest organizations, including the Greater Seattle Chamber of Commerce and King County United Way. In 1995, he founded the Technology Alliance, a cooperative regional effort to expand technology-based employment in Washington. He also has been a strong advocate for education for many years, chairing the Seattle Public School Levy Campaign in 1971 and serving as a member of the University of Washington's Board of Regents since 1997. Bill and his late wife, Mary Maxwell Gates, raised three children: Kristianne, Bill, and Libby. Now married to Mimi Gardner Gates, Gates continues his lifelong commitment to many civic programs, cultural organizations, and business initiatives.

ANTONIA M. GRUMBACH is a partner of the New York law firm of Patterson, Belknap, Webb & Tyler LLP. She has practiced in the area of tax exempt organizations for the past 25 years, and has served as a member of the Committee on Nonprofit Organizations for the Association of the Bar of the City of New York. She has also served on the Board of Advisors of the NYU Program on Philanthropy and the Law and is currently vice chair of that Board. She has lectured and written in the field of tax-exempt organizations and has published articles on fiduciary responsibility of directors, expenditure responsibility, foreign grantmaking of private foundations, and lobbying and legislative activities. Currently, Ms. Grumbach is also a trustee of several tax-exempt organizations, including two family foundations, as well as serving as co-chair of the Board of Trustees of Teachers College, Columbia University. Ms. Grumbach is also a director of the United States Trust Corporation and United States Trust Company of New York.

JUDITH K. HEALEY has been a professional in philanthropy for 27 years. She was executive director of the Minnesota Council on Foundations and later worked in senior positions at every type of foundation. Since 1989, she has been president of Executive Consulting, a firm specializing in planning assistance to family foundation boards. She has worked with more than 50 family foundations, given workshops to many more, and published widely in the field. Her novel, *The Lost Letters of Aquitaine*, will be published by William Morrow in 2003.

JONATHAN HOPPS is principal, Turning Point Consulting, Cumberland, Maine. Jonathan provides counsel to nonprofit organizations on board development, strategic planning, and fundraising. Stemming from his work with individual donors, Jonathan has been trained to work with individuals and families to conduct value-based estate planning. Jonathan's background includes alumni relations, major gifts, and campaign direction as well as marketing and communications. He has held senior positions at the Unitarian Universalist Association in Boston; Cambridge College, Cambridge, Massachusetts; and Reunion Productions, Watertown, Massachusetts. Jonathan earned a B.A. from the University of Vermont. and holds an M. Ed. From Cambridge College, Cambridge, Massachusetts.

TORY DIETEL HOPPS is principal, Turning Point Consulting, Cumberland, Maine. Tory has been a nonprofit leadership and resource development consultant since 1990. She has worked with educational, environmental, medical, and social service agencies to provide counsel on board development, strategic planning, and fund development. She has also provided start-up direction to launch several nonprofits, created new development operations, and worked on national and international campaigns. Her independent practice grew into Turning Point Consulting, LLC ™ in 1998. Tory earned a B.A. from the University of Vermont, and is a graduate of the Emma Willard School, Troy, New York.

BARBARA D. KIBBE is Director of Organizational Effectiveness and Philanthropy at the David and Lucile Packard Foundation. Ms. Kibbe brings more than 20 years experience in nonprofit management, philanthropy, and consulting to her work. Under Ms. Kibbe's leadership, the OEP Program provides nonprofit organizations access to tools and skills in planning, financial management, fundraising, communication, board and staff development, and executive transition to expand their capacity to pursue their missions. OEP also pursues goals to build and strengthen the field of nonprofit management and to foster effective philanthropy nationally. Ms. Kibbe is the co-author of two books: *Succeeding*

BIOGRAPHIES

with *Consultants*, published by the Foundation Center; and *Grantmaking Basics*, published by the Council on Foundations. She is a founder and serves on the steering committee of Grantmakers for Effective Organizations (GEO). Ms. Kibbe is a *cum laude* graduate of Wagner College (New York City) and earned her J.D. degree at Brooklyn Law School.

RUSHWORTH M. KIDDER is founder and president of the Institute for Global Ethics, a nonprofit, nonsectarian, and nonpolitical organization with offices in Camden, Maine; London, England; and Toronto, Canada. Author of eight books and scores of articles, his most recent book is *How Good People Make Tough Choices: Resolving the Dilemmas of Ethical Living*. Dr. Kidder is a trustee of the Charles Stewart Mott Foundation, and serves on the advisory council of the Character Education Partnership and The Conference Board Working Group on Global Business Ethics Principles, and the advisory board of Religion & Ethics Newsweekly on public television. He is a Fellow of the George H. Gallup International Institute and is a member of the advisory board of the Kenan Institute for Ethics at Duke University. An honors graduate of Amherst College, he earned a Ph.D. from Columbia University in English and comparative literature.

CHRISTOPHER M. PAYER is principal in The Wealth Stewardship Companies, a values-based estate and family legacy consulting firm. Chris received his B.A. from Skidmore College and then went on to 3 years of master's study at Cornell University. He is the president and founder of the Wealth Stewardship Institute, a national, multi-disciplinary, financial strategy think-tank providing research and training programs on wealth responsibility to advisors and families of affluence. He overseas the WSI Professional Mentorship Program and is currently finishing a book on his Wealth Stewardship Planning process. He is securities registered through Prime Capital Services, Inc.

JOHN SARE is a partner in the Trusts and Estates department of Milbank, Tweed, Hadley & McCloy LLP in New York. He advises a number of private foundations and public charities, and he counsels individual clients about estate planning, with an emphasis on charitable giving. He is a member of the adjunct faculty of the Columbia University School of Law, where he teaches the Seminar in Law and the Visual Arts. He has lectured and written on the private foundation rules, the 2001 estate tax reforms, gifts of copyright to charity, charitable giving generally, intermediate sanctions, the unrelated business income tax, and the public accountability rules applicable to charities. From 1998 to 2001, he was Secretary of the Committee on Nonprofit Organizations of the Association of the Bar of the City of New York. He previously served on that Association's Committee on Art Law. He received his B.A. from Southern Methodist University and his J.D. from Columbia University.

VINCENT STEHLE is the program officer for the Nonprofit Sector Support Program at the Surdna Foundation, a family foundation based in New York City with assets approaching $650 million. The Nonprofit Sector Support Program focuses on strengthening the policy and advocacy role of nonprofits, their internal management, and their ability to deal with a changing political, economic, and technological environment. Mr. Stehle is a founding member of the Board of Directors of the Nonprofit Technology Enterprise Network (NTEN) as well as a Director of ImpactOnline, which operates the VolunteerMatch online search service. Before coming to Surdna, Mr. Stehle worked for 10 years as a reporter for the *Chronicle of Philanthropy*, where he covered fundraising and management issues for the nonprofit sector. In addition, he has written extensively for other publications, including *The Washington Post*, *The Nation*, *Foundation News & Commentary*, and other magazines and journals.

DEANNE STONE is a freelance writer who specializes in writing about family foundations and family businesses. Her publications include *Sustaining Tradition: The Andrus Family Philanthropy Program*, *Grantmaking with a Compass: The Challenge of Geography*, *Creative Family Grantmaking: The Story of the Durfee Foundation*, *Hands-on Grantmaking: The Story of the Boone Foundation*, *Privacy and the Family Foundation: The Impact on Grantmaking, Family Issues, and Building Family Unity through Giving: The Story of the Namaste Foundation*. Her articles on philanthropy have appeared in *Foundation News & Commentary* and *Family Business* magazine. She holds an M.A. in education from the University of Chicago and a B.A. in sociology from Northwestern University.

PAUL YLVISAKER. A champion of cities and the urban underclass as a planner, government official, foundation executive, and educator, Paul Ylvisaker brought educational distinction to his public appointments and a hard-won understanding of the realities of urban poverty to his academic work. Lured from the Blue Earth County, Minnesota, Council on Intergovernment Relations to Harvard in 1944, Ylvisaker spent 10 years in academia before working for the Mayor of Philadelphia and then The Ford Foundation, where he put his ideas to work. As the creator of the Gray Areas Program at The Ford Foundation, Ylvisaker oversaw the allocation of more than $200 million in grants; these efforts led to major Kennedy and Johnson administration innovations, including the Community Action Program and the Model Cities Program. In the early 70s, Ylvisaker returned to academia, first at Yale and Princeton before becoming dean of the Harvard Graduate School of Education . Ylvisaker's teachings, writings, and mentoring about the field of philanthropy inspired then-CEO James A. Joseph to bring Ylvisaker on as a Senior Consultant to the Council on Foundations in 1982. For the next 10 years, until his death in 1992, he continued his work examining family philanthropy and the larger role of philanthropy in civil society. Ylvisaker's thoughtful and strategic work in the philanthropic community earned him the 1990 Council on Foundations Distinguished Grantmaker Award. Today, his work is honored with the Council's Paul Ylvisaker Award for Public Policy Engagement.

The National Center for Family Philanthropy and the editors and authors of *Splendid Legacy* gratefully acknowledge those who generously participated in the development of this book.

John Abele
Argosy Foundation

Arnold & Porter

Daniel Bader
Helen Bader Foundation

Mal Bank
The Cleveland Foundation

Nathanael W. Berry
The Sandy River Charitable Foundation

George Boone
Boone Foundation

Nancy Brain
Frances Hollis Brain Foundation

Nancy Bryant
Jerry Taylor & Nancy Bryant Foundation

Alexander (Sandy) Buck, Jr.
The Horizon Foundation

Christopher Buck
The Peter and Carmen Lucia Buck Foundation

Alice Buhl
Buhl and Associates

Andy Burness
Burness Communications

Butler Family Fund

Elli Carroll

Valerie Bayne Carroll

Carpenter Foundation

Stephanie S. Clohesy
Clohesy Consulting

Francie Close
Springs Foundation

John Colina
Colina Family Foundation

Susanna Colloredo-Mansfield
The Alces Foundation

Bill Conway
SandFair Foundation

John Craig
The Commonwealth Fund

John Straub Darrow
Wieboldt Foundation

Kim Dennis
D&D Foundation

David Dodson
MDC

Leslie Dorman
The Sterling Foundation

Nancy Douzinas
Rauch Foundation

John Edie
Council on Foundations

Erin Esposito
Fairview Scholars

Shirley Fredricks
The Lawrence Welk Foundation

Mary Jane Fredrickson
Family Office Exchange

Frees Family Foundation

Jonathan Frieman
JoMiJo Foundation

Frank Gibney, Jr.
Gibney Family Foundation

Hope Gleicher
Trellis Fund

Alison Goldberg
Robert P. & Judith N. Goldberg Foundation

Kathleen A. Good
Good Management Associates

Michele A. Goodman
J.W. & H.M. Goodman Family Charitable Foundation

Karen Green
Council on Foundations

Charles H. Hamilton
The Clark Foundation

Suzanne N. Hazelett
Randall L. Tobias Foundation

Hemenway & Barnes
Donor Services Office

Bruce A. Hirsch
Clarence E. Heller Charitable Foundation

Emily Tow Jackson
Tow Foundation

Hilary Joy
The Ken and Judith Joy Family Foundation

Leslie Kelly
The Haines Center for Family Philanthropy

Anne Marie Kemp
Greenlee Family Foundation

Harris and Eliza Kempner Fund

Charles F. Kettering, III
Kettering Family Foundation

Marion I. & Henry J. Knott Foundation

Judith Kroll
Council on Foundations

Thomas Kubiak
The Oliver B. Merlyn Foundation

Geri Kunstadter
Albert Kunstadter Family Foundation

Brian Laskowski
George Mason University

Jeffrey R. Leighton

Margaret Mahoney
MEM Associates

Phyllis Mailman
Mailman Foundation

Doug Malcolm

Maxine Marshall
The Marshall Fund of Arizona

Matrix Foundation

Kathryn McCarthy
Rockefeller & Co.

Curtis W. Meadows, Jr.
The Meadows Foundation

Mariann Mihailidis
Family Office Exchange

Milbank, Tweed, Hadley & McCloy

Claude Norcott
Consultant

The Nord Family Foundation

Penny Noyce
The Noyce Foundation

Don O'Keefe
The O'Keefe Family Foundation

Robert Owens
Tresorelle Foundation

Robin Platts
The Dresher Fund

Gerard E. Putnam
Dr. G. Clifford and Florence B. Decker Foundation

Robert A. Reuter
The Reuter Foundation

Z. Smith Reynolds Foundation

Gabby Rojchin
SUMO Creative

Bubba Self
Self Family Foundation

Self Family Foundation

Lisa Sobrato Sonsini
Sobrato Family Foundation

Christina M. Spellman
Mayday Fund

The Stocker Foundation

Robert Tobon
Helen Bader Foundation

Emily Hall Tremaine Foundation

David D. Weitnauer
The Rockdale Foundation

Richard Woo
The Russell Family Foundation

NATIONAL CENTER STAFF

Abby Cameron

Sally Jones

Marta Craig

Katie Nolan

Elizabeth Watkins

ADVISORY COMMITTEE

Virginia Esposito
National Center for Family Philanthropy

Sanford Cardin
Charles and Lynn Schusterman Family Foundation

Sarah Russell Cavanaugh
The Russell Family Foundation

Jessica Chao
Consultant

Beverly A. Cooper
The Reginald F. Lewis Foundation

William M. Dietel
Consultant

Robert Hull

Jane Leighty Justis
The Leighty Foundation

John W. Kunstadter
Albert Kunstadter Family Foundation

Jaylee Mead
Gilbert and Jaylee Mead Family Foundation

Nancy P. Roberts
Connecticut Council for Philanthropy

John Sare
Milbank, Tweed, Hadley & McCloy LLP

DESIGN AND PRODUCTION

Mary Ellis Fannon
Fannon Color Printing, LLC

Jennifer Higgins
Supon Design Group

Pum M. Lefebure
Supon Design Group

Melissa Yacuk
Supon Design Group

RESOURCES

From the National Center

The National Center for Family Philanthropy offers an array of printed resource materials to support you and your family foundation. For excerpts and additional information about the following resources, please visit the National Center's website at www.ncfp.org. If you have any questions about these publications, please contact the National Center at 202.293.3424. Publications may be purchased by calling or visiting the website. Additionally, several resources are available online including a monthly newsletter and information packets.

NATIONAL CENTER JOURNAL SERIES

Each National Center Journal is a complete reference on an important issue concerning family giving. The format of each Journal encourages quick access to topics of particular interest, or a more thoughtful consideration of issues in context.

Resources for Family Philanthropy: Finding the Best People, Advice, and Support. For the new family foundation, this Journal provides a helpful overview to topics such as managing your family's philanthropy; selecting and working with consultants, legal and investment advisors; and locating and connecting with the larger world of philanthropy. *Edited by Joseph Foote and Claude O. Norcott, 1999, 128 pages, $45*

Investment Issues for Family Funds: Managing and Maximizing Your Philanthropic Assets. This comprehensive guide unravels the issues that drive investment decisions of a family foundation and provides easy-to-understand answers to a full range of questions, including spending policies, investment guidelines, mission-related investing, and risk tolerance. *Edited by Jason C. Born, 1999, 169 pages, $45*

Living the Legacy: The Values of a Family's Philanthropy Across Generations. Donor Legacy remains one of the most distinguishing and distinctive themes in family philanthropy. This thoughtful compilation of stories and essays describes how families and foundations build and pass on a shared philanthropic legacy over time and across generations. *Edited by Charles H. Hamilton, 2001, 169 pages, $45*

Faith and Family Philanthropy: Grace, Gratitude, and Generosity. This collection of inspiring and informative essays provides a first-ever look into the motivations and religious traditions that guide many family philanthropists today. *Edited by Joseph Foote, 2001, 120 pages, $45*

NATIONAL CENTER WORKBOOK SERIES

National Center Workbooks are practical guidebooks for trustees, family members, staff, and advisors to family philanthropies. The content and design of the workbooks make them highly usable references.

The Trustee Notebook: An Orientation for Family Foundation Board Members. This orientation manual provides easy-to-understand explanations of the rules that govern private foundations trustees, and guidance on making good grant decisions and defining one's role in the activities of the foundation. *By Robert H. Hull, 1999, 85 pages, $45*

Voyage of Discovery: A Planning Workbook for Philanthropic Families. The reasons and moments for initiating a planning process are as varied as families and family foundations. Written by one of the most respected and experienced family foundation consultants, this is the first resource designed exclusively for families thinking about how to plan for the future of their giving programs. *By Judith Healey, 2001, 64 pages, $55*

NATIONAL CENTER MONOGRAPHS: PRACTICES SERIES

The Practices in Family Philanthropy series are guides to governance and management issues of particular interest to family giving programs.

Sustaining Tradition: The Andrus Family Philanthropy Program. When the Surdna Foundation decided it wanted to engage all of the members of the founding Andrus family, their goal was to involve nearly 350 family members in eight branches, spread over three continents. After three years of work, planning, and the creation of the Andrus Family Philanthropy Program, a larger purpose evolved — linking the larger family around concepts of service and education. *By Deanne Stone, 70 pages, $30*

Collaborative Grantmaking: Lessons Learned from the Rockefeller Family's Experience. Based on interviews and plenty of experience, this monograph profiles a series of collaborations initiated by members of the Rockefeller family, documenting how each was formed and organized, what problems were encountered, how these were resolved, and what was accomplished. *By Kimberly Robinson, 85 pages, $30*

Grantmaking With a Compass: The Challenges of Geography. Addressing one of the most significant challenges to family foundations, this monograph tells stories of how families have dealt with geographic dispersion of the fam

MONOGRAPHS continued

ily, including: honoring the legacy of the donor; defining a mission that accommodates individual interests and needs of different communities; maintaining high standards of grantmaking practices and evaluation strategies; and allocating funds equitably. *By Deanne Stone, 1999, 64 pages, $30*

Grantmaking With a Purpose: Mission and Guidelines. This publication describes what factors determine mission, how to develop mission and guidelines, and how they can be revisited from time to time. *By Virginia Peckham, 2000, 51 pages, $30*

Family Philanthropy and Donor-Advised Funds. Drawing on the personal experiences of donors and families, this monograph describes how they are meeting their charitable and family goals through donor advised funds, and includes a partial listing of organizations offering advised funds, sample documents for establishing a fund, and a bibliography of additional resources. *By Joseph Foote, 2000, 84 pages, $30*

NATIONAL CENTER MONOGRAPHS: PROFILES SERIES
Profiles in Family Philanthropy feature the stories of family philanthropies and the issues and circumstances they address.

Creative Family Grantmaking: The Story of the Durfee Foundation. This monograph chronicles the history and grantmaking of the Durfee Foundation. Considered by some a small foundation, this family has developed six distinctive and highly creative, trustee-driven programs. *By Deanne Stone, 1999, 40 pages, $20*

Community Kinship: The Story of the Springs Foundation. The experiences of the Springs Foundation are profiled in this monograph, chronicling how they have sustained their 50 years commitment of service to the citizens of South Carolina. *By Carol Robbins, 2000, 35 pages, $30*

PASSAGES: EXPLORING KEY ISSUES IN FAMILY GIVING
Available by subscription, the Passages series of issue papers features the latest in family giving research and practice in an accessible style and format.

Managing Conflicts and Family Dynamics in Your Family's Philanthropy. This paper introduces the causes and potential consequences of conflict in family philanthropy, and provides practical suggestions for preventing or assuaging conflict. *By Deborah Brody, June 2002, 8 pages, $20*

Opportunity of a Lifetime: Young Adults in Family Philanthropy. This issue paper addresses one of the most important opportunities in family philanthropy — encouraging young adults to take part in the family's giving process and to become philanthropic in their own right. *By Alison Goldberg, May 2002, 8 pages, $20*

PASSAGES continued

Supporting Organizations: Options, Opportunities, and Challenges. The considerations of why and how families establish supporting organizations are presented in a clear and non-technical context in this paper, with information on how SOs are typically structured and managed. *By Jason C. Born, December 2001, 12 pages, $20*

Discretionary Grants: Encouraging Participation... or Dividing Families? This issue paper looks at the common reasons that families use or opt not to use discretionary grants, and the typical process that is used to make these types of grants. *By Jason C. Born, September 2001, 8 pages, $20*

Board Compensation: Reasonable and Necessary? This comprehensive issue paper provides guidance on the legal regulations regarding compensation, suggestions for how to initiate a conversation among your board members about whether or not compensation is appropriate, and suggestions for how to develop a written policy based on this conversation. *By Jason C. Born, June 2001, 6 pages, $20*

PASSAGES: ARCHIVES EDITIONS
Archival editions of the National Center's Passages series are available for $5 apiece, or may be downloaded for free from the National Center's website at www.ncfp.org. Issues include:

- **Family Meetings: Preparing for an Effective Family Foundation Discussion**
- **The Donor Advisor: The Critical Role of the Advisor in Family Philanthropy**
- **Common Concerns: Current Issues Affecting Family Foundations**
- **An Introduction to Family Philanthropy**
- **Leadership and Continuity: Strategies for Effective Transitions in Family Foundations**

SPECIAL RESOURCES ON FAMILY PHILANTHROPY
Conscience and Community: The Legacy of Paul Ylvisaker. This collection of educator and philanthropic advisor Paul Ylvisaker's essays, speeches, and articles covers philanthropy, education, urban issues, and community. *Edited by Virginia M. Esposito, 1999, 392 pages, $35*

Family Foundations: A Profile of Funders and Trends. Family Foundations: A Profile of Funders and Trends is the first-ever study on the grantmaking and governance trends of a broad sample of the U.S. family foundation universe. *By Steven Lawrence, 2000, 55 pages, $19.95*

What Needs to Be Done: The History of the Ellis L. Phillips Foundation. This full-length history captures the spirit and values of the Phillips family's philanthropy and, particularly, the story of the founder, Ellis L. Phillips. *By Winston Emmons, 2001, 220 pages, $30*

RESOURCES

For Your Library

You may wish to create a set of references to complement *Splendid Legacy*. The following selective list of books and guides will help you develop a solid library of advice and information as you establish your family foundation. Please note that, while the list is organized by section, many of these resources cut across more than one of the topics and issues discussed in each of the sections.

I. CREATING YOUR FAMILY FOUNDATION

Cathedral Within: Transforming Your Life by Giving Something Back. Stories of extraordinary people who have used their private resources to improve public life.
AUTHOR: William H. Shore PUBLISHER: Random House
DATE PUBLISHED: 1999 PRICE: $15.00 PAGES: 294 pgs.
TO ORDER: Call 888.860.6101 or order online at www.amazon.com

Common Concerns: Current Issues Affecting Family Foundations. This essay details frequently asked questions by trustees and staff of family foundations including: the role of the donor; board selection; the role of nonfamily members; the role of younger family members; and the use of discretionary grants.
AUTHOR: Virginia Esposito
PUBLISHER: National Center for Family Philanthropy
DATE PUBLISHED: 2000 PRICE: $5.00 PAGES: 4 pgs.
TO ORDER: Call 202.293.3424 or available online at www.ncfp.org

Faith and Family Philanthropy: Grace, Gratitude, and Generosity. How does faith inspire and shape family philanthropy? How can giving become a spiritually fulfilling experience? These questions and others are addressed in this groundbreaking guide.
EDITOR: Joseph Foote
PUBLISHER: National Center for Family Philanthropy
DATE PUBLISHED: 2001 PRICE: $45.00 PAGES: 122 pgs.
TO ORDER: Call 202.293.3424 or order online at www.ncfp.org

Grantmaking With a Purpose: Mission and Guidelines. Using case studies from families, this guide describes how a mission statement can inform your decisionmaking process, and how program guidelines help ensure the integrity of the mission and the effectiveness of your family foundation's grantmaking. Describes how to develop mission and guidelines, what factors determine mission, and how mission and guidelines can be revisited.
AUTHOR: Virginia Peckham
PUBLISHER: National Center for Family Philanthropy
DATE PUBLISHED: 2000 PRICE: $30.00 PAGES: 51 pgs.
TO ORDER: Call 202.293.3424 or order online at www.ncfp.org

Inspired Philanthropy: Your Step-by-Step Guide to Creating a Giving Plan, 2nd Edition. This workbook provides advice on creating an effective giving program for donors with a few hundred dollars to give away, or those with a few million dollars. A mixture of philanthropic philosophy, personal accounts of how individuals have handled their giving, and exercises that lead you through the gift-making process.
AUTHORS: Tracy Gary and Melissa Kohner PUBLISHER: Jossey Bass
DATE PUBLISHED: 2002 PRICE: $24.95 PAGES: 304 pgs.
TO ORDER: Call 800.956.7739 or order online at www.josseybass.com

Living the Legacy: The Values of a Family's Philanthropy Across Generations. This seminal resource for family foundation trustees and staff considers the impact and importance of donor legacy, and how legacy can be transformed into a powerful living legacy. How does a foundation — and a family foundation in particular — describe and pass on its legacy over time and through generations? How is a donor's intent interpreted, maintained, adapted, and carried out by succeeding generations of trustees and staff? How do children and grandchildren blend their interests and a changing world with the donor's intentions, thereby creating a vital, ongoing philanthropy?
EDITOR: Charles H. Hamilton
PUBLISHER: National Center for Family Philanthropy
DATE PUBLISHED: 2001 PRICE: $45.00 PAGES: 220 pgs.
TO ORDER: Call 202.293.3424 or order online at www.ncfp.org

Wealth In Families. This helpful reference examines a series of fundamental questions surrounding wealth and its effects on family. The book places special emphasis on the value of family philanthropy, and includes several case studies of real families.
AUTHOR: Charles W. Collier PUBLISHER: Harvard University
DATE PUBLISHED: 2001 PRICE: $15.00 PAGES: 127 pgs.
TO ORDER: Call 617.495.5040 or order online at www.haa.harvard.edu

II. STARTING UP

Family Foundations and the Law. This important reference answers many of the most common questions on law relevant to the trustees, directors, and staff of family foundations.

AUTHOR: John A. Edie PUBLISHER: Council on Foundations
DATE PUBLISHED: 2002 PRICE: $55.00 PAGES: 80 pgs.
TO ORDER: Call 888.239.5221 or order online at www.cof.org

Foundation Desk Reference: A Compendium of Private Foundation Rules. This reference provides a checklist and descriptions of the rules relevant to the trustees, directors, and staff of private foundations.

AUTHOR: Benjamin T. White PUBLISHER: Southeastern Council of Foundations
DATE PUBLISHED: 1991 PRICE: $30.00 PAGES: 80 pgs.
TO ORDER: Call 404.524.0911 or online at www.secf.org/publications.asp

Harvard Manual on Tax Aspects of Charitable Giving. This comprehensive legal compendium provides guidance on donor options, tax law, and other related issues.

AUTHOR: Carolyn M. Osteen and David M. Donaldson
PUBLISHER: Harvard University DATE PUBLISHED: 1992
PRICE: $105.00 PAGES: 428 pgs. TO ORDER: Call 617.495.4647

Resources for Family Philanthropy: Finding the Best People, Advice and Support. A compilation of essays that offers family philanthropies guidance in reviewing and evaluating available resources. Addresses topics such as managing your family's philanthropy, selecting and working with consultants and legal and investment advisors, and locating and connecting with the larger world of philanthropy.

EDITOR: Joseph Foote and Claude O. Norcott
PUBLISHER: National Center for Family Philanthropy
DATE PUBLISHED: 1999 PRICE: $45.00 PAGES: 128 pgs.
TO ORDER: Call 202.293.3424 or order online at www.ncfp.org

Private Foundations: Tax Law and Compliance. This single-volume reference manual covers nearly all aspects of tax compliance for private foundations.

AUTHOR: Bruce Hopkins and Judy Blazek PUBLISHER: Jossey-Bass
DATE PUBLISHED: 1997 PRICE: $165.00 PAGES: 520 pgs.
TO ORDER: Call 877.762.2974 or order online at www.JosseyBass.com

III. ESTABLISHING A STRUCTURE

Board Member's Book. This orientation manual for nonprofits highlights the role and importance of board members. Discusses topics such as strategic planning, board and staff recruiting, and the evaluation of board members.

AUTHOR: Brian O'Connell PUBLISHER: The Foundation Center
DATE PUBLISHED: 1993 PRICE: $24.95 PAGES: 208 pgs.
TO ORDER: Call 212.807.2426 or online at fdncenter.org/marketplace

Family Foundation Retreat Guide. This resource manual provides an overview of how to think about and plan a family foundation board retreat. Includes guidance on format, process, and developing an agenda.

AUTHOR: Alice Buhl and Judith Healey PUBLISHER: Council on Foundations
DATE PUBLISHED: 1995 PRICE: $45.00 PAGES: 35 pgs.
TO ORDER: Call 888.239.5221 or order online at www.cof.org

Family Foundations: Now – and Forever? This monograph presents several examples of models from existing family foundations that are in the process of bringing on future generations of family board members.

AUTHOR: Paul M. Ylvisaker PUBLISHER: Council on Foundations
DATE PUBLISHED: 1997 PRICE: $25.00 PAGES: 27 pgs.
TO ORDER: Call 888.239.5221 or order online at www.cof.org

Family Issues. Using real-life stories and family systems theory, this guide provides helpful perspectives around topics such as understanding family dynamics, bringing on the next generation, and determining who is family.(Part of the Family Foundation Library.)

AUTHOR: Deanne Stone EDITOR: Virginia M. Esposito
PUBLISHER: Council on Foundations DATE PUBLISHED: 1997 PRICE: $65.00
PAGES: 141 pgs.TO ORDER: Call 888.239.5221 or online at www.cof.org

Family Meetings: Preparing for an Effective Family Foundation Meeting. This essay describes strategies for planning effective family meetings, including developing the agenda, choosing a location and setting for the meeting, facilitation, and follow-up. Includes a sample meeting agenda and "groundrules" for family discussions.

AUTHOR: Jason C. Born PUBLISHER: National Center for Family Philanthropy
DATE PUBLISHED: 2000 PRICE: $5.00 PAGES: 4 pgs.
TO ORDER: Call 202.293.3424 or online at www.ncfp.org

Foundation Trusteeship: Service in the Public Interest. This collection of essays discusses the roles of foundations and trustees, including the dynamics of effective boards, and the length and frequency of meetings.

AUTHOR: John W. Nason PUBLISHER: Foundation Center
DATE PUBLISHED: 1989 PRICE: $19.95 PAGES: 173 pgs.
TO ORDER: Call 888.239.5221 or online at www.cof.org

RESOURCES

For Your Library

III. ESTABLISHING A STRUCTURE continued

The Giving Family: Raising Our Children to Help Others. This guide is designed to help parents teach children, from toddlers to teens, how to use their time, talent, and, money to help others. Explains how parents, teachers, religious leaders and other adults can instill the spirit of giving and volunteering in children. Provides tips, exercises, and resources that are easy to use in any home.

> AUTHOR: Susan Crites Price PUBLISHER: Council on Foundations
> DATE PUBLISHED: 2001 PRICE: $19.95 PAGES: 120 pgs.
> TO ORDER: Call 888.239.5221 or online at www.cof.org

Governance. Based on interviews with hundreds of family foundation trustees, this overview provides guidance on many of the issues concerning the governance of a family foundation. (Part of the Family Foundation Library.)

> AUTHOR: Newell Flather, Mary Phillips, Jean Whitney
> EDITOR: Virginia M. Esposito PUBLISHER: Council on Foundations
> DATE PUBLISHED: 1997 PRICE: $65.00 PAGES: 193 pgs.
> TO ORDER: Call 888.239.5221 or online at www.cof.org

Investment Issues for Family Funds: Managing and Maximizing Your Philanthropic Dollars. Written for trustees and advisors, this resource addresses the broad array of issues involved in developing a set of investment policies and practices for your philanthropy, including spending policies, investment guidelines, time horizon, mission-related investing, and risk tolerance.

> EDITOR: Jason C. Born PUBLISHER: National Center for Family Philanthropy
> DATE PUBLISHED: 1999 PRICE: $45.00 PAGES: 169 pgs.
> TO ORDER: Call 202.293.3424 or online at www.ncfp.org

Management. This reference manual describes the key aspects of managing family foundations, from mission and board development, to accounting practices and evaluation. (Part of the Family Foundation Library.)

> AUTHOR: Martha Cooley EDITOR: Virginia M. Esposito
> PUBLISHER: Council on Foundations DATE PUBLISHED: 1997
> PRICE: $65.00 PAGES: 223 pgs
> TO ORDER: Call 888.239.5221 or online at www.cof.org

Preparing the Next Generations: A Workbook to Foster Intergenerational Involvement in Family Foundations. This workbook features suggestions for policies and activities to prepare and encourage next generations of family members to participate in the foundation.

> AUTHOR and PUBLISHER: Council of Michigan Foundations
> DATE PUBLISHED · UPDATED: 1998 PRICE: $10.00 PAGES: 64 pgs.
> TO ORDER: Call 616.842.7080 or order online at www.cmif.org

Responsible Family Philanthropy: A Resource Book on Ethical Decisionmaking for Family Foundations. This guide to ethical decisionmaking for family foundations includes answers to frequently asked questions, issue briefings, and an array of resource documents and references.

> AUTHOR: Michael Rion PUBLISHER: Council on Foundations
> DATE PUBLISHED: 1998 PRICE: $40.00 PAGES: 80 pgs.
> TO ORDER: Call 888.239.5221 or order online at www.cof.org

The Succession Workbook: Continuity Planning for Family Foundations. This workbook describes how to prepare the family foundation for the future by discussing relevant topics and issues the foundation may encounter.

> AUTHORS: Kelin Gersick, Deanne Stone, Michele Desjardins, Howard Muson, Katherine Grady PUBLISHER: Council on Foundations
> DATE PUBLISHED: 2000 PRICE: $110.00 PAGES: 112 pgs.
> TO ORDER: Call 888.239.5221 or order online at www.cof.org

Sustaining Tradition: The Andrus Family Philanthropy Program. This profile of the Andrus family describes how the family, after generations of limited involvement and low profile, managed to involve nearly 350 family members in the ongoing activities of the family's philanthropy.

> AUTHOR: Deanne Stone PUBLISHER: National Center for Family Philanthropy
> DATE PUBLISHED: 2001 PRICE: $30 PAGES: 69 pgs.
> TO ORDER: Call 202.293.3424 or order online at www.ncfp.org

Trends in Family Foundation Governance, Staffing and Management, 4th Edition. This study discusses trends in family foundation governance and management, and offers ideas about the future of the field.

> AUTHOR: Elaine Gast and Arica White PUBLISHER: Council on Foundations
> DATE PUBLISHED: 2001 PRICE: $60.00 PAGES: 92 pgs.
> TO ORDER: Call 888.239.5221 or order online at www.cof.org

The Trustee Notebook: An Orientation for Family Foundation Board Members. This orientation manual for new family trustee provides guidance on a number of important questions, including: What are the rules that govern trustees of private foundations? What is the process for making good grant decisions? How can new family trustees find and define their role in the activities of the foundation? The workbook's design allows you to create a basic trustee orientation handbook by including the governance and management documents of your own foundation.

> AUTHOR: Robert Hull PUBLISHER: National Center for Family Philanthropy
> DATE PUBLISHED: 1999 PRICE: $45.00 PAGES: 83 pgs.
> TO ORDER: Call 202.293.3424 or order online at www.ncfp.org

Voyage of Discovery: A Planning Workbook for Philanthropic Families. This resource provides a series of discussion questions to assist families thinking about the future of their giving programs. Includes discussion of key aspects of the planning process, and ideas for putting a plan in action.

> AUTHOR: Judith K. Healey PUBLISHER: National Center for Family Philanthropy
> DATE PUBLISHED: 2001 PRICE: $55.00 PAGES: 60 pgs.
> TO ORDER: Call 202.293.3424 or order online at www.ncfp.org

IV. GRANTMAKING AND COMMUNICATIONS

Collaborative Grantmaking: Lessons Learned from the Rockefeller Family. Profiles a series of collaborations initiated by members of the Rockefeller family, documenting how each was formed and organized, what problems were encountered and how these were resolved, and what was accomplished.

AUTHOR: Kimberly Robinson PUBLISHER: National Center for Family Philanthropy
DATE PUBLISHED: 2001 PRICE: $30.00 PAGES: 88 pgs.
TO ORDER: Call 202.293.3424 or order online at www.ncfp.org

Creative Family Grantmaking: The Story of the Durfee Foundation. With a relatively modest budget, the Durfee Foundation has developed an enormously creative and successful grantmaking program. How has this program evolved? What has made the work of the foundation so important to the family and the community it serves? This profile chronicles the history of the foundation and describes its six distinctive, trustee-driven programs.

AUTHOR: Deanne Stone PUBLISHER: National Center for Family Philanthropy
DATE PUBLISHED: 1999 PRICE: $25.00 PAGES: 48 pgs.
TO ORDER: Call 202.293.3424 or order online at www.ncfp.org

Discretionary Grants: Encouraging Participation... or Dividing Families. This issue paper looks at the common reasons that families use or opt not to use discretionary grants, and the typical process that is used to make these types of grants.

AUTHOR: Jason Born PUBLISHER: National Center for Family Philanthropy
DATE PUBLISHED: 2001 PRICE: $20 PAGES: 8 pgs.
TO ORDER: Call 202.293.3424 or order online at www.ncfp.org

Grantmaking. This reference is based on interviews with hundreds of family foundation trustees, and provides in-depth information on many elements of the grantmaking process. (Part of the Family Foundation Library.)

AUTHOR: Joseph Foote, Louis Knowles EDITOR: Virginia M. Esposito
PUBLISHER: Council on Foundations DATE PUBLISHED: 1997
PRICE: $65.00 PAGES: 131pgs.
TO ORDER: Call 888.239.5221 or order online at www.cof.org

Grantmaking Basics: A Field Guide for Funders. This manual provides insight and advice on a variety of grantmaking activities, including site visits, proposal review, and preparation for board meetings.

AUTHOR: Barbara D. Kibbe, Fred Setterberg and Colburn S. Wilbur
PUBLISHER: Council on Foundations
DATE PUBLISHED: 1999 PRICE: $55.00 PAGES: 115 pgs.
TO ORDER: Call 888.239.5221 or order online at www.cof.org

Grantmaking With a Compass: The Challenges of Geography. Using stories of families, this monograph offers examples of how families have dealt with issues of geographic dispersion, such as: honoring the legacy of the donor; defining a mission that accommodates individual interests and needs of different communities; maintaining high standards of grantmaking practices and evaluation strategies; and allocating funds equitably.

AUTHOR: Deanne Stone PUBLISHER: National Center for Family Philanthropy
DATE PUBLISHED: 1999 PRICE: $30.00 PAGES: 64 pgs.
TO ORDER: Call 202.293.3424 or order online at www.ncfp.org

Small Can Be Effective. This monograph offers ideas about the extensive array of opportunities available to small foundations. The author describes 20 "generic functions" of philanthropy for foundations with assets of less than $10 million, in four categories: financial, catalytic, conceptual, and community-building.

AUTHOR: Paul N. Ylvisaker PUBLISHER: Council on Foundations
DATE PUBLISHED: 1989 PRICE: $17.00 PAGES: 12 pgs.
TO ORDER: Call 888-239-5221 or order online at www.cof.org

V. COMMENCEMENT

The Charitable Impulse: Wealth and Social Conscience in Communities and Cultures Outside the U.S. This collection of essays explores how societies around the world have successfully cultivated the compassionate values that lead to private generosity and public benevolence.

AUTHOR: James A. Joseph PUBLISHER: Foundation Center
DATE PUBLISHED: 1989 PRICE: $24.95 PAGES: 210 pgs.
TO ORDER: Call 212.620.4230 or order online at www.fdncenter.org

Conscience & Community: The Legacy of Paul Ylvisaker. Few can inspire a generation the way that educator and philanthropic advisor Paul Ylvisaker did. This former foundation trustee has been described as the heart and soul of organized philanthropy. This collection of his essays, speeches, and articles touches on philanthropy, education, urban issues, and community.

EDITOR: Virginia M. Esposito PUBLISHER: Peter Lang Publishing
DATE PUBLISHED: 1999 PRICE: $35.00 PAGES: 392 pgs.
TO ORDER: Call 202.293.3424 or order online at www.ncfp.org

INDEX

INDEX

Encouraging family giving — Supporting philanthropic excellence

"We value the participation of individuals and families in private, organized philanthropy. We are committed to a mission and services based on our fundamental belief in the value of philanthropy and the ongoing participation of the donor and family."

— From the National Center's Statement of Values and Guiding Principles

The National Center for Family Philanthropy, a nonprofit 501(c)(3) organization, was founded to encourage families and individuals to create and sustain their philanthropic missions. It is the only national resource center that focuses solely on matters of importance to families engaged in philanthropy and their effective giving.

In doing so, we are guided by a set of values and principles that reflect our own understanding of the opportunity, character, and contributions of family philanthropy:

- We value the participation of individuals and families in private, organized philanthropy.
- We value the donor's right and ability to direct charitable assets through the philanthropic vehicles and to programs of choice.
- We value the personal acts of generosity that inspires private philanthropy, respecting both the issues of privacy and public trust that attend the decision to give.
- We value the pursuit of excellence in philanthropy.
- We value the role that philanthropy and philanthropic citizenship play in a civil society.
- We value the participation of new voices in our field.
- We value collaboration and respect our colleagues in this work.

The National Center serves donors and their families, their staff and advisors, and the organizations that work with them. We understand the special personal nature and professional issues of family philanthropy, including the critical moments in developing and sustaining a giving program. This understanding informs a broad range of publications, programs, and direct assistance as well as an appreciation for the best advice available in the field. The National Center maintains referrals to a nationwide network of resources and philanthropic service organizations.

Programs and Services

The National Center maintains an essential clearinghouse of information related to family philanthropy. Our library contains over 400 books related to the field, 750 annual reports from private and community foundations, and over 400 files of information (articles, policies and practices, samples, etc.) on a variety of topics of interest to donors, families, and advisors.

This clearinghouse provides the basis for many of the National Center's programs and services, including a library of publications (see From the National Center, page 246). Our commitment to developing the best and most current information for and about family philanthropy fuels an agenda of projects from the development of family foundations to the motivations and interests of new donors to the scope, scale, and practices of American donor families. The National Center designs and participates in more than fifty educational programs annually, many in collaboration with colleague organizations in the field.

How We Are Organized

The National Center for Family Philanthropy is governed by a Board of Directors representing donors, family members, trustees, staff and advisors to philanthropic families, and representatives of colleague organizations in philanthropy. A Washington, DC-based staff manages programs and operations. The National Center for Family Philanthropy is supported in four ways: by general support grants; by special project grants for its publications, programs, and research projects; by income earned from publications and educational programs; and by the "Friends of the Family" partners program — a leadership circle of family giving programs, related organizations, and individuals who share our belief in encouraging and supporting philanthropic individuals and families.